Internal Control:

A Fraud- Prevention Handbook
for Hotel and Restaurant Managers

by A. Neal Geller, MBA, PhD

Professor of Accounting and Financial Management
School of Hotel Administration
Cornell University

Internal Control:

A Fraud-Prevention Handbook for Hotel and Restaurant Managers

by A. Neal Geller

© 1991 School of Hotel Administration

Cornell University, Ithaca, NY 14853

Printed in the United States of America

ISBN 0-937056-06-5

The author wishes to express special thanks to the partners and staff of

Pannell Kerr Forster

for financial support of the research and writing phases of this book.

Dedication

This book is lovingly dedicated to my family:
Vivian, Bonnie and Larry, Amy and Bob,
and to my loyal writing companion, Allie.

Contents

List of Exhibits

Preface

Organization of This Book

This book is written in building-block fashion. Each chapter adds concepts and knowledge that are important and useful for later chapters. The book will be most useful if you read the chapters in order, even if you'd like to skip around or even ignore certain chapters completely. For example, hoteliers may wish to go right to chapter six, rooms-income control; or restaurateurs may wish to go right to chapter seven, food and beverage internal control. You will find, however, that to understand internal control completely in these income areas, the material in the first three chapters is important. In fact, knowledge of chapter two, cash receipts, is critical. Similar arguments can be made for the expense areas covered in chapters four and five. Likewise, the material in chapter nine, internal control with electronic data processing, also draws heavily on the discussion of income in chapters six and seven.

The chapters themselves are also constructed in building-block fashion. Each begins with background information, moves to the foundations of theories and concepts, and ends with practical applications. The beginning of each chapter has a list of objectives that will help you preview what you should expect to accomplish from the reading. Each chapter also contains a glossary of the key words that were introduced. There is also a combined glossary and an index at the end of the book.

Assumptions

Background and Prior Knowledge of Readers. The book assumes that the readers have some basic knowledge of the hospitality industry—either as practitioners or students. A basic understanding of the principles of financial accounting is helpful but not essential, and the book does not assume such knowledge. A cursory understanding of the basic workings of hotel and guest accounting—picked up by simply working in the environment—will suffice. The more work experience you have in the hospitality industry, the more useful this book will be. Students, particularly those in hospitality-management programs, will find that the book is a good learning and training guide that will be an excellent reference for their later careers.

The Buck Stops with the General Manager. Internal control can be applied at all levels—within the property, at the corporate level, or at the ownership level. This book presents internal control at the property level. The concepts and guidelines are explained as they apply to individual hotel or restaurant operations, with the primary responsibility resting with the property's chief executive—usually the general manager. The concepts discussed here can be applied at all levels, but the book assumes the viewpoint of the general manager, and the control structure is designed from the GM down through the property.

With the focus on the GM, it follows that the controls are designed for single properties. Although the basic principles for a multi-unit environment are similar, internal control at the chain level is beyond the scope of the book.

Ideal Internal Control. The book is written with the design and presentation of ideal internal control as the primary objective. All principles and concepts are presented in their most ideal form. That is, they are designed for the maximum level of internal control. Constraints, limitations, and trade-offs are discussed, but "ideal" remains the major design criterion, and it is left to you to decide when to back off from maximum control. If you are aware of the ideal control procedures in a given circumstance and the concepts and costs required to build those procedures, you will be in the best possible position to exercise judgment as to the level of control that is cost-effective for your property. At the same time, it is important to understand or measure the risks of backing off from ideal control. Such a level of understanding is also an important objective of the book.

Control-versus-Policy Trade-Off. The application of ideal internal controls often creates conflicts with other managerial policies—such as guest convenience or employee morale. An example might be where ideal control advocates severely limited access to liquor but a less restrictive access policy might make it easier and faster to serve the guests. Top management must confront such trade-offs and make the decision as to where to draw the control line. Such trade-offs are pointed out throughout the book, and discussed as fully as possible, so that management can develop the maximum amount of information before making such decisions.

Size of Operations. The most common trade-off operators will face is perhaps that between the cost of ideal internal control and the resources available for or benefits obtainable from such control. That trade-off is most common in smaller operations. Generally, the smaller the operation, the smaller the resources that are available for good controls—especially in terms of staff! Small operations simply have fewer employees, and, as will be seen in many areas of the book, having sufficient staff over which to spread functions is a basic tenet to good internal control. This problem is pointed out and discussed throughout the book. Generally, as operations get smaller, management must become increasingly involved with internal control procedures—even to the point of hands-on attention.

Coverage

Hotels as the Primary Model. The book uses the hotel as the primary model upon which to discuss and develop internal controls. There was no intention of neglecting such other important segments of the hospitality industry as independent restaurants or clubs. In the author's opinion, hotels provide the most general and complex examples upon which to build internal controls.

The other segments of the industry are either part of or closely related to hotel operations. Hotels contain restaurants, for example, and the internal controls designed for them are similar to those needed in free-standing restaurants. All chapters of the book, with the possible exception of chapter six, rooms income control, are relevant and important to restaurateurs.

For club operators, the entire book is relevant and applicable. Some areas of club management are not specifically covered (e.g., membership and dues management, assessments, pro-shop operations). The application of the principles developed and discussed throughout the book will work well in those areas, however.

In fact, the principles in this book will work well with all control issues encountered by readers, even when operations change because of the diversity of the hospitality industry or new technology. The basic principles of good internal control are sturdy building blocks that can be applied over and over again, even when the terrain changes!

Limited Scope. Like any technical work, the scope of this book is narrow so that its missions of developing, teaching, and implementing good internal controls could be accomplished. In most cases, discussions of detailed accounting or operating procedures were neglected in favor of those for internal controls.

Readers who wish to supplement or extend their knowledge are encouraged to review works on background or technique, such as principles of accounting, food and beverage control, front-office operations, or information systems. There is a selected bibliography at the end of each chapter and a full bibliography at the end of the book. Important references are also pointed out throughout the book via footnotes.

Appendices. The material in the appendices is no less important than that in the bodies of the chapters, but its coverage may be of interest to a smaller group of the readers. The appendices provide background, offer peripheral material, or give extended discussions of topics in the main text.

Acknowledgments

I would like to express my sincere thanks to several people who have provided assistance or support in the development of this book. Several of the partners and staff of the accounting firm Pannell Kerr Forster provided support and technical assistance. William H. Denham encouraged me, supported me, and was instrumental in obtaining the research grant that helped immeasurably in the preparation of this book. Greg Bohan provided encouragement, support, and technical assistance. Greg, as well as Henry A. Freire and Laurel Donnellan, reviewed the manuscript and suggested improvements. Special thanks are also due to the members of the Committee on Financial Management of the AH&MA, many of whom encouraged the work and made useful suggestions. In particular, John E. Nichols, vice president of internal audit for Omni Hotels, reviewed the manuscript and suggested improvements.

Special thanks are due to my editor, Glenn Withiam, of *The Cornell Hotel and Restaurant Administration Quarterly*, for an outstanding job of editing the manuscript. Glenn's knowledge of the hospitality industry, coupled with his superb editing skills, have made this book a far better work than it would have been from my writing alone.

Last, my colleagues at the Cornell University School of Hotel Administration were enormously helpful, providing numerous suggestions and much encouragement. Lorie Paulson, my former secretary, painstakingly transcribed tapes from my lectures in the course on internal control. Those lecture manuscripts were invaluable in writing the book. My most heart-felt thanks, however, are reserved for my students—particularly those who have taken the internal-control course over the years. They provided purpose, encouragement, humor, and innumerable suggestions, anecdotes, and cases. Their enthusiasm and *joie de vivre* are the main reasons I teach!

Finally, I would like to make it clear that any and all opinions expressed in this book are my own, and not those of the Cornell University School of Hotel Administration or *The Cornell H.R.A. Quarterly.—A.N.G.*

Chapter 1

Foundations of Control

Objectives

After completing this chapter, you should understand:

1. **What internal control is.**
2. **The characteristics that make the hospitality industry unique with respect to internal control.**
3. **The general principles that must be applied to ensure a good working environment for proper internal controls.**

What Is Internal Control?

To a hotel operator or manager internal control is the aspect of management that deals with prevention of fraud and embezzlement. Internal control is generally thought of as an accounting function or topic since it often deals with such items as money, records, and documents. The truth is that internal control is very much a function of the general manager and top management, because it deals with all aspects of the operation. Indeed, if a hotel is to develop and implement good internal controls, and thus be reasonably assured that it is preventing theft and embezzlement, top management must be thoroughly involved at all phases.

Here is an official accounting definition of internal control:

> Internal control comprises the plan of organization and all of the coordinate methods and measures adopted within a business to safeguard its assets, check the accuracy and reliability of its accounting data, promote operational efficiency, and encourage adherence to prescribed managerial policies. This definition is possibly broader that the meaning sometimes attributed to the term. It recognizes that a system of internal control extends beyond those matters which relate directly to the functions of the accounting and financial departments. A well-developed system of internal controls might include budgetary controls, standard costs, periodic operating reports, statistical analyses, a personnel training program and an internal audit staff.*

From that rather long-winded definition we can extract four central points that divide into two groups:

Accounting Controls

1. Safeguard assets, and
2. Ensure the accuracy and reliability of accounting data.

Administrative Controls

1. Promote operational efficiency, and
2. Encourage adherence to management's policies.

The purpose of this book is the prevention of fraud and embezzlement, so the controls discussed here will primarily be accounting controls. Administrative controls, particularly those that ensure adherence to managerial policy, are also important for internal control and the prevention of fraud and embezzlement. They entail the set of standard operating procedures (SOPs) that ensure that controls are properly implemented and adhered to. They must follow, however, well-developed accounting controls.

---

*American Institute of Certified Public Accountants (AICPA), Committee on Auditing Procedure, Special Report, 1949.

Conditions for Fraud and Embezzlement

There are three environmental conditions necessary for a fraud or embezzlement to take place. They are:
- Need,
- Opportunity, and
- Failure of conscience.

Need refers to the economic or psychological deficiencies that drive people to steal. It is an area that has received too much misguided attention over the years. Hotel and restaurant operators are constantly admonished to "watch their employees' life-styles" to assess whether they are "living beyond their means." Books on crime have dealt with the subject, even developing catchy phrases like "the three Bs" (booze, bookies, and babes).* I suppose that the advice was that when any employee indulged in one of the "Bs" he or she required special watching. Not only is the "three B" idea sexist and outdated, but it represents foolish advice. All employees, including top management, have economic and other needs. In fact, one could argue that economic needs drive good employees to produce! Focusing on the need condition puts managerial energy in the wrong areas—areas we as managers can do little about.

It is the second condition, *opportunity*, where management can exert some productive influence. If we can preclude the opportunity for stealing, then we can truly prevent fraud and embezzlement. The purpose of this book will be to help you set up accounting functions, revenue functions, cash functions, and other asset functions in such a way that there is no opportunity for theft. Clearly, the best way to prevent theft is to eliminate the opportunity.

The third condition, *failure of conscience*, involves conditions that allow a thief to rationalize the act of stealing. People need to rationalize theft. They need to convince themselves that they are somehow justified in taking what does not belong to them. Unlike economic and psychological needs, however, management can have some indirect influence on this need. That influence comes from creating an environment where it is difficult to rationalize acts against the operation. One way to accomplish this is to apply our internal-control principles firmly but evenly throughout the organization, and having the same rules for top management as for other employees. In this way, we preclude

---

*See: Norman Jaspan, *The Thief in White Collar* (Philadelphia: J.B. Lippincott, 1960).

discriminatory feelings and grumbling on the part of the line staff. If all managers are required to sign a check for food and drink in the same manner any hotel guest would, an atmosphere of control and record-keeping prevails. If management, on the other hand, simply picks up a soft drink or pastry in a casual manner, the atmosphere that prevails may well be one of "the boss takes what he or she wants, why shouldn't I?" Similar situations exist for such issues as steward's sales (when merchandise is sold to staff at reduced rates), searching packages at the door, and punching-in at the time clocks. The important notion is that we apply the rules evenly everywhere, thus precluding one important avenue of rationalization.

In summary, there are three environmental conditions necessary for fraud and embezzlement to take place. The condition upon which management can exert the most influence is opportunity, so it makes the most sense to concentrate on precluding or preventing the opportunity as the key control objective. Most of the principles of control that follow in this book have as their primary goal removing all opportunities for theft.

Hospitality Industry Characteristics

All businesses have areas of weakness and vulnerability to fraud and embezzlement. Hospitality businesses have the same general control weaknesses that affect all enterprises. The hospitality industry has some general operating characteristics that render it relatively more vulnerable to theft, as the following list attests.

- Many cash transactions,
- Small business,
- Relatively low-skill jobs,
- Positions with low social status,
- Items having relatively high value (e.g., wine), and
- Use of commodities.

Cash. Much has been said in the popular and business press of how the world is moving to a "cash-less" society. With the widespread use of hotel charge accounts, credit cards, debit cards, and in the near future, "smart cards," it is true that far less cash changes hands in many hotel transactions. Most hotels today require guests to present a major credit card for registration and for the establishment of credit regardless of how the guest wishes to settle the bill. In spite of that fact, hotels still need to maintain and deal with a great deal of cash. For one thing, the guests expect it. Guests want easy access to cash for tipping, shopping, entertainment and recreation, and for foreign exchange. Most hotels also have numerous revenue outlets that are open for long hours, requiring many more cashier shifts and cash banks than businesses that have a single revenue outlet operating only from nine to five.

Size. Even though many properties are large and many hotels are part of a chain, a hotel operates primarily like a small business. Even large hotels are aggregations of many relatively small revenue outlets. In a large, modern, full-service hotel, the rooms department may be a fairly large revenue center, but there will be many bars, restaurants, and other revenue centers that are individually small operations. Thus, the critical mass or economies of scale that help larger operations with efficiency and control are often lacking.

Job status. A service business that operates 24 hours a day, seven days per week, the hotel industry comprises many unskilled, low-paying jobs. Most revenue dollars are brought in by wait staff, food and beverage cashiers, and front-office clerks. The high turnover and low social status that often comes with that type of employment does little to help the internal-control environment. Automation is raising the skill levels necessary in many of these jobs, but it will be a long time before growth and economic viability raise the overall standard.

Commodities. The items of inventory we use in the hospitality industry are commodities, that is, goods that our employees would normally need and buy for their own consumption. We are, after all, providing lodging and food, and most people need to provide lodging and food for themselves and their families. At the same time, our inventory items are also of high value relative to their size and weight. Seafood, steak, good wine, and other items can have considerable cost and sales value, yet do not take a good deal of space and are easily concealed or consumed.

General Principles of Good Internal Control

Exhibit 1.1 lists ten general principles of internal control. These principles apply to all business enterprises. As I explain them, however, I will particularly point out the way these factors apply to the hospitality industry. In addition to these general principles, there are two mechanical processes that are important in a general way to all

EXHIBIT 1.1
General Principles of Internal Control

1. Maintain division of duties
2. Fix responsibility with one individual
3. Limit the number of employees with access to assets
4. Keep cash banks and stores to a minimum
5. Make internal control preventive, not detective
6. Perform surprise counts by independent employees
7. Bond employees with access to cash, records, or stores
8. Require vacations and rotate employees
9. Schedule frequent external audits
10. Use cost-benefit analysis

internal-control procedures. These are the concepts of the audit trail and accounting documentation, both of which I will also discuss in this chapter.

1. Division of Duties

Division of duties, also referred to as separation of duties and segregation of duties, is the single most important principle of internal control. It is also the most pervasive concept, so I will discuss it specifically in nearly every chapter of this book.

Division of duties is a simple but powerful concept. Here's how it works: No one individual should have total control over any transaction. If there are two or more people involved with each transaction, it would take collusion (i.e., a conspiracy) between those two (or more) persons in order to falsify or otherwise change that transaction. One important way to actuate the principle of division of duties would be to keep the custody of assets separate from the record-keeping or accountability for those assets. In a hotel, we keep cash handling separate from bookkeeping. Front-office cashiers, for example, have constant custody of large sums of cash. Why can't they simply take a handful? Because in a well-controlled operation they have custody of the cash, but they do not have access to or control over the accountability for that cash. Their original bank, or float, is issued by another person who records the amount and shift time of that issue. The individual banks are also recorded in the general ledger by yet another person. The transactions that change the cashier's bank over the shift—e.g., revenue collections—may be posted by the cashier, but are likewise not under his or her total control. As we will see in later chapters, revenue generation and recording, whether in rooms, food and beverage, or other areas, are fairly complex transactions involving several persons. So, our cashier has custody and access, but cannot control the accountability. An income auditor may have access to the audit trail and accountability, but should not have access to the cash. As transactions get more complicated, there are usually more and more people involved, making collusion more and more difficult.

The essential preventative role that division of duties plays is that when there are several people involved in a transaction (i.e., no one person has complete control) then collusion becomes a necessary condition to fraud or embezzlement. Collusion is a difficult and fragile process to achieve. When two or more people must collude to perpetrate a fraud, the probability of that fraud's coming to fruition is far smaller than if one of the individuals had complete control.

Limitations. Division of duties, by itself, is not sufficient to prevent internal-control problems. The division must be an effective one. If a hotel puts two relatives (or two life-long friends) on a transaction, the separation may not be effective. Division of duties also can be expensive, and I generally do not recommend adding staff strictly for the sake of accomplishing it. As I wrote in the preface, when operations are small and effective division of duties may be difficult to cost justify, management must assume more of the duties. If duties must be combined, moreover, such combination should involve management personnel. More discussion of that concept will appear in later chapters.

Division of duties must be combined with other principles to yield effective internal controls. In the chapters that follow, where specific internal-control principles are discussed, division of duties will appear again—usually as the first item of discussion—and the specific divisions of tasks will be explained.

2. Fix Responsibility in One Individual

Where practical, responsibility for a given activity should always be designated to a single individual. In that way, the person can be informed of his or her responsibilities, be given a set of standard operating procedures, and be expected to adhere to them. If the responsibility is given solely to one individual, then management knows where to start looking when there is a problem. This principle should also be viewed from the employees' perspective, however. The employees are held responsible for assets or actions, so they need the conditions to allow them to carry out their responsibilities. For example, a front-office cashier should be solely and fully responsible for his or her bank. Consequently, no one but that individual should have access to that bank. No sharing of banks! No sharing of custody! It is unfair to make a person responsible for a bank and then give others access to it.

3. Limit the Number of Employees with Access to Assets

The more people with access to cash or merchandise inventories the greater the risk of losses—whether by actual theft, or by simple mismanagement. This principle is common sense. The principle also fits well with the one above: fixing responsibility. Responsibility for an asset cannot be fixed to a single individual (or the smallest group) if there is unlimited access to the asset. Limiting access, however, has some operational trade-offs.

4. Keep Cash Banks and Stores to a Minimum

The principle of keeping banks and inventories to a minimum improves control perspective in much the same way as limited access does: namely, it lowers the risk. It also has the added advantage of fitting very well with the modern management tools of cash management and inventory management. Those concepts help lower costs and increase profits by the scientific management of cash and other assets.*

Minimizing cash banks and stores and limiting access to them, however, will force management to make operational trade-offs. I call these "control/policy trade-offs," a term we will encounter throughout the book and a recurring problem in the field of internal control. A

---

*See, for example: Raymond S. Schmidgall, *Management Accounting for the Hospitality Industry,* Second Edition (East Lansing, MI: Educational Institute, American Hotel & Motel Association, 1991).

conflict or trade-off often exists between good internal controls and operating policy—especially operating policy that is geared toward good guest service and ease of operation. While limiting access and minimizing stores provide better control, those procedures may make it more difficult or complicated to provide excellent and fast service. For example, we are more likely to run out of a guest's favorite brandy if we minimize stock. And then we'll compound the problem by requiring several signatures, including that of the general manager, to gain entry to the liquor storeroom for another bottle! Similarly, minimizing the size of cash banks makes sense from a control perspective, but the hotel's image may suffer if a clerk needs to tell a guest that he or she does not currently have enough cash in the drawer to change a $100 bill!

Thus, a trade-off often exists between ideal control and the policies of management that may have as objectives good or fast service, good employee relations, or simple cost savings. We will encounter such trade-offs frequently in this book, and I will discuss them as they arise. The general rule, however, is to strive for the most ideal control and then have management modify the control procedures as necessary. Management must always be aware, however, of the increased control risks involved in stepping away from ideal controls.

5. Make Internal Control Preventive—Not Detective

The nature of internal control and the fact that it deals with frauds and embezzlement—crimes for sure—lead a lot of managers to want to play detective. After all, if you are concerned that your employees are stealing from you, you want to catch the thieves! There is nothing wrong with a wish to ferret out and punish thieves. A far more effective program, however, is one that prevents the thefts in the first place. Remember that the primary objective of an internal-control program is to preclude the opportunity for theft. That is prevention, and in the long run it is far more productive and cost effective than detection. In fact, with the proper prevention, there will be nothing to detect! Throughout the balance of the book, I will make prevention my primary goal. You'll see, however, that this goal can also cause some conflicts.

6. Perform Surprise Counts by Independent Employees

Surprise counts of cashier shifts, merchandise, storeroom inventories, and bars should be performed frequently enough so that they become expected. The word "surprise" refers to the exact timing and location of the counts. They are random, but not unexpected. In fact, if the counts were truly unexpected, they would be in direct conflict with the principle that internal control should be preventive not detective. The fact that surprise counts are made frequently and are written up in job descriptions and SOPs is what turns a normally detective endeavor into a preventive one. Cash-handling, inventory-handling, and accounting employees should expect surprise counts or shut-downs of their shifts on a random basis. Obviously, if such counts were made systematically, they would be useless. For example, if you count the cash bank in the rooftop bar every fourth Thursday of the month precisely at 4:00 PM, you can almost guarantee that it will be fine! The random counts should be performed by independent employees who do not normally count that cash or take that inventory. It is a good idea, for instance, for top management to get involved occasionally with this important part of the internal-control program.

7. Bond Employees with Access to Cash, Records, and Stores

All accounting, cash-handling, inventory-handling, and top-management employees should be bonded through an insurance policy called a "fidelity bond." A fidelity bond is a type of insurance that protects the hotel against losses from employee dishonesty. Like fire insurance, when the hotel experiences a loss, the bonding company reimburses it for the amount of the loss (up to the limits of the policy). In fidelity bonding, the losses are those related to employee dishonesty.

In addition to loss recovery, fidelity bonding is a strong deterrent to fraud and embezzlement by employees. That aspect, other characteristics of fidelity bonding, and the legal environment in general are discussed in greater detail in Appendix 1.1, at the end of this chapter.

8. Schedule Mandatory Vacations and Rotate Employees

It is a good idea to establish mandatory vacations as part of the hotel's personnel policies. Aside from the human-resources issues, this policy has important internal-control implications. Particularly for accounting, cash-handling, and other clerical employees, the idea that at some time in the year they must relinquish their work to someone else is a healthy one. It allows fresh perspectives to surface, and sometimes uncovers unhealthy or weak situations. In many of the cases of actual frauds and embezzlements that I am familiar with, the fraud's discovery took place when someone unexpectedly left his or her duties. Many of these cases of internal-control failure appear throughout the book. That notion sounds detective rather than preventive, but if mandatory vacations are SOP, they will, indeed, be preventive.

A comparable procedure involves the rotation of employees where it is feasible. Cashier, clerk, and other clerical positions are generally good candidates for rotation. Some of the same benefits are obtained as those stemming from mandatory vacations. Additionally, the rotated employees have a chance to experience a wider sample of the hotel's operations. There are sometimes difficulties with rotation as skill requirements are not necessarily interchangeable. Where practical, though, rotation is a useful part of an overall internal-control program.

9. Conduct Frequent External Audits

It is essential to have frequent independent audits performed by an external audit firm. The independence and objectivity brought to the audit process by an outside auditor are extremely valuable. It is also important for the top management of the hotel—the general manager and the controller, for example—to discuss the state of the hotel's internal controls with the outside auditors. As part of their audit process, outside auditors assess the general strength or weakness of the operation's internal controls. This assessment is one of the ways in which auditors determine the scope of their audit. It is a good idea for management to ask for feedback on that process, and to use that information to improve apparent weaknesses.

It is also important to recognize that having external audits means neither that the hotel is fraud-proof nor that all frauds and embezzlements will be discovered. The objectives of the outside auditor are much broader than fraud detection alone. Those objectives, the procedures, and the implications of audits—both external and internal—are discussed in much more detail in Chapter 10. Although outside audits do not guarantee that a hotel is fraud-proof, they are a strongly recommended part of the overall internal-control program.

10. Use Cost-Benefit Analysis

This final principle is an important one: internal-control programs must be subject to the same cost-benefit analysis as any other investment or part of the hotel operation. To be feasible, the cost of internal-control procedures should be lower than their benefits. The problem with that type of analysis for internal control is that the benefits are hard to measure. The costs are usually fairly cut and dried, but the benefits are stated in terms of possible or anticipated losses prevented. If all works well, we will experience no losses, yet we must estimate what fraud or embezzlement exposure we face so as to project anticipated benefits of internal control. Cost-benefit analysis is essential because it is easy for internal-control programs to run up high costs—particularly for the labor required to obtain proper division of duties and to maintain checks and balances. Management, therefore, must do its best to cost justify all control programs.

Building Blocks of Internal Control

The Audit Trail

The audit trail is defined as a reference in an accounting transaction to an underlying source or document. For auditing and internal control, the audit trail is more than simply a reference. It is a trail in the true sense of a path or road of the history of accounting transactions that can be followed, mapped, recreated, or traced. It consists of all of the evidence of the transactions including their source documents. Source documents can be documents dealing with external parties (e.g., invoices, guest checks) or strictly internal documents (e.g., vouchers, journals, ledgers).

It is convenient to think of an audit trail schematically as a circular path that traces all transactions from their inception to their conclusion. In an accounting sense, the trail leads from the point of occurrence to the financial statements. It consists of processes as well as source documents. Such a trail is pictured in Exhibit 1.2, using rooms revenue as an example.

An auditor needs to be able to enter the circle at any point and move in either direction to reconstruct transactions. If any source document or transaction-processing point is missing or becomes otherwise unreadable, it should be possible to reconstruct the entire transaction by moving around the circle in both directions. That procedure and the evidentiary documentation it implies are invaluable to good internal controls.

EXHIBIT 1.2

An Audit Trail for Rooms Revenue

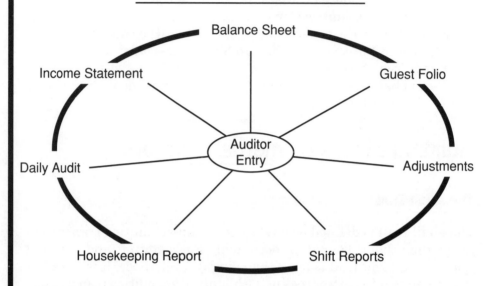

The audit trail is, in effect, a circular series of transaction documents. An auditor can enter the circle at any point and move in either direction, using one document to verify or reconstruct the information in another document.

Accounting Documents

The principle of accounting documents is an important concept that is pervasive throughout internal control. The following are the key characteristics that describe most accounting documents.

- They are numbered serially;
- They have multiple parts or copies;
- Their distribution is controlled by the accounting department; and
- They must be accounted for periodically by serial number.

Serial numbers are exactly what the name implies. Each document is printed with a number one step higher than the one preceding it, so that the individual documents can be accounted for. The concept of unique serial numbers is a critical attribute of the audit trail and the audit process. It is particularly important with revenue documents.

Having **multiple parts** or copies is also a straightforward concept. Most accounting documents are printed in duplicate or triplicate. Some may have as many as six or seven copies. The number of copies necessary will vary with the process. I will discuss the numbers of parts needed for different transactions in the relevant sections of the book.

Distributed by accounting. Accounting documents are under the control of the accounting department regardless of the fact that they are used by other departments. The accounting department orders the documents, specifies their design (in consultation, of course, with the users), assigns numbers, receives them, inventories them, stores them, and issues them to user departments. The documents should be issued to user departments in blocks with a permanent record of the serial numbers issued. Final copies ("back copies" or "hard copies"), in most cases, will be returned to accounting for audit and filing.

Accounting, then, is charged with the cradle-to-grave responsibility for these documents, as implied by their final attribute, **accounted for periodically** by serial number. The accounting department has recorded the serial numbers at receipt, in inventory, at issue, and at final turn-in. Periodically, in most cases monthly, the integrity of the numerical sequence must be verified. This is accomplished by a combination of inventory and audit. Specific examples will appear throughout the book.

Appendix 1.1:

Fidelity Bonding

Using fidelity bonding is one of the general principles of internal control. In this appendix, I will explain those aspects of a hotel's legal environment that increase the importance of fidelity bonding. The characteristics of the general types of bonds and the advantages of

The legal environment governs what hotels may and may not do in terms of personnel policies for screening and testing their employees. A partial list of those practices (in alphabetical order) that pertain to internal-control protection are:

- Bonding,
- Fingerprinting,
- Lie-detector tests,
- Questions about prior criminal record,
- Search of packages, and
- Search of persons.

With two exceptions, bonding and search of packages, most of the above items may not be practiced by hotels. *Fingerprinting* of employees, as a condition of employment, is not legal.

Lie detectors are extremely unreliable, and such testing may not be used as a condition of employment. In fact, recent legislation makes it illegal for private firms even to perform lie detector tests on their employees. *Questions about prior criminal record* generally may not be asked as part of the application or screening process. With probable cause, a hotel may check into prior records but may only ask about convictions. That is, you may not ask whether a person has been arrested. Since probable cause would be difficult to presume with prospective employees, questions about prior convictions are not useful as screening devices.

You are allowed to *search packages* as they leave the hotel, under the doctrine known as "rule of the house." Rule of the house means that the hotel establishes a rule whereby all packages that leave the hotel are subject to opening and search. The key word is "all," and internal control is better served if everyone—from the general manager down—is subject to the same rules. While the practice of searching packages is allowable, I recommend that you eliminate the need for such searches by not allowing steward's sales. Steward's sales are a nice benefit to employees, but can create internal-control problems beyond their value to employees. It is better to negotiate with other businesses to offer discounts for employees.

Search of person is another matter completely. Generally, persons may not be searched without probable cause. If probable cause does exist (e.g., a theft has taken place and some employees are suspected), the hotel management is well recommended not to get involved with searches or any other investigatory acts. Instead, call the police. Hotel managers should not hesitate to bring in the police to do any investigations—searches included. Incidentally, the law holds that purses are part of person, and are not packages. So, while packages may be searched, purses may not be. That fact has caused some hotels to make rules about the size and type of employees' purses.

The bottom line is that hotels are not allowed to maintain most of these practices as conditions of employment or as screening tools, except for search of packages, which is not a screening device anyway. In contrast, bonding is perfectly legal as a condition of employment. In other words, a hotel can require fidelity bonding for individuals holding any of its positions. The hotel must purchase a bond for each employee or position, but the burden of "being bondable" is at that point placed on each individual seeking employment. Bonding companies have wider latitude and greater access to information about criminal backgrounds and other screening data than hotel companies do. Moreover, these firms are very professional at the task and accomplish it far better than a hotel could. Bonding companies also share data with each other so that a person who is found ineligible to receive a bond from one company because of a prior fraud will find himself or herself ineligible with any bonding company.

Bonding companies also practice a rule called "prosecution as a matter of course." That means that they will always prosecute a fraud—regardless of whether restitution is offered or other "plea-bargaining" takes place. That practice is important as a strong deterrent to fraud and embezzlement. If employees know that bonding companies will always prosecute, they will be more reluctant to steal. Hotels, when operating on their own, may be reluctant to prosecute because of negative publicity and because they hope for restitution of the stolen money. Of course, with bonding, the hotel gets its money back anyway!

Fidelity bonding, then, confers three important advantages upon hotels:

1. The chance for recovery of stolen funds;

2. A deterrent to embezzlement; and

3. Greater latitude in screening.

The chief disadvantage to fidelity bonding is its cost. That cost will depend on the company, the hotel's geographic location, the experience of the industry in that region, the types of positions covered, the type of bond, and the amount of coverage. The individual hotel has control only over the last three items, with the amount of coverage being the most flexible. Hotels must weigh the positions to be covered and the amount of coverage against the cost of each. The final decision must be based on an analysis of costs and benefits.

Bonds are available in two general types: individual and position. They can be single (i.e., for each person or each position) or they can be purchased in groups, known as "schedules." Blanket bonds, which cover all employees in a particular hotel, are also available. The broader the coverage, the more expensive the bond. Blanket bonds, therefore, are expensive, but sometimes they are useful when purchased with a small limit (one or two thousand dollars per employee, for example).

For accounting and cash-handling positions, where larger amounts of coverage are required, position or name bonds are more practical. Position bonds are usually more expensive per dollar of coverage than name bonds, because the hotel has more flexibility in filling the positions and the bonding company has a correspondingly larger risk. The amount of coverage for each position also requires careful study. Attempts should be made to calculate average exposure, as it is usually too expensive to insure for peak exposure.

There are also rules for documentation, timing of losses, and many other key factors. For those reasons and because this book has just scratched the surface of fidelity bonding, while ignoring other insurance and risk management completely, readers are urged to discuss fidelity and theft insurance in detail with experts provided by their insurance agent or carrier. There are also some selected references in the bibliography that deal with casualty insurance and risk management.

Glossary

Accounting Controls—Procedures that are concerned with safeguarding assets and ensuring the accuracy and reliability of financial records.

Accounting Documents—Forms that are numbered serially, have multiple parts or copies, whose distribution is controlled by the accounting department, and are accounted for periodically by serial number.

Administrative Controls—Procedures to ensure operational efficiency and adherence to management's policies.

Audit Trail—The path or road (consisting of entries and accounting documents) of history left by accounting transactions, which can be followed, mapped, recreated, or traced.

Cash Management—A systematic and scientific approach to the control of inflow, outflow, borrowing, and investment of cash and other short-term assets so as to minimize cost and maximize return.

Control/Policy Trade-Off—A description of the conflict that develops between ideal internal control and management's operating policies. Often one can be improved only at the expense of the other.

Custody of Assets—Having physical control or guardianship of assets; also used in the context of having responsibility for the assets.

Deterrence—The process of preventing, discouraging, or inhibiting an act, usually by intimidation or fear of the consequences.

Division of Duties—The segregation or separation of tasks among several employees so that no single individual has complete control over an entire transaction or process.

Embezzlement—The act of an employee or other insider fraudulently converting property to his or her own use; employee theft.

External Audits—Having the firm's accounting books and documents periodically examined by an outside accounting firm.

Fidelity Bond—A casualty-insurance policy that insures the firm against employee dishonesty.

Float—In the internal-control context, the original stake or initial cash given to a cashier for use in his or her shift. In a cash-management context, to describe the difference in cash balances between the company's books and the bank's books.

Fraud—The intentional distortion of the truth to acquire property that belongs to another; the intent to deceive; trickery.

Internal Control—The methods and measures adopted within a business to safeguard its assets, check the accuracy and reliability of its accounting data, promote operational efficiency, and encourage adherence to prescribed managerial policies.

Inventory Management—A systematic and scientific approach to the purchasing, storing, and issuing of inventories so as to minimize cost and maximize return.

Opportunity—In the current context, a set of circumstances allowing or facilitating embezzlement.

Probable Cause—A reasonable ground for supposing that a criminal charge is well-founded.

Rationalize—To find reasons that theft or fraud would be reasonable or appropriate.

Record Keeping—The process, usually attributed to a hotel's accounting office or department, of analyzing data and making entries or recording transactions into the accounting records.

Standard Operating Procedures (SOPs)—Methods of completing tasks and functions within the operation that have become routine or have been stated in formal rules.

Steward's Sales—A procedure whereby hotels sell products to their own employees so that the employees obtain the benefit of better quality or lower price.

Trade-Off—A balance. In this case, the balance between committing scarce resources and achieving optimum internal control.

Selected References

Bruce H. Axler, *Security for Hotels, Motels, and Restaurants* (New York: ITT Educational Publishing, 1974).

W.B. Connolly, Jr., and M.J. Connolly, *A Practical Guide to Equal Employment Opportunity* (Law Journal Seminars Press, 1989), Vol. 1, Ch. 2, Sec. 2.01-2.02

Bob Curtis, *Security Control: Internal Theft (3rd Printing)* (New York: Chain Store Publishing Corp., 1977)

Davidson, Stickney, and Weil, *Accounting: The Language of Business (4th Edition)* (Glen Ridge, NJ: Thomas Horton & Daughters, 1979)

Philip Gordis and Edward A. Chlanda, *Property and Casualty Insurance* (New York: Rough Notes Co., 1982).

Mark R. Greene and James S. Treischmann, *Risk and Insurance (7th Edition)* (Cincinnati: Southwestern Publishing, 1988).

Roger H. Hermanson, James Don Edwards, and R.F. Salmonson, *Accounting Principles (1987 Special Edition)* (Plano, TX: Business Publications, Inc., 1987).

Norman Jaspan, *The Thief in the White Collar* (Philadelphia: J.B. Lippincott Co., 1960).

Raymond S. Schmidgall, *Management Accounting for the Hospitality Industry(Second Edition)* (East Lansing, MI: Educational Institute of the American Hotel & Motel Association, 1991).

John E.H. Sherry, *Legal Aspects of Foodservice Management* (New York: John Wiley & Sons, 1984), Ch. 6, pp. 90-92.

John E.H. Sherry, *The Laws of Innkeepers (Revised Edition)* (Ithaca, NY: Cornell University Press, 1981).

Wanda A. Wallace, *Handbook of Internal Accounting Controls* (Englewood Cliffs, NJ: Prentice-Hall, 1984).

C. Arthur Williams, Jr., and Richard M. Heins, *Risk Management and Insurance (6th Edition)* (New York: McGraw-Hill, 1989).

Chapter 2

Cash Receipts

Objectives

After completing this chapter, you should understand:

1. **The principles for the proper receipt of cash.**
2. **The head cashier's function.**
3. **Proper mail-receipt procedure.**
4. **Check-cashing procedure.**
5. **Procedures for turn-in and banking.**

What Are Cash Receipts?

If I were writing this book using strictly accounting terms, I would title this chapter "revenue receipts" or "revenue operations" since the processes I will describe involve controlling the taking-in and recording of all the hotel's receipts. A modern hotel receives payment for its services in a variety of ways: cash, checks, credit and charge cards, and by directly billing its customers—referred to as accounts receivable. Hereafter, when I refer to "cash receipts" I am referring to the broader meaning of all the hotel's receipts.

In this chapter, I will focus on the receipt side of revenue transactions. In later chapters on rooms revenue and food and beverage revenue, I will discuss controlling the revenue-generation side of the transactions.

Principles

Division of Duties. The most important control device for cash receipts is division of duties. As I explained in Chapter 1, any employee with cash-handling responsibilities should not have access to the bookkeeping or other accountability functions for that cash. Likewise, bookkeeping or other accounting employees should not have access to cash. By structuring your operation this way, you maintain the overall principle that no single employee has control over the entire transaction.

Head-Cashier Function. Every hotel should have a head cashier to act as the chief cash-handling employee. The head cashier is in charge of all cashiers, pick-up and turn-in of banks and shifts, custody of the cash banks, maintenance of point-of-sale and credit-card devices, scheduling of cashier hours, and all of the physical aspects of banking—preparing deposits, requesting change, and supervising the transit.

In an ideal world, that person is completely independent of the accounting department. In practice, however, the accounting department is often in charge of cashiers and cash handling. At minimum, the head cashier reports to the controller or other top accounting officer. Since the world is rarely ideal, most hotels will have to live with some reduction in division of duties in these functions. In larger organizations, it is acceptable for the head cashier to report to the controller as long as there are other accounting executives without cash-handling responsibilities that also report to him or her. In smaller organizations, someone from management—an assistant manager or resident manager—should assume the duties of the head cashier.

The important issue in all cases is that the separation between cash handling and bookkeeping must be maintained. The specific method by which that division is accomplished can vary according to your organizational structure and resources.

Limit Access to Receipts. Cash and other receipts should be strictly limited to *bona fide* cashier stations. In most hotels, that means the front-office or food and beverage cashiers. In larger or more complex hotels, there may be such revenue centers as a garage or golf course that could also have cashier stations. Receipts for receivables and deposits for advance bookings coming in the mail can be controlled with the adoption of the mail procedure discussed below. The key issue in restricting receipts to *bona fide* cashiers and the mail is the maintenance of the division of duties between cash handling and record keeping. If cash receipts are limited to the cashiers, there will be no opportunity for record-keeping employees or others to have access to cash.

Mail Procedure. All mail should be opened by someone other than a cashier or a person with accounting responsibilities. Large organizations may have a mail department, but in most hotels the mail should be opened under the control of the general manager (usually his or her secretary) and then routed to the relevant departments. The key control matter involves payments received. Checks or other payments received in the mail should be listed (in modern practice that means photocopied) and sent directly to the head cashier for deposit at the bank. Thus, another potential means of access to cash by accounting or other record-keeping employees who should not have such access is avoided. Two copies of the checks received should be made—one sent to accounts receivable for posting, and one to the auditor or general-ledger bookkeeper for verification and audit.

Deposit Receipts Intact Daily. The head cashier should deposit each day's receipts intact daily. By intact, I mean that the amount turned in by each cashier shift is discrete and identifiable. For practical reasons, turn-ins can be aggregated as long as there are adequate records to verify each turn-in separately. The total of the day's receipts, however, must remain intact. That is, one day's receipts cannot be aggregated with those from another day, but rather they must be deposited daily. If geography or other factors make daily deposit impossible, the daily receipts should be left intact and deposited in a batch as soon as possible.

Aside from the obvious cash-management and interest-earning issues, there are strong internal-control reasons for depositing receipts daily. Allowing several days' receipts to accumulate at the hotel permits the opportunity for the type of fraud known as "lapping." In lapping, the perpetrator "borrows" from one day's receipts to cover shortages in another. Typically, lappings occur at the end of the month. An employee may have "borrowed" money for personal use. If several days' receipts are available at the end of the month, the employee can borrow from the future, effectively close the month without detection, and be safe until the end of the next month. Of course he or she must repeat the process on each successive month—unless the money is paid back. Depositing each day's receipts intact daily prevents the opportunity for such lapping.

Another procedure that can help prevent lapping in both cash receipts and cash disbursements is occasionally to request "cut-off" bank statements from your hotel's bank. Banks typically prepare and send business bank statements at the end of the calendar month. Such statements record all deposits and withdrawals for the full month. For a cut-off statement, the bank prepares an additional statement for a portion of the month—say, at the fifteenth or twentieth of the month. The cut-off statement should be sent directly to management, out of the normal channels of distribution. If an employee is practicing lapping, a cut-off statement will clearly show the shortages. The major problem with cut-off bank statements is that they are detective not preventive. If the procedure is practiced routinely and consistently, however, it can become preventive. Most external auditors require cut-off statements as a regular part of their audit procedure.

Point-of-Sale Devices. Cash registers or other point-of-sale (POS) devices should always be used to record sales and receipts of cash and other payments. The hotel should never allow a cash-box operation. In the chapter on food and beverage revenue, I will discuss the implications of modern, electronic point-of-sale devices. It is sufficient here to point out that modern technology has made available fairly sophisticated and quite inexpensive devices to act as cash and revenue registers. They should be used for all occasions!

Three important principles govern the use of POS devices:

- Totals should be permanently locked (never cleared);
- Shift readings should be taken by an accounting (not cash-handling) employee and recorded indelibly; and
- Independent readings should be taken periodically.

The issue of permanently locking totals is best understood with the example of older, but still popular, mechanical cash registers. Those devices typically have several keys—for operation, for taking readings, and to "zero-out" the register. My advice is to throw away the "Z" or zero-out key. Daily or shift totals can be calculated by reading the register, recording the amount, and subtracting the earlier shift's reading to arrive at the current shift totals. While it may seem easier simply to total the machine, record the number, and set it back to zero for the next shift, the internal-control dangers far outweigh the expediency.

There are four control reasons to read a register but never clear its totals. First, an employee with access to a "Z" key could actually re-create a fictitious tape to cover up a theft. The idea is a bit bizarre, but it's been known to happen.

Second, a permanent audit trail is created when you simply read the machine. If you zero the register, you effectively destroy any audit trail. Auditors—internal, external, or governmental—greatly prefer a permanent audit trail. It allows re-creation if documents are lost, and vastly simplifies the verification process.

Third, when the register is never cleared, the would-be embezzler is forced to carry any of his or her manipulations forward. If some peculation is performed in the cash-receipts function, it will become part of the permanent record—making ultimate discovery more probable and, hence, thievery riskier.

Finally, clearing registers renders independent readings useless. The purpose of taking independent readings is to give management an opportunity for further checks on the system and for additional decision-making information. A manager or the controller might take a reading once a month or once a week. To use that reading, you subtract from it the figures from the last independent reading and you have a total for the interval. For example, if you took an independent reading six days ago and take another one today, you can subtract the six-day-old reading from the current one and you get a total for the six days. That six-day total can be compared with recorded revenue or bank deposits for the six days, giving an excellent and independent control check. When registers are cleared, that entire process is precluded and the notion of independent readings is rendered useless!

Daily shift readings should be taken by an accounting employee and not a cashier or room manager. The primary reason for this policy is to maintain a division of duties, but developing an audit trail and ensuring proper recording of revenue also play important roles. The primary source of revenue that is recorded in sales journals comes from

POS-device readings. Detailed source documents like guest checks and register tapes are important for verification and audit, but the actual revenue record comes from the readings. That record then plays important accounting and internal-control roles when cash receipts, accounts receivable, and costs are compared to it.

The advent of the modern electronic point-of-sale device may modify some of these procedures. The general rule, in my opinion, is that these newer machines increase accounting and internal-control opportunities for management, and thus their development has been a positive step for our industry.

Check Cashing and Exchange

Most hotels find that they need to cash personal and traveler's checks for the convenience of their guests. Guests expect that service. They are by definition away from home when staying at a hotel, and they have previously established credit upon check-in. Any hotel managers who have a policy of never cashing their guests' checks might wish to skip the next two sections of the book. We are assuming, however, that most hotels do cash checks and need a safe and effective internal-control policy for dealing with the process.

Never Cash a Check Made Out to the Hotel! Few rules in this book are "golden rules" in the sense that they are never to be violated. This is one such rule, however. Never exchange a check that is made out to the hotel for cash. Checks made out to the hotel are presumed to be for goods, services, or payments for past indebtedness. They should be deposited in the bank accounts of the hotel. This principle seems simple enough, and it is the route that most checks travel. The danger lies in creating a process whereby checks can be converted to cash. In most businesses, including retail operations that accept checks for payment of goods and services, checks are not cashed for the customer. If checks need to be cashed for the customers' convenience, then we establish a separate process for converting checks to cash. If a single check made out to the hotel is cashed or allowed into this process, then any checks made out to the hotel could slip in. The best single way to avoid the dangers—and over time many individuals in the hotel will have ample access to checks made out to the hotel—is never to allow such checks to be cashed. We want to isolate checks that we may cash for the convenience of our guests from all other checks.

The best way to accomplish that isolation, and to do so with a clear audit trail, is through the process that follows.

Check-Cashing Procedures

- Have the guest make the check out to "Cash";
- Ask the guest to endorse the back of the check;
- Immediately stamp the back to end negotiability;
- Post the transaction to a permanent record; and
- Clear cashed checks each shift by the "Exchange Process."

Checks made out to "Cash." At first look, the notion of checks made out to "cash" appears shocking, if not dangerous. It must be remembered that the danger is not in checks made out to cash, but in cashing checks made out to the hotel! We avoid that danger and create the isolation we want for checks cashed for convenience by having them made out to "cash." It is a good idea for hotels to limit check cashing to the front-office cashiers. When this process takes place at a *bona fide* cashier station—where cash of all denominations is kept and handled— a check made out to "cash" is no more dangerous than a $100 bill! In fact it is less dangerous because we can end the check's negotiability by stamping it "for deposit only." No such device exists to protect the $100 bill.

Guest's endorsement. Before the guest is given his or her cash, the cashier should request that the guest endorse the back of the check. The check has been made out to "cash" and the guest's signature on the back is evidence that the guest received cash for the check and that the check was not for the payment of goods, services, or indebtedness. This part of the process protects the hotel from the type of fraud perpetrated on the hotel by guests whereby the guest receives cash for a check and later claims the check was in payment for services. This type of fraud is extremely rare but the prevention technique is simple and relatively painless.* Again, the more serious danger comes not from cashing guests' legitimate convenience checks, but from checks that should be for payment being fraudulently cashed.

Immediately stamp the back. Good cashier training should include the habit of immediately stamping all checks with the hotel's "deposit only" rubber stamp. That act ends the negotiability of the

---

*In the many cases I have seen, only one fraud of this type has been detected. See Case 2.1.

check, and, with a properly designed stamp, ensures that the check will end up in the correct bank account.

Post to a permanent record. It is a good control practice to set up a permanent audit trail of all check-cashing transactions. Various methods work well—separate check-cashing cards, the back of the folio, the back of the registration card, or the computer file in fully automated front offices. Many of the automated systems do not have such a separate capability, and the transaction must be treated as a "paid-out." The author prefers not to use paid-outs for convenience check cashing, and recommends the back of the registration card in those cases. All that is necessary is a simple grid or matrix to contain the date, the amount, and the clerk's initials. The guest information and credit history are already part of the front of the card. The back of the card is also a convenient place to emboss the guest's credit card for credit verification and signature-on-file purposes. Some of the credit-card companies guarantee their members' checks when cashed. I'll discuss these matters further in the chapter on rooms-income control.

Clear checks from the shift bank by exchange. The process of clearing these cashed checks is an important one. First, as checks are cashed for our guests' convenience we deplete the cash in the cashier's bank, and it will need replenishment. Second, as was stressed earlier, we want to ensure that only convenience checks have been cashed. A process that we will call the "exchange process" will accomplish both of these objectives.

The head cashier processes the various shift cashiers' turn-ins (discussed in more detail in the next section). In that process, the head cashier records the turn-in, prepares a revenue report for the audit staff, prepares the bank deposit, replenishes the original bank with useful denominations, and checks any discrepancies. The process also requires removing any "exchange" items (checks and traveler's checks that have been cashed) and replenishing an equivalent amount of cash. The term "exchange" is used because the items are not new revenue, nor payment of past indebtedness, but rather items we cashed for the guest. We exchanged the guest's check for cash to the guest, and now we have to exchange it again to replace the cash we gave out. The way we accomplish that is to deposit those checks (remember they were stamped "for deposit only") in the hotel's bank account, and draw a check called an "exchange check" that we cash at the bank. That cash replenishes what was consumed by cashing guest checks. It sounds complicated, but it really is not. It's a fairly simple process—we cash

Case 2.1

Cancelled Checks Are Poor Witnesses

The following incident occurred in a city-center hotel:

A party of two persons registered with an abundance of baggage and presented to the manager a letter of credit. The restaurant and other departments in the hotel were well-patronized by the couple, and purchases were charged to their front-office account. Theater tickets and other non-hotel items were also paid for by the hotel on their behalf and charged to their guest folio.

On the second day of their visit, they requested that a check for $100 be cashed. This request was granted, and the check was verified by the bank; thereafter, the couple cashed checks about every other day, and the hotel advanced cash to them several times, as it seemed that their credit was good.

The couple stayed ten days, and their bill amounted to $2,640.50. At check-out, they requested that the bill be mailed to their address as given on the register. This was done. A week later, the hotel received a letter stating that the bill had been paid and that the writer held cancelled bank checks as evidence.

The hotel brought suit for collection. In court, the former guest produced a number of checks made to the order of the hotel and endorsed by the hotel, totalling $2,640.50, the amount of the couple's city-ledger account. As these checks showed no evidence that cash had been received for them, the court's decision upheld the defendants' claim that their cancelled checks were sufficient evidence of payment of the account.

Discussion

This is the only case I am familiar with (out of dozens) where the guest was the perpetrator, and the check-cashing mechanism was used directly to effect the fraud (front-end rather than back-end!)

The court had to realize that the guests were ripping off the hotel, but its hands were tied in that the hard evidence was all against the hotel. The guests had established credit, and, in fact, were good credit risks. They were just wise guys who intentionally took advantage of weak controls at the hotel.

The hotel should have had a check-cashing procedure that required the checks cashed for guests be made out to cash—to distinguish them from checks for payment for goods or services and to flag them as having been cashed. Also, the guests should have been required to endorse the back—as direct evidence that they received the cash. This last item, alone, would have brought the opposite verdict in the court. Finally, a permanent audit trail should have been established for checks cashed by entries to the registration card, or similar form, and through the exchange-deposit mechanism discussed here.

someone's check, deposit that check in our bank account, and withdraw a check to "cash," which we then cash at the bank to "pay us back." The exchange check that we draw on the hotel's bank account should be made out to "cash–exchange." It is a good idea to formalize the process, in advance, with the hotel's bank, and to use the opportunity to remind the bank, in writing, that it is never to cash checks made out to the hotel.

The advantages of the process far outweigh the small amount of extra time the head cashier and management may spend on the process. A permanent audit trail is established allowing us to trace all checks cashed and all cash movement within the hotel's cash banks. When the head cashier makes up the bank deposit, he or she lists (including the duplicate deposit slip) and deposits the exchange items separately. The head cashier is also responsible for drawing (or requesting, in more complex operations with separate payables systems) the replenishment or exchange check. Management's role is to verify the documentation and sign that check. In the case of exchanges, the documentation consists of the exchange items prepared for bank deposit. Management should look them over, verify that they are all legitimate exchange items, and make sure no checks made out to the hotel have slipped in. This additional step affords some extra division of duties and serves as a check on the head cashier.

The hotel accountant will also need to record the exchange trans- actions in the cash-receipts journals in much the same way that all other cash receipts are recorded. The difference is that a ledger account called "exchange" is used. That account is a wash account. It is credited when the exchange items are deposited, and debited when the re- plenishment check is drawn. It always ends up with a zero balance.

A concluding note on the exchange topic is in order. The process may seem somewhat cumbersome—especially in light of the fact that it seems easier just to "cash" the exchange items with other cash in the turn-in. For example, a typical front-office cashier's turn-in may have many thousands of dollars in cash, checks, and credit-card vouchers. The checks may contain some "exchange" items that were cashed. Why not simply deposit the exchange items combined with the other checks? You would not need to deposit all the cash because you could replenish the banks right on the spot. The reason we do not do that is that it is very poor internal control. It allows no separation between items cashed and items received for payment and it leaves no audit trail. In fact, after such a transaction is accomplished, there is no trace and the check-cashing mechanism could conveniently be used for frauds—defeating the whole purpose of setting up good internal controls.

Credit policy and miscellaneous items in check cashing. Credit policy encompasses management's role in decisions involving the extension of credit to our guests—namely, how, where, and how much to extend. In the check-cashing arena, credit policy involves limits on check cashing, the credit requirements (i.e., identification, license, credit card, guest registration) and the cashier training necessary to ensure smooth and ongoing implementation. Many hotels limit the dollar amount or the frequency of guests' check cashing. These issues apply to all checks—those accepted for the settlement of accounts as well as those cashed for convenience. Credit policy and the internal-control-related details of the credit manager's function are discussed in the next chapter.

The final issue in check cashing involves traveler's checks. Some hotels treat them much like cash, and others treat them like personal checks. I think the best approach is to treat them like personal checks. Certainly, traveler's checks are less risky from the perspective of whether or not they are good. In this case, however, we are not primarily interested in credit-worthiness. The issue is one of internal control and preventing fraud. For that purpose, traveler's checks should be treated like any other check.

Cash Turn-In and Banking

The head-cashier function is a critical one for good internal control. The job description and division-of-duties aspects were discussed earlier in the chapter. Some important details of that position as they relate to internal controls are:

- Structural requirements,
- Turn-in procedure,
- Pick-up procedure, and
- Banking.

The *structural requirements* need to be reviewed in the context of the control principles. I strongly recommend that turn-in always be made to a person (preferably the head cashier) or, at least, witnessed by a second person. In other words, turn-in simply placed in a "drop box" of some sort should be avoided. Most hotels, of course, are 24-hour

Exhibit 2.1

Cashier Pick-Up Procedures

1. These procedures and policies apply to all hotel cashiers—food and beverage and front office.
2. All cashiers must qualify for bonding and must pass the screening process designated by the hotel's insurers.
   a. Any violation of the bond or any other fraudulent act will be prosecuted fully.
   b. The hotel will conduct surprise counts of banks including surprise shift shut-down and turn-in.
3. Cashiers will be responsible for their assigned banks and turn-ins.
   a. A bank is the initial cash that a cashier is given for the purpose of making change.
   b. Banks will be of a fixed amount in designated denominations.
4. Cashiers are responsible for reporting to the head cashier approximately one-half hour prior to the start of their shift to pick up their banks.
   a. Banks will be stored in a "till drawer" in a safe-deposit vault in the counting room.
   b. Keys to the individual vaults will be kept in a key box in the counting room.
   c. Opening individual vaults will require a vault key and a guard key kept by the head cashier.
   d. Cashiers will verify the amounts of their banks.
   e. The head cashier will witness this count and sign off on a bank pick-up report.
   f. Cashiers will keep their vault keys in their tills until the end of their shifts.
5. If a cashier needs change or bank replenishment during a shift, he or she will call the head cashier for delivery. The bank will be raised and will stay at the new amount until turn-in, when it will be reduced to the original amount.

operations with late food and beverage outlets. Since it would be prohibitively expensive to have three head-cashier shifts, seven days per week, most properties will need to have drop safes and other procedures.

It is important to have a professionally built drop safe installed—like the ones used at banks. When the drop is placed in an open drum or chamber, the safe itself is inaccessible. When the chamber is closed or rotated, the drop falls into the safe, but during that operation the

EXHIBIT 2.2

Cashier Turn-In Procedures

1. Turn-in will take place in the counting room and will be witnessed and verified by the head cashier.
2. Count complete till.
3. Record all coin, currency, checks, and credit cards on turn-in sheet. (For checks and various credit-card vouchers, an adding machine tape may be attached and used in place of a detailed listing.)
4. Subtract original bank on turn-in sheet.
5. Separate amount of original bank preserving the most logical denominations, place bank in till, and lock till in vault.
    a. Front-office cashiers will make a separate turn-in for exchange items (checks made out to cash and travelers checks).
    b. The original bank for front-office cashiers will be reduced by the amount of exchange items before it is locked in the vault.
6. Place balance in turn-in envelope along with key to vault, change, and supply-request form.
7. The head cashier will verify the turn-in, initiate any necessary discrepancy report, and fill the request order for currency, coin, and supplies. The head cashier will periodically audit the banks and perform surprise counts and audits, in conjunction with the audit staff.
8. The income controller will prepare summary reports of revenues and other payment streams for each cashier shift (e.g., accounts receivable or advance deposits) and audit those against the turn-in. Reasonable attempts will be made to reconcile discrepancies, and overages or shortages will be permanently logged. Cashiers with consistent and continuing discrepancies will be subject to retraining and, ultimately, disciplinary action.

drop itself is no longer accessible.

From a control perspective, the drop safe is used only for turn-in shifts at those times when no head cashier is present. The turn-in should not be simply "dropped," but should be witnessed by another cashier or someone from management.

The *procedures for turn-in,* and its counterpart *pick-up,* are shown in detail in Exhibits 2.1 and 2.2. Conceptually, there are two approaches to turn-in. One is to allow the cashier to read the register and make

Case 2.2

The Sidetracked Refund

A public utility company decided to refund a deposit to a hotel. The notice to that effect was received by one of the hotel's accountants. Realizing that the management knew nothing about the refund, the accountant instructed the utility company to hold the check and he would pick it up. He did so, and then drew an exchange check for the exact amount of the refund, deposited the utility company's check, and cashed the exchange check. He entered neither item on the hotel's books. The exchange check was cashed at the bank without question, though it bore only the hotel's stamped endorsement. Since the refund check was deposited in the usual fashion, the utility company had no reason to suspect wrongdoing. The auditor himself made the reconciliation of the bank account with the books, and was in that way able to conceal the manipulation temporarily.

The scheme unraveled, however, when the hotel's external auditors unexpectedly arrived ahead of schedule. In making the reconciliation of the bank account with the hotel's books, they noted the transaction on the bank statement, but couldn't locate the exchange check in question. The hotel's management later found it in the accountant's private papers.

Discussion

This case describes a fraud perpetrated on the hotel because its check-cashing and exchange procedures were not tight enough. It is also a classic example of the violation of division of duties between accounting and cash handling. Although technically those duties were divided, the accountant in this case was able to have access to cash because of lax check-cashing procedures. It is a typical example of the "back end" use of this weakness.

The fact that the hotel cashed guests' checks facilitated the fraudulent conversion of a check made out to the hotel and meant as payment for money due the hotel (a utility deposit in this case). The principle violated here is that checks made out to the hotel should never be handled by an employee with accounting responsibilities. The problem was compounded by the fact that the exchange mechanism was lax. If done correctly, someone from management would review the documentation—consisting of all exchange items—before signing an exchange check. In such a review, the manipulation of the utility's deposit check would stand out.

In addition to the weaknesses in the check-cashing procedure, the hotel's auditors should periodically have checked the status of deposits owed the hotel and interest accrued or paid on them. Also, when a vendor that is normally paid by the hotel owes the hotel money, it is a good idea to request a credit toward the hotel's account rather than to accept direct payment.

certain that his or her actual turn-in equals that amount. The other approach, the blind turn-in, is far superior. In a blind turn-in, cashiers count their total drawer, list all items, subtract their original bank, and turn the balance in as their shift turn-in. During this entire process they have no access to their register readings, so they turn in what they have, without knowing what they are supposed to have. The argument for allowing cashiers access to their registers is that discrepancies can be traced and worked out on the spot with the shift cashier. With blind turn-in, in contrast, someone else must balance the turn-in and try to solve discrepancies later. It is sometimes argued that with blind turn-in the hotel cannot make the cashiers responsible for shortages since they were not informed or did not know about them at turn-in time. It is hard to know what is meant by "making cashiers responsible," but better internal control is obtained with blind turn-in. It is difficult for a cashier or other employee to perpetrate a fraud when they have no access to the register readings and do not know what they should turn in. As can be seen in Exhibits 2.1 and 2.2, there is also better division of duties with the blind turn-in approach. I strongly recommend the blind approach and have personally observed it to work well in many hotels and restaurants—both small ones and larger and more complex ones. The increased level of internal control far outweighs some of the arguments against blind turn-in.

The *banking* aspects of the head-cashier function are fairly straightforward. The head cashier does all of the hotel's banking. As was discussed earlier, division of duties requires that accounting personnel do not handle cash, including banking. In smaller properties, where having a separate head cashier is infeasible, management takes over the function. Someone from management with no accounting responsibilities should be designated to do the banking.

The banking procedures involve custody of all cash banks, replenishing those banks and the overall hotel cash bank with useful denominations of coin and currency, handling the exchange items, preparing all deposits, and supervising or arranging for transit to and from the hotel's depositories. In larger hotels, and even for small operations in larger cities, transit can often be arranged by armored car service.

The preparation of the deposits plays an important internal-control role. The head cashier handles the deposit of cash, including payments that have come in the mail, ensuring division of duties. The head cashier should list all items (modern and inexpensive photocopying and microfilming make this task easier in large or high-volume operations) and prepare a duplicate bank deposit slip. Multi-part forms are easily available, or an alternative would be to have the bank send a duplicate slip or listing. The duplicate slips and listings give the audit or accounting staff the data they need to audit or post, while allowing them no access to the actual cash or checks. Similar care and procedures should be taken with credit-card vouchers— both the type deposited at the bank and those that must be mailed to the credit-card companies for redemption. Credit-card vouchers should also be given the added control feature of being accounted for by serial number. I will discuss handling credit-card revenue in the next chapter on accounts receivable.

Audit of Cash Balances

The final issue involving cash receipts is the need for a periodic audit of all balances of cash on hand. The chief accounting officer, usually the controller, should personally supervise the periodic counting and recording of all cash balances at the hotel, including all register tills. At least one other accounting person should participate in the counts in order to ensure objectivity and division of duties. The periodic count (preferably monthly, but at the minimum quarterly) should be indelibly recorded in a ledger specifically for that purpose and compared to the amount for "cash on hand" in the general ledger. Discrepancies should be recorded in the ledger ("over" and "short"). Significant discrepancies must be vigorously investigated.

Glossary

Accounts Receivable—A claim or debt due to the hotel from a guest or customer for services rendered.

Blind Turn-in—The process of having cashiers count and list their total cash drawer, subtract the original bank, and turn in the balance—all without having access to the readings of their shift totals.

Bona Fide—Sincere or genuine; made in good faith.

Cut-Off Statements—Statements (usually checking-account bank statements) prepared at a random or specially selected time other than the end of the month.

Daily Intact Deposit—The procedure of depositing each shift's receipts separately and daily in the hotel's bank.

Documentation—The process of writing down all of the procedures for a given task or function in such detail that someone unfamiliar with the task could perform it from the written record alone.

Emboss—To press in a manner that leaves an imprint. In financial transactions, to imprint a credit card on a hotel document or record of charge.

Exchange—The act of trading one item for another. In hotels, trading customer's checks that the hotel cashed for them for cash to replenish the house banks.

Head Cashier—The hotel's chief cash-handling employee, in charge of all cash handling and custody, banking, and management of shift cashiers.

Indelible—A marking that cannot be erased.

Lapping—A type of embezzlement where assets or other resources from one period are used to cover shortages or manipulations from another period. A fraud of "over-lap."

Pick-Up—The procedure whereby hotel cashiers obtain their starting banks and other supplies and sign-in for their shift.

Point-of-Sale (POS) Device—A register or terminal where sales are recorded and bills are settled with customers.

Signature-on-File—The procedure whereby hotels post charges to a guest's credit-card account without the guest's actually having signed a charge voucher. Generally that guest's account number and signature were otherwise obtained—for example on the registration card.

Source Documents—The documents of evidence associated with transactions, usually with outside parties: typically, sales slips, invoices, register tapes, time cards, and receipts.

Turn-in—The procedure whereby hotel cashiers deposit their accumulated receipts, starting banks, charge vouchers, and excess supplies with the head cashier and sign-out for their shift.

Selected References

Laurent Caraux and A. Neal Geller, "Cash Management: A Total System Approach for the Hotel Industry," *The Cornell Hotel and Restaurant Administration Quarterly*, 18, No. 3 (November 1977), pp. 46-55.

A. Neal Geller and Lloyd C. Heath, "Solvency, Financial Statements, and the Importance of Cash-Flow Information," *The Cornell Hotel and Restaurant Administration Quarterly*, 22, No. 3 (November 1981), pp. 45-51.

Paul J. Beehler, *Contemporary Cash Management • Principles • Practices • Perspective* (New York: John Wiley & Sons, 1978).

Jarl G. Kallberg and Kenneth L. Parkinson, *Current Asset Management: Cash, Credit, and Inventory* (New York: John Wiley & Sons, 1984).

Chapter 3

Accounts Receivable and Credit-Policy Issues

Objectives

After completing this chapter, you should understand:

1. **Accounts receivable.**
2. **The principles for the internal control of accounts receivable.**
3. **The credit manager's function.**
4. **The concepts of bad debts, collections, and write-offs.**

Accounts-Receivable Procedures

Accounts Receivable. Accounts receivable is the term for money owed the hotel that has not yet been paid. In accounting, it is considered an asset and is found in the balance sheet right after cash. In practice this account appears in the general ledger and is called "accounts receivable–control." It represents the total owed the hotel at any time. Most firms also simultaneously keep another set of accounts called "accounts receivable–subsidiary," which is made up of all the individual customer's amounts owed. Naturally, the total of the two accounts should be the same.

In hotel practice there is sometimes confusion with these terms. Most hotels call their live listing of guests' charges, belonging to guests currently in the house, the "guest accounts receivable" (also known as the "bucket," "bin," "tub," or "tray"). When a guest with previously established credit checks out without settling with the traditional cash, check, or credit card, but rather wants a bill mailed, we often call that transaction "city ledger." It is sometimes referred to as "direct billing" or "a direct-bill customer," but the accounting entry is a transfer to the "city ledger." That city ledger is the traditional accounts receivable.

The internal control for accounts receivable is an important area even if a hotel does not have a large amount of direct-bill business. Accounts receivable is an area subject to frauds of its own, and sometimes it is used as a facilitator of or cover-up for other frauds. If your hotel never does any direct billing, then this section can be skipped, but do pay attention to the next section on credit-policy issues.

Accounts Receivable: Principles of Internal Control. The major internal-control principles for the accounts-receivable function are:

- Division of duties,
- Aged trial balances,
- Rotation of clerks, and
- Systematic write-off procedures.

Division of Duties. Division of duties for receivables requires separating the following tasks:

- Billing,
- Receiving cash,
- Keeping ledgers—control and subsidiary,
- Credit policy and collection, and
- Authority for making allowances.

This five-way separation (or six, if you separate the keeping of subsidiary and control accounts) appears to be costly. When we look at it more closely, however, it normally turns out not to require any extra personnel. The important separation, as with all internal control, is between cash and record keeping.

Billing. Billing is the process of making up or typing customer invoices, drawn from the subsidiary ledger, and the process of supervising their dispatch in the mail. Any clerical or secretarial employee can be designated this task, as it is usually a short, part-time one. It should not be done by any cash-handling employees, including front-office clerks. It should also be separated from the clerks who keep the ledgers. In small operations with few clerical employees, management may need to get involved in the process. In all cases, a management employee should supervise the actual mailing of the bills.

Receiving Cash. No person receiving or otherwise handling cash should have anything to do with the accounts-receivable functions. Cash is received in the accounts-receivable process when customers make payments on their accounts. Most of those payments come in the mail. (Occasionally a customer will make a payment in person. In that case, we should insist that such payments be made only at the front desk where the clerks can ring it up as a payment to city ledger.) For payments received in the mail, we have the mail procedure discussed in Chapter 2. In this way, we stick with the overall principle that we receive cash only at a *bona fide* cashier station or through the mail. Checks are sent directly to the head cashier, and copies are used by the accounts-receivable clerks to post the ledgers.

Keeping Ledgers. The process of keeping ledgers is bookkeeping or record keeping that must be separated from cash handling. The processes of allowing credits and making collections, discussed below, must also be separated from the record keeping. To obtain ideal internal control, the posting of subsidiary ledgers (the individual customer accounts and the primary source of the billings) should be kept separate from the control ledger account. This separation is not a problem in large hotels as there are often several accounting employees, one of whom usually does all the general ledger work. There are other subsidiary clerical tasks that can be safely combined with the accounts-receivable subsidiary ledger, such as payroll and accounts payable.

In smaller properties, it may not be cost effective to separate subsidiary posting from general-ledger posting. In those cases, internal control is accomplished by the other separations discussed and by management's being extra vigilant in checking and supervising the billing.

Credit Policy and Collection. The functions of developing credit policy—establishing limits, requirements, etc.—and collecting overdue accounts are in the job description of the "credit manager," discussed in detail in the next section. The important control issue is that the credit-management functions must be separate from billing, record keeping, or receiving cash. Only large hotels have a separate credit manager, but the functions of that office always exist and need to be accomplished by other management employees.

Authority for Making Allowances. When allowances or credits are authorized, we are simultaneously reducing our revenue and the customer's account. It should be obvious that such authority must be kept separate from those employees who are billing, posting, or receiving cash. Otherwise, a fraudulent credit or allowance would be an easy way to cover an embezzlement. This separation is not an expensive one, because it is a management function anyway and one that does not require a great deal of time. The procedures for granting allowances and recording them via allowance vouchers is discussed in detail in Chapter 6 (rooms income).

Aged Trial Balances. The preparation of the aged trial balance, usually known by the more familiar name "Aged Accounts Receivable," is an important on-going management tool. It is prepared monthly by the clerk who is in charge of the accounts-receivable control account. The aged receivable account should be carefully scrutinized by management each month. It is simply a summary of the accounts receivable control, stratified by age. It contains only the totals of each age group, usually as follows:

- Current (usually 30 days or less),
- 31 - 60 days,
- 61 - 90 days,
- 91 - 120 days, and
- Over 120 days.

It is also a good idea to attach a separate schedule with the listing of the names and amounts owed for those accounts over 90-days old to help you make decision about extending credit. The aged accounts receivable is a useful management tool for cash-management and credit-policy purposes. It also has an internal-control consequence in that it forces management continually to scrutinize the amounts and patterns of their accounts receivable. Changes in the patterns should be thoroughly investigated as they may indicate internal-control problems. The economic climate, pricing, and changes in our customers or their spending habits can also affect the receivables aging pattern.

Rotation of Clerks. Rotation of employees was discussed in Chapter 1, and is a useful idea with receivables clerks—providing it can be cost justified.

Systematic Write-Off Procedure. Establishing a systematic procedure for collection and write-offs is an important element in internal control. This procedure is discussed in detail in the next section.

Credit Policy, Bad Debts, and Write-Offs

The Credit Manager. All hotels need a credit-manager function, but only large hotels can afford to employ a person solely to be credit manager. In small properties the function is sometimes shared by several people, including top management. The credit-manager function includes two major areas: credit policy and collection. Credit policy involves developing the procedures and rules for the extension of credit. It includes such items as how much credit guests are allowed, what identification or cards will be required at check-in or to establish credit, when settlement must be demanded, credit limits, time limits, check acceptance, and check-cashing procedures.

These tasks often include the types of decisions that top management needs to be involved with. Credit-policy decisions can affect who comes to the hotel, how the sales department can sell, how space is reserved, and which corporate clients get credit. Clearly these are items that the general manager himself or herself must review. That is why the credit manager's function is sometimes divided up over several top-management people. There is no internal-control problem with that, except that the credit-manager function should be separate from accounting and record keeping. In hotels where there is a credit-manager position, that person often reports to the controller or chief accounting officer. There is not a major control problem with that practice, as long as the credit manager has no actual accounting responsibilities. Where no credit manager is hired but the duties are divided up, care must be taken that the collection part of the credit-manager function is absolutely separated from any accounting tasks. Similarly, the record-keeping portion of bad-debts procedure and collection must be maintained by an accounting person, with no access by the credit manager or any cash-receiving employees.

Collection is the other half of the credit manager's function. It involves the administration of bad debts and the efforts to collect both bad debts and bad checks. The detail of the collection function, as well as those of systematic write-off, are discussed in the section below.

Bad Debts and Bad Checks. Bad debts are accounts receivable that have become old and are possibly uncollectable (definitions and policies vary, but generally accounts over 90 or 120 days are considered bad debts). Bad checks are checks that we accept and deposit, but are returned to us by our bank as uncollectable. Except for the early steps to be taken with bad checks, the two are treated in the same fashion. After all, if we have a check that has bounced several times, we have at best an account receivable—and most likely a bad debt.

Bad checks come back from the bank in the mail. You should have an established mail procedure for incoming payments, and it is used in the same way for bad checks. The secretary who opens the mail sends the checks to the head cashier for deposit. The same should apply to checks that come back: they go to the head cashier for re-deposit. The routing of copies varies slightly. The audit copy still goes to the audit office—in this case, to serve as a flag for setting up an audit trail. The copy normally earmarked for receivables should instead go to the credit manager to act as a flag for action.

The action at that point is to simply contact the payor to let him or her know that the check has been returned and that the hotel is putting it back in for deposit. At this time, the accounting department should set up only a temporary audit trail (e.g., a "tickler" file).* Bad checks often will clear the second time when there is some contact with the payor.

If a bad check comes back for the second time, it can truly be viewed as a bad debt and more formal treatment can begin. The bad check comes in the mail, so the same routing through the head cashier takes place. When the head cashier gets the bad check this time, it is held in the hotel safe until it is collected or written off. This time, the auditor's copy serves as signal to set up the permanent bad-debt file, and the credit manager's copy serves as a signal to begin more formal collection efforts (for the check plus any bank service charges). From this point

---

*An entry will need to be journalized for this transaction, of course, as follows: Accounts receivable is debited to reflect the customer's debt and to establish it on the books. Cash is credited to reflect the reduction in the hotel's bank account by the bank returning the check. Finally, any bank charges incurred should be added to the customer's account.

Case 3.1

A Case of Cashier Collusion

In a new city hotel catering almost exclusively to commercial travelers, the policy was to cash the guests' personal and business checks after satisfactory credit information had been obtained. During the course of a year, quite a number of checks cashed by the hotel and drawn on good bank accounts were returned due to errors, such as insufficient funds. These checks were readily corrected and collected through correspondence by the credit manager.

The credit manager's office was allowed to keep the bad checks and the delinquent-accounts ledger.

At the end of the accounting year, the credit manager presented the accountant with a list of delinquent and bad-check accounts amounting to nearly $8,000 that the manager considered uncollectible. These accounts were written off as bad debts without further investigation by the accountant.

When the external auditor examined these accounts, the auditor made a routine request that the returned checks be produced for inspection to support of the claim that the accounts were uncollectible. The credit manager was unable to comply, claiming that the checks were in the hands of several collection agencies. Not to be rebuffed so easily, the auditor requested that the agencies return the checks. But the collection agencies stated that none of the checks mentioned had ever been given to them to collect.

Upon cross-examination, the credit manager admitted that he had cashed $6,000 in checks that had been made good and also those made in payment of the delinquent accounts. To arrange the transaction, he worked with one of the front-office cashiers, who was in collusion with him.

Discussion

This hotel had a failure of division of duties. Specifically, the credit manager had custody of the bad checks, kept the delinquent-accounts ledger, and directly accepted payments from collections. The credit manager's function must be kept separate from cash and record keeping. The accounting department should have custody of the delinquent account register including detailed records of all transactions and collection efforts. As for any payments received, they should be made only through the hotel's normal cash receiving channels—at a *bona fide* cashier's station or in the mail.

The mail procedure, discussed in Chapter 2, provides that checks—good or bad—go to the head cashier for deposit (in the case of bad checks the head cashier holds them as evidence for write-off). Copies of the checks will go to accounting for record keeping, and to the credit manager for collection action.

In this hotel, the procedures for write-off were also lax. A systematic, periodic write-off should be conducted, with the top manager having the sole authority for approval. Written approval should come only after careful review and cancellation of all of the documentation, including a history of all collection efforts.

Finally, the check-cashing and exchange procedures were violated, allowing checks made out to the hotel to be cashed. The only checks ever cashed are those cashed for the convenience of the hotel's guests—and those should be made out to cash (the check-cashing procedure is discussed in detail in Chapter 2).

---

in the process, bad checks and bad debts are treated essentially the same way.

Permanent Record. A designated member of the accounting staff sets up a permanent record for each bad item. It doesn't matter whether the record is a bad-debts ledger or register, a card file, or a computer file. The important issue is that we establish a permanent record of each bad item that will trace its history from inception to full collection or write-off. That bad-debt file will remain in the custody of the accounting department. Thus we have a three-way division of duties: the head cashier has custody of bad checks and receives any payments, the accountant has the records, and the credit manager takes actions, including implementation of the hotel's credit policy (e.g., cutting that particular guest off at the front desk, or flagging that guest as "cash only" or "fully authorized credit card only").

Collection. Logically, the next step in the process would be to try collecting the debt. To begin the discussion of collection, I must warn you that self-collection has become a complicated and somewhat dangerous endeavor. In 1978 Congress passed the Consumer Credit Protection Act (1978 Public Law 95-109). This legislation was needed to protect consumers from harassment from unscrupulous collection agents. In fact, it was supported by the major associations of collection agencies. An important implication of the act is that it is difficult and potentially dangerous (in the financial sense) for amateurs to become collectors.* Readers are urged to see the suggested readings and to consult with their legal counsel before starting any collection program.

With that warning in mind, you can begin the collection process. The internal-control implications involve payment and record keeping. Payment, even if generated at the urging of the credit manager, should

---

*See: Walter H. Page, "Credit Where It's Due (You)," *The Cornell Hotel and Restaurant Administration Quarterly,* 21, No. 2 (August 1980), pp. 27-42; reprinted as appendix 3.1.

be accepted only through the mail or at the front desk. If the credit manager has a "hot prospect" that wants to pay an old bill, he or she must bring the prospect to the front desk (or other *bona fide* cashier station at the hotel) to make payment. Otherwise, the client can mail it in. In that way we preserve the division of duties and also keep in place our normal mechanisms for recording payment and maintaining the audit trail. Any payments, whether internally or externally generated, and all collection efforts should be recorded by the accounting department in the bad-debt file.

Know your local and state laws regarding bad checks. The hotel may have to obtain what is known as a "formal protest" from or with the help of the bank. In most jurisdictions writing a bad check is a crime, and local police agencies or even the district attorney's office may help businesses collect bad checks.

There are two ways to proceed externally with collection efforts of both bad checks and bad debts. One is to use a collection agency and the other is to use an attorney. In all cases, the bad-debt file should be updated and custody of bad checks should remain with the hotel. If the outside agency insists on the original bad item, a receipt should be obtained and kept with the bad-debt file.

It is often wise to use a reputable and licensed collection agency. These agencies usually operate on commission, so there is little or no cost if they do not collect. If they do collect, they usually take one-third to one-half of the debt as their fee. Attorneys also can be effective. Often a letter from an attorney is enough to get a person to begin making payments. If a hotel is going to use an attorney for collections, it should use one that specializes in that work. The decision on whether to use a collection agency or an attorney is an individual one, often made on a cost-benefit basis. Large hotels or chains that have attorneys on full-time retainer can do some collection with little additional cost. Using an attorney solely for collection or going into litigation for collection will be expensive. Again, the cost-benefit principle must be applied.

Write-offs. Writing off bad debts is a serious and potentially problematic endeavor. Any time we have an internal accounting entry (i.e., one without a transaction with an outside party) that reduces revenue or assets, we are especially vulnerable to fraud. As in many other transactions, a proper audit trail and division of duties can prevent possible problems. The write-off process should be systematic rather that haphazard—say, monthly or quarterly depending on your volume. The write-off must also have the general manager's specific approval. The accounting department should prepare the documentation, consisting of the bad-debt file with all its history of collection efforts, the bad check itself or original folio in the case of a bad debt, and any legal documents. The general manager should check the documentation for authenticity and to gain some knowledge about the hotel's credit and collection policy, and then authorize the write-off by signing and indelibly cancelling the documentation. That cancellation is important because frauds have occurred where the same documentation was used more than once! After the general manager approves the write-off the accounting department should proceed with the entries, and file the documentation.

Appendix 3.1

Credit Where It's Due (You)

by Walter H. Page, *American Credit Control*

Adapted from: Walter H. Page, "Credit Where It's Due (You)," *The Cornell Hotel and Restaurant Adminstration Quarterly,* 21, No. 2 (August 1980), pp. 27-42.

This appendix will introduce you to proven techniques of credit management. Whether you handle collection activities yourself or hire a professional collector, the suggestions offered here will help you to establish better controls, elicit prompter payments, and improve your profit margin. They will also show you how to stay within the bounds of legal restrictions pertaining to credit, although these general guidelines should be supplemented with counsel from your attorney. Finally, they will impress on you the importance of approaching credit matters with both common sense and imagination, because no two accounts or situations are alike.

Know the Law

Congress has been explicit in defining acceptable and unacceptable debt-collection practices. The following overview of the pertinent sections of the Consumer Credit Protection Act* will give you some familiarity with the basic concepts of collection law,

*Public Law 95-109, an act of Congress effective March 20, 1978.

but you should consult your attorney for answers to specific questions and for information on regulations pertaining to collection in your state. Note that these laws apply not only to collection agencies you engage, but also to any representative of your firm who participates in collection efforts.

Section 804

- The consumer is guaranteed privacy in the collection effort. If you communicate by telephone or the mails with a third party—while attempting to locate the debtor, for example—you are prohibited from mentioning or indicating in any manner that the consumer owes a debt.
- In mailed communications to debtors, you are not allowed to use any language or symbols on the outside of the envelope that could indicate the envelope's contents relate to a debt. A firm named Ace Collection Agency, for example, could not use its name on an envelope.
- The use of postcards for collection notices is specifically prohibited.
- If asked, a collector talking with a third party for the purpose of locating a debtor must identify his firm. Under such circumstances, it is acceptable to reply, "I am Mr. Johnson of Acme Credit Service." However, you cannot say that the consumer owes a debt; you can only say, "This is a business matter," or, "This is a personal matter."
- If the debtor has turned the matter over to an attorney, and you receive notice that the attorney has been engaged, you may not communicate with anyone other than the attorney, unless the attorney fails to respond to your communications within a reasonable length of time.* If you receive written or oral notice that an attorney is representing the debtor, you should ask whether the attorney is representing the consumer in the matter of your account. The attorney may actually be representing the consumer on an altogether different matter, rather than protesting the account.

Section 805

- The collector is not allowed to make phone calls to the debtor at unusual hours, on holidays, or on Sundays. The allowable time is from 8 AM through 9 PM (in the *debtor's* time zone) during business days. If the consumer has indicated he works odd hours and cannot be reached by phone during the permissible calling hours, you may be allowed to place calls during the hours the debtor is available.
- You may not call the debtor at his place of employment unless he agreed at an earlier time to accept phone calls at work (do not even consider this option unless you have the debtor's permission in writing). You may write to a consumer at his place of employment as long as you adhere to the regulations pertaining to written communications.
- The Truth-in-Lending Law permits the consumer to tell you he will not pay the debt and that he does not want any further communications from you. In such cases, the debtor should send you written notice of his intent not to pay and specify his reasons. Upon receipt of the notice, you must stop collection efforts but can notify the debtor that legal action will be taken. You may say this only if you intend to take legal action; you may not use it as a threat or an attempt to coerce the debtor into paying.

---

*What constitutes a reasonable time period was left to the courts. In any situation involving an attorney, try to establish a time limit within which the attorney must report a decision to you.

- You may not abuse or harass the debtor. Abusive language, repeated phone calls, and threats of physical harm are prohibited.

Section 806

- You may not make an inordinate number of calls to the debtor, because repeated phone calls may be construed as harassment.
- When you call or visit the debtor, you may not represent yourself as someone other than yourself.

Section 807

- You may not add charges to the debtor's account or represent that additional charges will be levied if the account is turned over to a collection agency or to an attorney—unless the amount of collection charges is specified in the original contract.
- If you notify a debtor that he is about to be sued for nonpayment, you must sue him. *You cannot send a notice of intent to sue unless you will take the action.* Such a notice should specify the date that action will be taken.
- You may not furnish false information to a credit-reporting bureau for the purpose of discrediting the debtor.
- If an account routinely monitored by a credit bureau is disputed (see "Disputed Accounts," below), you must so advise the credit bureau. Failure to inform the bureau may lead to a violation of the consumer's rights—and perhaps allow the consumer to sue you for recovery of damages.
- You may not charge interest unless the amount to be charged is expressly mentioned in the contract and permitted by law (see "Interest," below).

Any person performing collection activities must adhere to the foregoing regulations. Failure to comply in any respect can result in penalties, fines, and lawsuits.

Extending Credit

Anyone who extends credit is, inevitably, vulnerable to some losses. In addition to the straight dollar amount of bad debts, slow accounts are expensive in a number of ways. You can limit your credit-related losses by taking a systematic, consistent approach to the extension of credit. Credit is a privilege, not a right, and granting it should be based upon such factors as the consumer's ability to repay, his current solvency, his past performance in repaying credit accounts, his present employment, and the amount of the transaction.

The most common type of credit extension is the acceptance of credit cards issued by banks and other entities. You can also extend credit yourself. By applying the principles set forth in the following section, those who wish to extend credit to consumers will be able to (1) increase their business and (2) make money on the credit they extend.

Interest: The Extra Earning Power of Credit Sales

Credit sales are essential to hotels because so many guests expect to settle their accounts with a credit-related transaction. You are entitled to charge a fee for extending credit. A typical service charge is 18 percent of the transaction amount annually, or 1.5 per-cent per month.*

You can add service charges only if you consistently advise customers of the conditions under which such charges are levied and the amount to be charged. Printing a statement like the following on your invoices provides sufficient notice:

Payment terms: 30 days. Service charges are assessed in the amount of 1.5 percent per month (18 percent annually) on all past-due accounts.

If you intend to assume the risks attendant upon extending credit, you should also take advantage of the additional profits available to you through service charges.

The Credit Application

The first step in credit management is the prudent evaluation of persons asking for credit. You need complete information about each credit applicant, both to judge the applicant's ability to pay you and to help you locate the debtor if problems arise later.

Establish a set policy for extending credit, and adhere to it at all times. Have credit-application forms or cards printed, and ask every credit applicant to complete one. Make no exceptions. The form should ask for the applicant's name, address, phone number, place of employment, bank, credit references, and signature.

- Ask for the applicant's complete name; require a full *residence* address; and it is especially important to get the applicant's phone number. If a debtor ignores your statements, you will need a way to contact him.
- Require the applicant to identify his place of employment, and verify the information through a phone call to the employer.
- A bank reference is always desirable, and when large sums are involved it is mandatory.
- Ask for three credit references, advise the applicant they will be checked, and follow through. Ask the references about the applicant's performance in repaying his accounts.

In collecting this information from an applicant, remember that the sole criterion for extending credit is the applicant's ability to repay the account.

Special Cases: Women, Senior Citizens, Teenagers

It is illegal to deny credit on the basis of an applicant's gender. Because a woman's credit history may require special treatment—if all records of payment are in her husband's name, for example, or if she has worked exclusively as a homemaker—ask the loan officer at your local bank to explain the bank's procedures in evaluating women who apply for credit.

---

*In calculating the service charge, remember that you add 1.5 percent of the original purchase price only; although the outstanding balance for a given purchase will grow each month as service charges are added, the monthly service charge and the principal remain constant. For example: For an account of $100, a service charge of $1.50 is added for the first month past due (total due: $101.50). The second month, the service charge is 1.5 percent not of the total outstanding—$101.50—but of the original purchase price ($100). Hence, $1.50 is added again in the second month, bringing the account to a total of $103; the third month, the outstanding balance is $104.50.

Another applicant who may require special consideration is the senior citizen. If a retired debtor defaults on an account, collection will be difficult; although you can take legal action for recovery, you cannot attach a Social Security, pension, compensation, or disability check. A rule applicable to any extension of credit is especially important here: start with small transactions, monitor the debtor's repayment, and govern further extensions of credit accordingly.

Many creditors are reluctant to extend credit to teenagers, but as a look at the record of nonpayment among adult customers will reveal, young people have no monopoly on delinquent accounts. If yours is a business serving the needs of younger customers— who, incidentally, have enormous spending power—don't force them to take their business somewhere else; just take reasonable precautions.

In extending credit to a person younger than 18, you must have a parent or legal guardian sign a written agreement stating that in the event of nonpayment the parent or guardian will be liable for payment (and check the parent's credit references). Consult your attorney for information on state regulations pertaining to the extension of credit to young people. Granting credit to a responsible young person can be a sound investment in your future business.

The Order Form

By law, all credit transactions must be authorized via a signed order form. As is true of the information requested on the credit application, the information provided on the order form must be complete, including: the purchaser's full name, complete (street) address, and phone number; a list of all items purchased (including serial numbers, if applicable) and the price of each; the total amount of the purchase and any sales tax; and the purchaser's complete signature.

If a purchase is made in a company's name, rather than to be charged to an individual, you should also obtain the following information:

• The name of the individual responsible for payment;
• The names, titles, home phone numbers, and home addresses of the company's
    officers or principals;
• The signature of the head of the company, authorizing purchases;
• The name of the company's bank, if a new firm; and
• Recent credit references (make a phone call to verify them).

When purchases are made in a corporate name, none of the corporation's officers is legally responsible for the payment of monies due; when purchases are made on behalf of a partnership or company, the owners are liable for business debts incurred, either individually or collectively.

Requesting complete information from credit applicants is prudent not only from the standpoint of facilitating collection activities at a later date: it also forewarns consumers that you take credit transactions (and their repayment) seriously.

Although the Truth-in-Lending Law is specific in stipulating how credit transactions should be handled, it is your privilege to extend credit only when in your considered opinion the resulting transaction would be good. Set a credit policy, establish criteria, and apply them consistently—without exception.

Accounts Receivable: Getting Your Money

It's easy to neglect accounts receivable—there are always plenty of other matters requiring immediate attention. But if you allow too much time to elapse before examining your books, or wait until you need money for some purpose of your own, you are making a critical mistake.

In my experience, a businessperson with, say, $20,000 in accounts receivable ranging from six months to two or more years past due is often not especially concerned about the magnitude of those receivables because the operator labors under the misconception that he or she can recover all of the money due at any time just by exerting a little effort. A good fifth of those accounts receivable are probably uncollectible. Develop the habit of checking your accounts, and your accounts receivable will rarely get out of control.

Every day a past-due account remains on your books, the value of its recovery and the likelihood of its recovery grow slimmer (see the chart above). It is therefore imperative that collection efforts start at an early stage in the delinquency. Create a filing system for receivables—color-coded or organized in some other way that will allow you to determine at a glance, as part of your work day, the accounts that may prove to be collection problems. Monitoring your accounts may yield valuable insights for your future credit policies, indicating areas in which you should modify the way you handle the extension of credit. As a general rule, at the end of three months of billings you should be prepared to commence collection efforts.

...by Mail

You should send statements to consumers in accordance with an established billing schedule—at least once every 30 days, so that you can add the service charges as they accrue. A notice specifying the amount of the charge must be clearly printed on all statement forms; you are not permitted to rubber stamp, type, or write the charges on individual statements (this regulation is intended to prevent inconsistent application of the charge). The notice most often reads as follows:

NET Cash:
A 1 1/2% per month service charge, or 18%
annual fee, will be charged on all accounts
30 days past due.

Whatever the words you use, however, they must appear on *all* statements.

On your second statement, write or stamp the word "Please"—nothing more. If this tactful approach produces no results in 15 days, you have a collection problem, and your next statement should be more forceful. A series of suggested collection letters is shown on the facing page. Collection letters should be individually typed or, if this is not practical, they should at least be typed and duplicated in such a manner that they have the appearance of individually typed letters.

All collection correspondence should be typed on your letterhead. It is not legal to make up a different company name for the purpose of implying that a third party is now involved. State a time limit (10 or 15 days) for the debtor's response on all collection letters—and then act on it. Unless you consistently follow up on the due dates you set, the debtor will not take your statements seriously and your collection efforts will be wasted.Remember that if you send the debtor notice that you intend to sue, you must do so.

If the amount of the debt is small, you may be able to take the matter to Small Claims Court, where you need not use the services of an attorney. In some states only matters involving $500 or less can be heard in Small Claims Court, while in other jurisdictions the ceiling is $1,000. When possible, it is to your advantage to use the Small Claims Court. Be prepared with two copies of a complete, typed, itemized statement, showing all debits, credits, and service charges. If the debt exceeds $1,000, obtain professional help.

A Word About Envelopes

You can enlist the aid of the U.S. Post Office in locating debtors by including the phrase "Address Correction Requested" on the envelope of every statement you send out. If a debtor moves and files his forwarding address, the Post Office forwards your mailing piece to the debtor and sends you the debtor's new address on its Form 3547 (shown below). You are charged first-class postage for every address correction sent to you, and must pay a small fee for the correction service, but the investment is well worth it: obviously, you cannot collect from someone you can't locate.

Because the Post Office keeps address changes on file for a limited time, transfer new addresses to your ledger cards immediately. If you receive notice of an address correction, you can be reasonably sure that the debtor received the statement; you therefore need not send another statement for that month and should wait for the next billing cycle.

What if the envelope is returned to you and marked "Unknown" or "Moved—Left No Address"? If you followed the procedures outlined earlier in this article, you know the debtor's place of employment. You may call the place of employment and ask whether the consumer has informed that office of his new address; if so, forward the statement to the new address. If you do not receive Form 3547 from the Post Office, you can assume the statement was delivered. Your other option is to send a statement to the employer's address in a plain white envelope. You *must* mark the envelope "Personal" in bright red. If you fail to do so, and the envelope is opened by a third party, you may be open to a lawsuit for invasion of privacy or, in the case of a disputed account, for dissemination of false information.

You can help ensure that the debtor will open the envelope by using stamps, rather than a recognizable postage-meter imprint, and by listing your postal-box number as the return address. (If you rent a postal box, register its number as one of your addresses on the forms you file for return of Form 3547 to ensure you are informed of debtors' new addresses, regardless of the address you use on your envelope.)

...by Telephone

The telephone is an especially effective tool in collecting accounts when used properly. Remember when communicating with debtors to speak in a modulated voice and to avoid annoying mannerisms. Prepare what you have to say—and say it pleasantly but firmly, using short and easily understood phrases. Although it may be difficult, remain courteous.

EXHIBIT 3.1

Sample Collection Letters

You should begin this series of collection notices when the debtor has failed to respond to three billings. All of these letters should be typed on your letterhead. You may find that typing the notices in uppercase letters is effective in getting the debtor's attention.

First effort

> Amount Due   Due Date
>   (10-15 days)
>
> We find your account to be past due. Please remit promptly so that we are not required to take further steps.

> Amount Due   Due Date
>   (10-15 days)
>
> Your merchandise (goods, services) was (were) given to you in good faith.
>
> To date, no payment has been received.
>
> We will expect your remittance by return mail.

Second effort

> Amount Due   Due Date
>   (10 days)
>
> Since we have not received payment on your account, we wonder whether there is some problem of which we are not aware.
>
> Please communicate with us and advise.
>
> Your failure to respond will lead us to believe that payment is being avoided.

Third effort

> Amount Due   Due Date
>   (From Letter 2)
>
> A judgment can be taken against you for non-payment of your past-due account.
>
> All court costs and interest will be added to the account. To avoid a judgment, and to prevent this matter from becoming a matter of public record, pay your account now.

Note that in the third letter you are only notifying the debtor that an action can take place—you are not saying that it will.

If you intend to take legal action

Amount Due   Date

A legal action will be taken against you for nonpayment of your past-due account.

All court fees and interest charges will be added to the account.

This action will be taken 10 days from the date of this communication if we receive no response from you.

This letter can be used only when you intend to take the legal action.

Amount Due   Date

FINAL NOTICE

Unless payment is received within 10 days on your past-due account, it will be referred for collection.

If you receive no response to this communication within 10 days, you must turn the account over to a collection agency or an attorney.

Amount Due   Date

YOU WILL BE SUED

If you intend to avoid this action, it is imperative that you remit immediately and notify us that payment is on the way so that this action can be stopped.

By law, if you receive no response to this letter within 30 days, you must turn the account over to a collection agency or an attorney.

Keep in mind that making phone calls costs money and takes time. Collecting the account on the first call is ideal, of course, and additional calls are simply repetition. As a rule, never say anything on the telephone that you would not write in a letter. Following this simple rule should protect you from criticism (and worse). Keep the conversation on the proper level. Be persistent, but understanding; tactful, but direct.

After a short period of working the telephone, you should be able to determine from the debtor's tone of voice whether the account will be paid without any difficulty. Experience will allow you to judge which debtors will require additional pressure, and what actions will enhance the probability of collecting on a given account.

If the debtor will not commit to a payment schedule after two or three calls, you should consider taking legal action or engaging a professional collection service for recovery. Obviously, the account must be large enough to warrant an action of this type. If the account is small, it may be best to write the matter off as a bad debt.

A few rules for making collection calls:

- Always have records of the account at hand when you make phone calls. Know what you are going to say, and say it clearly and with conviction.
- Control the interview.
- Set a time limit on all calls—five minutes at most.
- Remain professional, not emotional.
- Speak only to the debtor or to a member of the debtor's immediate family (spouse or sibling). You may also leave a message with a son or daughter old enough to understand what you are saying.
- If an individual not in the immediate family answers, ask when the debtor will be available, and make the call then.
- After each call, record the results of the call on the ledger card. Attempting to record results after making 15 or 20 calls can only lead to confusion and unnecessary repetition of calls.

When you reach the debtor, get right to the point. You might say, "My name is Robert Johnson and I am calling for Ace Hotel. We have billed you on your account for $300 four times, and have had no response from you. I would like to know *right now* what arrangement you are going to make to pay the account in full." Always use the word "arrangement"; if you say "arrangements," you are implying that time payments can be made.

Then just wait for the debtor's response before saying another word. Very often, the debtor agrees to pay the account in full on the first call. If the debtor says he is having financial difficulties, ask why he did not tell you so. Why did you need to make a call to find out? This approach puts the debtor on the defensive. If the debtor tells you he is unemployed, *always* ask how long he's been without a job. If your account is four months old, and he has been unemployed only a month, ask why he did not pay you while he was employed. You are also allowed to ask the debtor to pay you from his unemployment benefits.

In any call to a debtor, ask whether he is still employed with the same company and make a note of his response (including the date).

To the extent possible, you should insist that the debtor repay the amount in a single payment, if that was your original agreement. It is better to remain flexible, however, than to sacrifice the possibility of payment by being unwilling to negotiate.

If payments are to be made in installments, always ask the debtor to make his first payment at once. If you establish a payment schedule, find out precisely when the debtor intends in remit the first payment—and repeat the date, to ensure he understands what you expect. Ask the debtor to send the payment to your attention. Advance the account in your files to three days beyond the due date—and if the debtor has not remitted by that time, call him immediately to find out why not. Even after receiving collection calls, some debtors ignore the situation, presumably in the hope that the account will be forgotten. Maintain a rigid schedule of phone calls, especially on follow-up calls, and keep track of all calls you make in a chronological file or daybook.

Suppose you call a debtor and, reaching his spouse, learn that he is not available. Ask the spouse when the debtor will be available—and, if the hours are such that you cannot call him then, leave a message that he should call you. Calls of this type can be both frustrating and unproductive, because you may have no way to get beyond the spouse to the debtor.

You should call not only debtors who have failed to remit *any* payment but also those who are making payments more slowly or in smaller amounts than agreed upon. Emphasize the terms of the credit agreement, reminding the debtor of the size of the payment required and the due date. Also remind the debtor who submits payment inconsistently or in reduced amounts that the service charges added to the account each month are increasing the amount he must ultimately pay. If you and the debtor agree to a new payment schedule, send a written notice confirming that future payments will be expected on or before the new due date.

A debtor making very small payments on the account can sometimes be induced to increase the size of the payment. Point out to the debtor how long is will take to pay the amount due.

In making telephone calls pertaining to delinquent accounts, you will need to make a good number of off-the-cuff judgments. There is no standard answer to all collection problems. Each debtor has a unique personality; some react badly to pressure, while others will respond to it by paying promptly. It is important to remember that successful collection often requires negotiation. If a debtor is genuinely unable to pay the account at the time you call, insisting that he pay will not produce a check. In fact, being too rigid may lead the debtor to refuse to pay an account he would have been happy to settle as soon as he was able. In such cases, if the amount due is too small to justify legal action or professional collection efforts, you have failed completely in your objective.

Be flexible: take a little, and sometimes give a little. This approach is more productive in the final analysis.

Disputed Accounts

If a consumer disputes a debt, ask him to communicate all the details of the dispute to you in writing. If he does so, you have an opportunity to take steps toward a resolution of the dispute. If he does not, however, he has not abrogated his rights and his failure to respond is not legally considered an admission of liability. Send him written notice that you will wait 30 days for him to attempt to resolve the matter in dispute. If he does not respond within that time, you may resume collection efforts (you still won't know whether his complaint was legitimate, but you have no alternative but to proceed).

The Kinds of Debtors and Debts

Not all debtors are incorrigible deadbeats. There are four major categories of delinquent payers: the victim of circumstance, the staller, the slow payer, and the credit thief.

• **The victim of circumstance:** Unemployment, personal illness, illness in the family, fire, automobile accident, and other circumstances may constitute valid reason for nonpayment of an account. In such cases, be patient; the debtor will generally come up with the money as soon as he is able.

If a debtor has experienced misfortune, bear in mind that pressing the issue is not likely to resolve the matter, and will only antagonize the debtor. If you are understanding, the debtor may well make payments to you before paying his other creditors.

• **The staller:** Some debtors voice all kinds of complaints about real or imagined problems in an attempt to stall payment. The best way to cope with such debtors is to listen to all they have to say, and then ask for your money. You will be surprised at the number of times this straightforward approach produces results.

If the debtor's complaint is valid, take steps to correct the problem at once—then send the debtor a letter explaining the corrective measures taken and asking for payment in full of the balance due.

• **The slow payer:** It is difficult to induce a slow payer to settle his account in full. If you exert some pressure, he will usually send a payment, but most often it is a minimum amount used as a delaying tactic. Accounts of this nature can be extremely expensive to handle. If the amount due justifies it, you can always resort to legal action, and you are able to notify the debtor that such action is being considered.

• **The credit thief:** Some debtors who execute transactions on credit have absolutely no intention of paying. They are so deeply in debt, and have so many judgments against them, that there is virtually no possibility of recovering any money from them. They are considered judgment-proof because they have little or no income and they own no property that could be attached to satisfy a judgment. The only way to avoid extending credit to such individuals is to obtain complete information at the time of application and verify all references.

When you learn that a debtor is a credit thief, and your efforts to collect fail, accept that the account is a bad debt.

The Check Is in the Mail

Many debtors will tell you their accounts are paid. Some are telling the truth; others are just stalling. It is difficult to resolve a situation in which the debtor maintains he has paid because you must always entertain the possibility that you failed to record a payment.

To determine whether the debtor is bluffing or has perhaps made an honest error, you should ask him for proof of payment in the form of either a receipt or a cancelled check. If the payment was allegedly made by check, ask for a copy of both sides of the check. Even if it was cashed, a copy of the front of the check can prove nothing unless the bank marked it "Paid." Because some debtors write checks for the sole purpose of pretending they've made payment, obtain a copy of the check's reverse side, upon which the bank's cancellation mark will appear if the check was cashed.

If the consumer refuses to produce documentation of the account's payment, and you have examined your books and records carefully, you have only one recourse: turn the matter over to your attorney for his evaluation and suggestions for the resolution of the account. Be certain to advise him that the consumer claims he has paid. Legal action should be taken only when the amount of the account warrants the time and effort required to resolve it.

The Rubber Check

Procedures for handling returned checks vary from state to state, so you should consult your attorney for advice in this area. [This book discusses the control aspects of returned checks in Chapter 3.]

When a Debtor Goes Bankrupt

If you receive a court or legal notice that a debtor is filing a petition in bankruptcy, you are required to cease all collection efforts aimed at the debtor. If you receive such a notice directly from the debtor, either in writing or by phone, ask immediately what attorney is representing the debtor. Send the attorney and the court an itemized statement of the account by certified mail and request a return receipt.

Never take for granted that a bankruptcy petition will be filed simply because the debtor has told you so. Many individuals who intend to file never go through with the bankruptcy action; others will tell you they are going bankrupt just to stall your collection efforts. If you are unable to determine the name of the debtor's attorney, proceed with collection efforts until this information can be obtained.

The Way of Judgments

A judgment is a legal record issued by a court of proper jurisdiction. It avers that a given sum is indeed owed to you by the debtor. Many people assume that, when a judgment is awarded, the total due will automatically be paid. In fact, many judgments are never paid. The process of collecting a judgment can be long and time-consuming, requiring a number of legal steps. Consult your attorney for advice on the procedures required to collect on a judgment.

The length of time that a recorded judgment remains in effect varies from one state to the next (see the exhibit on the following page). After the specified period has elapsed, a judgment is no longer enforceable and you have no means to effect collection— although the term of a judgment can be extended in most states for a small fee.

When the Debtor Disappears

Professional collectors refer to efforts aimed at finding relocated debtors as "skip-tracing." Locating a debtor who has moved from his original address is an art requiring considerable patience, a little luck, and in some instances the detective abilities of Sherlock Holmes. Skip-tracing also requires tact, for you will be in contact with people who you hope will help you locate the "skip." Nonetheless, you should make an all-out effort to track down relocated debtors—or accept the considerable cost of leaving numerous accounts unpaid.

The procedures outlined earlier in regard to the credit application provide a logical starting point for skip-tracing. Begin by calling the telephone number given on the credit application. If the debtor has moved within a reasonably small area, he may have retained the phone number when he changed his address. If a new number has been assigned, the telephone operator will often give you the new number automatically. If not, call the director assistance and ask whether a new number has been assigned to the debtor. You should specifically advise the operator that it is a new number you seek.

If these calls yield no information, call the employer listed on the credit application. When you reach a member of the organization who may have a record of the employee's erstwhile address, your remarks should be limited to the following: "My name is John Spelvin, and I am calling for Spelvin Caterers. I am attempting to verify employment for Mr. George Smith. Is he still employed with you?" If the answer is affirmative, ask to check the address on record at the place of work against the address recorded on the application. If you are asked to state the purpose of your call, merely reply, "It is a personal matter." If the debtor is still at the place of employment, but the employer has not been informed of a change of address, you may forward mailings to the debtor at the place of employment. Adhere to the rules governing mailings: mark the envelope "Personal" and include no exterior indication that the contents relate to a debt.

Some companies will not give out information on the phone, and require that you send a letter formally requesting information. If this is the method you must use, you should phrase the letter as follows:

May we please verify the employment of the person named below:

Mr. James Jones

1234 Main Street

City, State, Zip

The address indicated is the one we have on file. If you have a more recent address for Mr. Jones, we would appreciate your so advising us.

Thank you for your cooperation. A stamped, self-addressed envelope is enclosed for your convenience in replying.

It may be useful to call the credit references listed on the credit application. Other creditors may have learned the debtor's new address. Even when talking to other creditors, however, do not say you are attempting to locate the party in the matter of an unpaid bill. If you learn the debtor's new address, attempt to reach the debtor by telephone. If you are unable to contact him, send a statement to the new address in an envelope with "Address Correction Requested" imprinted on it. This device insures that the invoice is delivered and allows you to verify the address, for if the Post Office does not return an address-correction card, you may assume that the debtor has received the billing.

If you are a member of a local credit bureau, see whether the debtor's new address is on file at the bureau—and, if not, ask to be notified when the bureau learns of the new address. In the process of moving, many people purchase furnishings and other household goods, and these transactions require credit. If a credit check is made, a new address and a new place of employment may be identified.

A "criss-cross" telephone directory may be a good investment if one is available in your area and if you have a substantial number of accounts. This type of directory contains a wealth of information. All named listings are in alphabetical order; all streets are listed in numerical order; the names of tenants are given; tenant ownership of the residence is indicated; and telephone numbers are included. A criss-cross directory helps you call the persons residing on either side of the debtor's residence. These individuals may be able to give you the debtor's new address or phone number.

Suppose you have taken all the foregoing steps and have not been able to trace the debtor. File the account and, when new city directories are available, check to see whether the debtor is listed. Your local library will have copies of the directory. You can also consult directories going back two or three years for helpful information.

In applying each skip-tracing technique, record on the ledger card the steps you have taken, the dates, and the results.

The Hanging Account

A "hanging account," as described in this section, is extremely expensive to carry on the books and can be the most difficult account to resolve.

A hanging account often involves a debtor who is on friendly terms with the creditor. The creditor feels uneasy about mentioning the unpaid balance, for the debtor is still doing business with the company, and there is a natural reluctance to interfere with a personal relationship. In many instances, the creditor fears the possible loss of the debtor's friendship or business.

It is a mistake to assume that simply because a customer continues to do business with you, he will eventually pay the outstanding balance on his account. Many creditors are inclined to allow familiar customers to build up their accounts this way, even though the unpaid balance at the end of the month or year is substantial.

The hanging account amounts to a "no-win" situation for the creditor—especially when it comes time to ask that the account be paid. The debtor, on the other hand, suffers no compunction about running up the account, and always acts highly indignant when the creditor sees fit to ask for the amount due to him. The debtor may interpret the creditor's request for money as an affront to his integrity.

The longer a hanging account remains unpaid, the less apt the debtor is to recognize the total amount due, and the more likely he is to decide that there must have been errors in the creditor's accounting; after all, the debtor *knows* the account is not that large.

A hanging account requires hours of arguing and bickering, poring over ledger sheets, and discussing service charges. Records of the account inevitably include charge slips without a signature and without clear indication of the goods purchased, so the creditor may need to remember transactions that took place two or three years ago in defending his records to the debtor. Because many of the transactions cannot be explained to the debtor's satisfaction and because the creditor does not have adequate documentation of the purchases to support his claims, the end results of hanging accounts include lost money and lost customers.

If these were not sufficient reasons to avoid hanging accounts, consider the cost of carrying such accounts on the books year after year. Suppose that a customer owes you $6,000 at the beginning of the year, purchases an additional $3,500 worth of goods and services during the year, and pays you $3,000 on his account during that time. The unpaid balance to be recovered is $6,500—in fact, more than the amount owed you at the beginning of the year. Debts accumulate quickly in accounts of this type, but because the creditor receives *some* payment, he is rarely concerned about the balance. The creditor may also find the hanging account expensive in lost service charges. This type of account is not usually conducive to adding such charges, and because the creditor may not issue statements on a regular basis, he will often neglect to calculate the applicable service charges. Moreover, even if service charges *are* added, they may never be recovered if the balance is not paid.

If any misunderstanding should arise between debtor and creditor in respect to the amount owed, the creditor generally finds that his records of the account are inadequate. The informality of hanging-account transactions complicates the task of recovering the full balance due the debtor.

Consider some of the circumstances that can render a hanging account uncollectible:

• **The death of the debtor:** How do you explain to an attorney and the probate court the amount of money the debtor owed you if your only records are incomplete, unsigned sales slips? It is unlikely that you will be able to support your claim for the unpaid balance with such flimsy evidence.

• **The debtor sells out,** goes bankrupt, or goes out of business for another reason: How do you protect your interests? Your informal handling of a hanging account will make it difficult to establish the amount due. If litigation is required, you will incur additional expenses for attorneys and court fees, even if the legal action is successful (which is not often the case).

• **The death of the creditor:** If you die, the procedures required to settle accounts will cost dearly. The Internal Revenue Service will tax the entire amount listed on the books as "Accounts Receivable," even though many of the accounts will never be paid. Most of the accounts will be turned over to an attorney for collection at a cost of 33 1/3 to 50 percent of the receivables. It is not uncommon to find an estate of $500,000 in accounts receivable reduced to $100,000 after estate taxes, probate, and collection costs.

You can resolve some of your existing hanging accounts by sending debtors a letter of the type shown below. The letter should be typewritten, signed, and sent in a plain white envelope. There should be no indication on the envelope that it is being sent by your company; using a stamp rather than a postage-meter imprint, and even mailing the letter from a town other than the one in which your business is located, will help ensure that the debtor at least opens the letter out of curiosity. The letter informs the debtor, in a manner that does not offend, that you perceive his account as a problem.

This letter essentially asks the debtor to bring his account up to date. If you followed the suggestions regarding typing and stamping the envelope, you can be reasonably sure that the debtor opened the envelope, and any debtor who does not respond to the letter in some fashion should be regarded as a possible problem.

If any debtor objects to the letter, say, "We didn't *want* to send it, but our supplier (or bank, or any other third party) told us we had to because they said our accounts receivable were too high." You might also make the following additional comments: "You know you owe the account, I know you owe the account, and *I* know you will pay, but *they* (the bank or supplier) are in the driver's seat. So why don't you make an arrangement with me to pay something each month on the balance we now have, and

Amount of the Account

Dear _____:

This letter is of vital concern to us, so please give it your careful consideration. We wish that we could visit with you, and explain this matter in person; however, time does not permit a personal call.

Our accounts receivable have grown so large that we have not been able to stay within our credit terms with (name of supplier or bank). Their terms with us are 10 days. Our terms with you specify payment by the tenth of the month following the receipt of a statement—in other words, a maximum of 40 days. This means that we must pay a staggering sum during the interim: a sum that we cannot afford if our customers allow their accounts to go past the due date on our credit terms.

We are writing to explain the tremendous load that we must carry, so that you will have a better understanding of our situation, and we ask you to make your payments promptly—in accordance with the time limits of our extension of credit to you.

Very truly yours,

(Signature)

pay for any new purchases? That way, you'll reduce the balance, and I can get these people off my back, and yours too. Okay?" Then proceed to negotiate the payments.

Always mention that you will expect a payment each 30 days on the past-due amount because your banker or supplier will be in every month to check the accounts. You thereby imply that any further actions to be taken are out of your hands. In other words, you shift the blame to someone else and preserve your image as a friend who is willing to help.

You should be aware that many debtors deliberately take advantage of creditors' willingness to extend credit on a hanging account. It's a means of advancing their own business enterprises at the expense of yours—often without incurring any additional cost for failure to pay.

If You Need an Attorney

Most attorneys do not perform collection work as a regular part of their practice. If there is an attorney in your area who specializes in collection work, he is the individual most qualified to help you handle collection efforts.

If you are already represented by an attorney in the conduct of your business, as a matter of courtesy ask him whether he can handle your collection problems. Do not expect him to take on this added responsibility as a favor; if he is in general practice, he almost certainly does not have the time to provide complimentary services, and your accounts will be neglected in favor of work that is more lucrative to him.

Do not refer $20 accounts to a collection lawyer; they only waste the attorney's time for a negligible reward. Accounts of at least $100 justify a professional collection effort. Expect to pay a commission of 33 1/3 to 50 percent of the amount due, varying with the amount collected and the age of the accounts.

When you first contact the attorney, ask him what he considers the smallest acceptable account. As a practical matter, he must apply as much effort to collect on a $50 account as on a $500 account, and the returns to you and to him are much smaller on the $50 account.

Selecting a Collection Agency

As an alternative to using a collection attorney, you can engage a professional collection agency. An agency is paid only for accounts actually collected; there is no charge for unsuccessful efforts.

A collection agency can also refer an account to a collection attorney for legal action in the event its efforts fail. By doing business with a collection agency, you also have the availability of a collection attorney. Finally, a collection agency will generally be able to collect some of your smaller accounts. Commission fees are higher on small accounts, but any amount you receive is better than nothing.

The representatives of a collection agency will be entrusted with your money, so it is essential that you learn as much as you can about an agency before you select one. How long has the agency been in business? How many employees does it have? Go to the agency's office and examine the physical layout of its facilities. Ask for references, and check them. You should engage an agency whose track record and employees inspire your confidence.

Conclusion

No one enters a place of business and says, "Give me that, but I am not going to pay for it." Instead, the customer may say, "Bill me the first of the month," or, "I'll send you a check." Unfortunately, these promises are often broken.

Far too many members of the business community are guilty of laxity in extending credit. They fail to ask for the money due them, and they fail to examine their accounts receivable on a consistent basis. This unsystematic approach to credit can entail substantial losses.

The typical creditor actually seems afraid of asking for his money, out of fear of offending the debtor and losing the debtor's business. What he fails to realize is that, if he does not ask for his money, he has not only lost the customer—who will generally make purchases elsewhere if his unpaid balance is substantial—but his money too.

The most important component of credit management is the painstaking evaluation of the credit application. Routine monitoring of your accounts receivable and a regular billing series will also prevent small problems from developing into large ones. When these procedures fail, applying the techniques set forth in the foregoing pages will help you recover the money that is due you.

INTERNAL CONTROL

3

Glossary

Accounts Receivable—Control—The balance sheet (general ledger) account representing the total accounts receivable due to the hotel; the sum of all the individual (subsidiary) accounts receivable.

Accounts Receivable—Subsidiary—The individual guest accounts representing the monies each individual owes the hotel; the sum of the subsidiary accounts receivable equals the control account.

Aged Accounts Receivable—A listing of the accounts receivable-control account, stratified by age, usually from current to over 120 days.

Bad Checks—Customers' checks that the hotel has accepted and deposited in the bank but that have been returned by the bank as uncollectible, usually because of insufficient funds.

Bad Debts—Past-due accounts receivable that have become old (over 90 or 120 days), and are probably uncollectible.

Billing—The portion of the accounts-receivable process concerned with typing or producing statements from the subsidiary accounts receivable, and mailing those statements to the customers.

Bucket (bin, tub, or tray)—The guests' accounts receivable, or total charges incurred by guests currently in the house, as represented by their folios. Also used to describe the physical files containing the guests folios.

City Ledger—Hotel jargon for the subsidiary accounts receivable of guests who have settled their folios by transferring them to prior-approved direct billing. It is probable that the historical origin of "city ledger" evolved from use of the hotel's facilities by local customers (i.e., those from the "city").

Collection—The process of attempting to receive payment from customers on past-due accounts or bad checks.

Collection Agency—An outside firm that specializes in collecting bad debts or bad checks for the hotel for a fee usually based on a percentage of the amount collected.

Credit Manager—A member of the hotel's management team whose responsibilities center around the formulation and administration of credit policy, as well as the collection of accounts.

Credit Policy—Those aspects of the hotel's operating policies that deal with the extension of credit to guests, and the procedures, rules, and training required to successfully accomplish that extension of credit.

Guest-Accounts Receivable—The total charges-to-date incurred by and posted to the folios of guests currently in the house.

Protest—The legal procedure necessary to establish evidence of the fact that a returned check is officially uncollectible. Usually performed by the hotel's bank and evidenced by a notarized document.

Write-off—A process consisting of internal accounting entries whereby a hotel removes uncollectible accounts (assets) from the books and transfers them to expense (through an allowance account).

Selected Reference

Walter H. Page, *Extend Credit and Collect—Professional Credit Management* (Cortland, NY: Walter H. Page, 1979).

Chapter 4

Purchasing and Expense Control

Objectives

After completing this chapter, you should understand:

1. The attributes and documents important for purchasing.
2. The function of the purchasing department.
3. The function of the receiving department.
4. The internal control of purchases and other expenses.
5. The control of petty-cash disbursements (Appendix 1).
6. The principles of inventory and its control (Appendix 2).

Verification of Invoices

The key management-control issue when paying for the goods and services that the hotel consumes is whether the correct bill is being paid. What is meant by the correct bill? Several questions come to mind: did we receive all of what we ordered? Does the bill reflect what was received? Was our staff satisfied with the quality? Did we get the best price? Is the bill calculated with the prices that we were promised or agreed to? Is the math correct?

All of these questions can be satisfactorily answered if the control process is designed to verify three key attributes:

- Price,
- Quality, and
- Quantity.

Price refers to the item prices that appear on the invoices we receive from our suppliers. The price on the invoices must correspond to the price we thought we were to be charged when we agreed to the purchase.

Quality refers to the condition of the goods and services that we received and how well the product matches what we specified when we agreed to the purchase. Quality control involves inspection and examination of the products upon receipt and follow-up as to how they held up in use. Some correlation must also be made to the specifications agreed to at the time of the original purchase.

Quantity can refer either to quantity ordered or quantity received. As we will see later in the discussion on receiving, quantity ordered is important from the perspective of the purchasing department as it works to ensure sufficient supplies to meet needs. The more important issue for internal control, however, is quantity received. The quantity stated on the invoice—the amount we are billed for—must agree with the quantity that we actually received. Therefore, receiving staff must check on quantities received by counting and weighing items and the recording of those counts and weights or at least noting any discrepancies on the delivery tickets. More detailed discussions of this process, and that of checking quality, appear in the section on the receiving department.

In addition to verifying price, quality, and quantity, a system of paperwork should be designed to integrate the verifications in the accounting and disbursement processes, to ensure a beneficial division of duties, and to minimize the payroll costs. This system operates through a unique application of the concept of "management by exception." Before this application can be described, however, some accounting and audit-trail foundations must be built.

You may recall from the discussion of accounting documents in Chapter 1 that accounting documents are:

• Serially numbered,
• Multi-part or multi-copy,
• Controlled by the accounting department, and
• Accounted for periodically by serial number.

I am repeating these characteristics because they are so important to purchasing and expense control. For the key accounting documents used in purchasing and expense control, the accounting department records the serial numbers at receipt, in inventory, at issue, and at final turn-in. Periodically, in most cases monthly, the integrity of the numerical sequence must be verified. This is accomplished by a combination of inventory and audit. These attributes are presumed for all the documents that follow.

Internal Control of Purchasing

The role of the purchasing department in hotels is important from the perspectives of cost and quality control, as well as internal control. Although every hotel has a purchasing-department function, only large hotels have complete purchasing departments with a purchasing manager and staff. In smaller hotels there may be only one purchasing person, while in very small operations someone in management will be designated to do the purchasing—perhaps the chef, an assistant manager, or even the general manager.

An important internal-control issue surfaces when the role of the purchasing manager is reviewed. Frauds that involve the purchasing function usually center around the purchasing officer's accepting money or other reward from vendors so that the hotel will purchase overpriced or substandard items. That type of fraud is extremely hard to prevent. Normal internal-control procedures and divisions of duties are designed to preclude the opportunity for internal fraud. Purchasing problems involve collusion with persons outside the hotel—the suppliers. The quality of the goods is easier to assure, as we will see in the section on receiving. There is still the issue, however, of correlating the quality received with the prices we have been charged. The suitability of the prices (i.e., getting the best possible price) is almost impossible to check even with the best internal control procedures.

The best control on price adequacy is top-management involvement in the process. As we will see later in the section on disbursements, the general manager must review all invoices and supporting documentation, and sign the checks for payment. As part of that process, it is an excellent idea for the manager to review the prices, speak with chefs and others about quality levels, and occasionally call around personally to shop some prices. That shopping, coupled with occasional review of the competitive-bidding process, is an important control measure that can help ensure the adequacy of the purchasing function.

The primary functions of the purchasing manager are to procure the goods and services needed by the hotel and to obtain the highest possible quality at the lowest possible prices. The purchasing manager's function must be kept separate from receiving, storage and inventory, and the accounting for and ultimate payment of invoices. There is not usually a problem with maintaining separation in accounting, but in practice the purchasing manager often works with or even supervises the receiving or storeroom personnel—a combination that should be avoided. These product-handling employees should report to the accounting department or directly to top management.

Purchasing is most effectively accomplished by a process known as competitive bidding. Competitive bidding can be formal. In that process, written specifications are sent out, closed (secret) written bids are received and all opened at once, and the purchase is awarded to the low bidder. This formal type of bidding is typical of governmental and other public institutions. It is complicated and expensive, particularly in the specification-writing process.

A less formal but still effective approach to purchasing can be as simple as getting at least three competitive prices before making the purchasing decision. That approach is typical in most hotels, and creates sufficient control if top management stays involved with the process and occasionally checks prices—making sure that the purchasing manager knows it!

Purchase Orders. Purchase orders (POs) are multi-part accounting forms that play several vital roles in the internal-control process for purchasing and expense control. Exhibit 4.1 shows examples of typical hotel purchase orders.

Exhibit 4.1

Sample Purchase Orders

PURCHASE ORDER

PAGE _____ OF _____

DATE ORDERED _____

EXPECTED DATE OF RECEIPT _____

SUPPLIER'S NAME _____

PURCHASE ORDER #

QUANTITY	SHIPPING UNITS	ITEM NAME & SPECIFICATIONS	REMARKS

SMALL ORDER FORM

CORNELL UNIVERSITY
ITHACA, N.Y., 14853

DATE	S.O. NUMBER	ACCT. NO.
	L- 46534	

DELIVER TO AND MARK FOR:

TO:

MATERIAL OR SERVICE	QUANTITY	UNIT PRICE	TOTAL

VENDOR: SHIP AND BILL ITEMS IN STOCK. CANCEL BALANCE.

TOTAL COST

NOTICE: This order is valid only with suppliers previously authorized by Cornell Purchasing Department to accept special orders. Only expendable supplies shall be furnished and charges on a single order may not exceed $300.00. FURNISH ITEMS FROM STOCK — NO BACK ORDERS ACCEPTED.

E B Pirko
PURCHASING MANAGER
CORNELL UNIVERSITY

AUTHORIZED SIGNATURE

BILLING COPY

ORDER PLACED BY:

RECEIVED BY:

WHITE - Original Order   YELLOW - Accounting Copy   PINK - Vendor Copy   000035

First, the purchase order authorizes the purchase. Under our legal system, any employee of the hotel can call a supplier and order goods. If we accept receipt of them, we are bound to pay for them. A letter should be sent to all suppliers and even potential suppliers stating that the hotel will not be responsible for (i.e., will not pay for) any goods or services except those ordered with a properly executed purchase order. That letter is also an excellent opportunity to state who in the hotel is authorized to make purchases, explain any limitations that may apply to those persons, and provide sample signatures. That type of notice limits and controls purchasing at the hotel to those employees whom management wishes to have such authority. The power to purchase should be limited to the purchasing staff and to selected members of management (who can step in and order in last-minute or emergency situations).

Second, the purchase order provides key portions of the documentation used to pay invoices. In this function it plays a role in verification of all three attributes of purchasing. The purchase order is the key source of the prices we agreed to at the time of the purchase. It is also a source of information about quality, because it specifies the quality or grade of items ordered. It also specifies quantity ordered. As we will see, the receiving function is more important in ascertaining actual quality and quantity, but the purchase order is the key document for verifying price. One copy of the purchase order goes directly to the accounting office, where it becomes part of the overall documentation, and is used in the monthly verification of serial numbers.

Operationally, the restriction of all purchases to those accompanied by a purchase order may seem cumbersome. Many items—fresh fruits and vegetables, for example—are ordered and shipped daily. They often are ordered by telephone at 5:00 AM for delivery later that morning. Many of these items are ordered frequently in high volume, so filling out a purchase order for each and every one, daily, may also seem cumbersome.

These problems, however, can be alleviated and even turned into control aids rather than hindrances. In practice, suppliers will generally be willing to ship on a telephone order if they are speaking to an authorized purchaser and are given the purchase order's serial number. The hotel must follow up by quickly mailing the fully executed confirming purchase order. If it is a few days late, the purchasing manager can expect to hear from a nervous supplier!

The problem of too much paperwork for the purchasing department

EXHIBIT 4.2

Sample Quotation Sheet

STEWARD'S MARKET QUOTATION LIST

QUOTATIONS				ON HAND	ARTICLE	WANTED	QUOTATIONS				ON HAND	ARTICLE
					FISH (Cont'd)							**Vegetables (C**
					Carp							Estragon
					Codfish, Live							Egg Plant
					Codfish, Salt Boneless							Garlic
					Codfish, Salt Flake							Horseradish Roots
					Eels							Kale
					Finnan Haddie							Kohlrabi
					Flounders							Lettuce
					Flounders							Lettuce, Ice Berg
					Flounders, Fillet							Lettuce, Place
					Fluke							Leeks
					Haddock							Mint
					Haddock, Fillet							Mushrooms
					Haddock, Smoked							Mushrooms, Fresh
					Halibut							Okra
					Halibut, Chicken							Onions
					Herring							Onions, Yellow
					Herring, Smoked							Onions, Bermuda
					Herring, Kippered							Onions, Spanish
					Kingfish							Onions, White
					Mackerel, Fresh							Onions, Scallions
					Mackerel, Salt							Oyster Plant
					Mackerel, Spanish							Parsley
					Mackerel, Smoked							Parsnips
					Perch							Peppermint
					Pickerel							Peas, Green
					Pike							Peas
					Porgies							Peas
					Pompano							Peppers, Green
					Redsnapper							Peppers, Red
					Salmon, Fresh							Potatoes
					Salmon, Smoked							Potatoes, Bermuda
					Salmon, Nova Scotia							Potatoes, Idaho
					Scrod							Potatoes, Idaho
					Shad							Potatoes, Sweet
					Shad Roes							Potatoes, New
					Smelts							Potatoes, Yams

Courtesy: William Allen & Co.
Form 6032

INTERNAL CONTROL

4

Exhibit 4.3

Sample Grocery Form

nescafe								
newburgh sherry								
noodles, ABC								raisins
noodles, broad								ravioli
noodles, egg								raspberry preserves
noodles, fine								relish, dill
noodles, Lazangina								relish, sweet
noodles, Med.								rice, bag
nuts, salted								rice, box
nuts, sliced								rice krispies
nutmeg								ritz
								rosemary leaves
								rolled oats
								rum flavor
								ry krisp
oatmeal								
oil, cooking								
oil, salad								
okra								
olives, cocktail								saffron
olives, ripe								sage
olives, stuffed								salt, cooking
olives, Queen								salt, table
onion, cocktail								salmon
onion, sm. white								saltines
orange juice								sardines
oysterettes								sauerkraut
								sauerkraut juice
								sanka Ind.
								shades, egg
								shades, tom.
paprika								shortening
pastes, blue								shr. wheat
pastes, green								spaghetti
pastes, red								spaghettini
peanuts								spice mixed
peanut, butter								strawberry jam
peas #2								stringbeans
peas #10								sugar, brown
pear halves								sugar, ind. envelopes
pear, red-green								sugar, gran.

Courtesy: William Allen & Co.
Form 8192

can be alleviated and the process of competitive price shopping can be helped and encouraged by the addition of some easy-to-use forms. I believe that if we can turn the paperwork, often resented by non-accounting employees, into something that makes their jobs easier, they will welcome it rather than resent it. An example of this axiom can be seen with the purchasing function. The purchase orders shown in Exhibit 4.1 resemble invoices in that there are columns for quantity, description of the item, unit price, and total price, and there is a row or line for each item. Filling out all of that data for everything we need in a busy hotel is time consuming. Exhibits 4.2 & 4.3 are samples of standard quotation sheets. They list most of the typical food items used in hotels, and they have columns for several price quotations. Forms of this type or simpler ones that can be made up to fit your individual hotel are quite useful as shopping lists of what needs to be ordered, while they also are quotation sheets for prices. After all the quotes are received, the purchasing manager can decide where to buy each item and then flag them for each supplier (by circling, highlighting in different colors, or any other simple flagging schemes).

Writing a purchase order becomes simple. The purchasing agent fills out the top portion of the PO and writes "see attached form" in the product section. The purchaser then simply staples a copy of the annotated quotation sheet to the PO, calls in the order, gives the vendor the PO number, and drops the PO into the mail. Thus we have supplied, with one simple form, a shopping list, a quotation sheet, and the specifications for the purchase orders. This is a prime example of making paperwork easier and more helpful to the employees, while ensuring necessary documentation.

Internal Control in Receiving

The receiving department plays a key internal-control role by checking on quality and quantity of goods ordered. All hotels must have a receiving function—that is, someone must accept goods that are shipped. In larger properties, a receiving department comprises a receiving manager, material handlers, and storeroom clerks. In smaller operations there may be only a receiving clerk—and he or she may work part-time or be shared with other functions such as accounting, security, or payroll. The primary responsibility of the receiving person is to check all orders for quality and quantity as they enter the hotel. That process

EXHIBIT 4.4

Sample Receiving Report

RECEIVING REPORT — (DAILY and WEEKLY)		INVOICE NO. OR DATE	TOTALS		MEAT	FISH	POULTRY	PRODUCE	DAIRY	BAKED GOODS	UNIT NAME		UNIT NO.		DAY OF WEEK	GI
	VENDOR NAME		INDIRECT	DIRECT												
-	YESTERDAY'S WEEK-TO-DATE	(LINE 42)														
1																
2																
3																
4																
5																
6																
7																
8																
9																
10																
11																
12																
13																
14																
15																
16																
17																
18																
19																
20																
21																
22																
23																
24																
25																
26																
27																
28																
29																
30																
31																
32																
33																
34																
35																
36																
37																
38																
39																
40																
41	TOTAL TODAY															
42	TOTAL WEEK-TO-DATE															
43	% TO SALES															

Courtesy: William Allen & Co. Form 9514

is documented by a serially numbered accounting form known as the receiving report.

Questions usually arise in hotels as to what type of skills a receiving clerk needs and to whom he or she should report. Since the most complicated part of quality assurance involves checking foods and beverages, the clerk needs the skills necessary to evaluate those items. The problem with that notion is that a person with a level of food and beverage skill high enough to judge food quality will not remain a

Case 4.1

A New Method of Recycling

An accountant employed at a 300-room hotel kept the general books, drew all checks, handled petty cash, and made all deposits. The checks were signed by the manager and countersigned by the accountant. The manager never questioned or examined any bills. The checks, after being signed by the manager, were returned to the accountant's office for mailing.

Immediately after being hired, the accountant secretly ordered a new checkbook from the bank, which was identical in all respects to the one the hotel was using. The number sequence for the duplicate book started with the nearest hundred preceding the real checkbook, so the accountant had a substantial supply of duplicate checks. He abstracted from the files bills of the same month of the previous year that bore approval signatures of department heads still in authority. After changing the year, the accountant entered these bills in the purchase journal, drew a check payable to the dealer, attached it to the bill, and presented the check, complete with supporting paper work, to the general manager for signature. The bogus bills were mixed in with legitimate checks and bills. Also in the stack was a check from the duplicate checkbook with the same amount, date, and numbers as the duplicate dealer's check, but made payable to the chief accountant, "for exchange." This check was supposed to be necessitated by the cashing of guest checks in excess of the day's receipts and was supported by a duplicate deposit slip, which was made up, stamped, and initialed by the accountant instead of the bank teller.

The exchange check and fictitious deposit slip were placed on top of the bills and checks ready for signature, while the dealer's check was near the bottom, so that the two identical amounts would be less likely to attract suspicion.

After the bills and checks were returned to the accountant's office for mailing, the accountant would take the exchange check to the bank and have it cashed. He would hold the fake dealer's check until the end of the month, and then call personally at the bank for the statement and cancelled checks. The exchange check would be removed from the cancelled checks and replaced by the dealer's check, which the accountant suitably endorsed, perforated, and cancelled to simulate the check-clearing process.

The accountant's systematic method of stealing lasted several months, until it was time for the outside audit. When arrangements were made for the audit, the manager was advised to instruct the bank to forward the bank statement and cancelled checks to the external auditor's office at the end of the month—the critical time window for the accountant's scheme. After reconciling the cash with the bank statement, several exchange checks were found in the cancelled checks of the previous month. They had not been entered in the cash book, but in their place were similar amounts entered as payments to dealers. The auditors then inspected the bills supporting the payments and uncovered the scheme.

Discussion

In this case, the accountant secretly ordered a duplicate check book. Care should be taken in purchasing procedures—and especially in letters to vendors concerning purchase orders—to ensure that accounting documents have an extra measure of purchase control, including top-management approval.

The check-cashing and exchange mechanisms were also used improperly to cash the fraudulent checks. These procedures are fully discussed in Chapter 2.

Those two weaknesses are important, but they are not the central issues in the case. The duplicate check book and the weak check-cashing mechanism made it more convenient to perpetrate the fraud, but it could have been achieved without them. It is quite easy to convert checks by depositing them in a remote bank account and waiting for a period of time before withdrawing the cash. The perpetrator could open such a bank account in a city different from the hotel, and clear checks.

The key issues in the case are division of duties and the lax disbursement procedures for approving and paying bills. The accountant should have no access to cash, including the exchange process and the checks to be mailed to vendors. Checks for vendors, once approved, should not be returned to the accounting department, but rather should be mailed under the control of the authorized signor.

The disbursement procedure calls for the authorized signor (preferably the general manager) to scrutinize the documentation carefully (including the original purchase order, receiving report, and invoice—all matched), cancel that documentation to prevent its re-use, and ensure that the check is properly made out and mailed to the vendor at the correct address. The general manager should also apply a similar high level of scrutiny to the exchange process and to checks made out to exchange.

Also, the periodic use of cut-off bank statements by management—as was done by the external auditor in this case—is a good preventive measure.

---

receiving clerk or will not work at the salary we can afford to pay a receiving person. Moreover, receiving plays an extremely important role in purchase documentation, and a person familiar with accounting would be valuable in assuring that the audit trail is complete. Therefore, I usually recommend that the receiving person have good clerical skills and that he or she report to the accounting department. As for the food and beverage skills needed to evaluate product quality, I recommend that the receiving person solicit the help of chefs and other food preparers. The hotel gains the advantages of allowing those that work with the product to evaluate its quality, plus some additional division of duties.

Quantity checking is critical to the control process. The receiving clerk has the prime responsibility for checking all orders for quantity received by counting and weighing the items. Needless to say, if a product is charged for by the item, it should be counted, and if it is charged for by weight, it should be weighed. All deliveries should be so checked, and the counts and weights should be noted on a receiving report that is turned in to the accounting office daily.

Exhibit 4.4 is a sample of an individual receiving report. Some hotels use a large daily receiving log on which all deliveries for the day are recorded. Again, as with the purchasing function, we would like to make the paperwork helpful and easy to use. The receiving report shows the accounting office the quality and quantity of goods received. Any way in which that can be accomplished will suffice. A receiving report such as the one in Exhibit 4.4 can often be filled out only at the top with the body stating: "see attached invoice." Then, the delivery ticket or shipping invoice that accompanied the goods can be stapled to the receiving report. Most shipping invoices already list the quantities, and the receiving report can be used for the exceptions, those counts and weights that disagree with the original order. When there are exceptions, the receiving clerk must get the delivery person to agree with the new count or weight, and to sign the receiving report (or a credit memo or any type of exception document). In that way the accounting office can notify the vendor of the discrepancy, and of the fact that the delivery agent verified it.

Some hotels simply affix a large rubber stamp to the shipping invoice, which, in effect, becomes the receiving report. There is no major internal control problem with that shortcut, except that it provides no separate mechanism for reporting and verifying discrepancies. Changes must be written alongside the original count or weight and initialed by both parties. It would seem that a separate receiving report is more satisfactory. Remember, the receiving report must be sent to the accounting office to become part of the overall accounting documentation.

A final issue with respect to receiving is whether to have "blind receiving." As with blind turn-in, blind receiving means that the receiving person tallies all deliveries without knowing what to expect. The argument for blind receiving is that the receiving person is apt to do a more careful job of checking the order when he or she does not have a PO to refer to. In the opposite case, a copy of the purchase order is sent to the receiving department in advance. In that way they know what to expect. With that approach, the receiving person will know if an order does not come in or if the quantity received is different from the quantity ordered. The disadvantage could be that a person with a PO is likely to check the order casually against the shipping invoice, rather than performing an item-by-item check. Both arguments have some validity, and the internal-control ramifications of blind receiving versus checking against a PO are not significant, albeit more ideal internal control is achieved with blind receiving. The decision of which method to use is based on the personal preference of management.

The Role of the Accounting Department

The primary function of the accounting department in purchase and expense control is to record the transactions and thus simultaneously establish the hotel's indebtedness to suppliers, while posting expenses to their proper account categories. While accomplishing those standard bookkeeping functions (notably accounts payable), the accounting department can also play some important internal-control roles—and do so with no additional expense.

The "accounts-payable clerk" (the bookkeeper who handles accounts payable) has the responsibility of assembling and checking all of the documentation associated with purchasing and payment. As we saw earlier, copies of the purchase orders and receiving reports come into the accounting department. The POs contain the information on the prices that we should be charged, while the receiving reports convey the quantities actually received and the items' quality. We can presume the items are acceptable in the absence of exception flags. The hotel's suppliers or vendors will typically mail invoices stating the actual prices and quantities to the accounting department.

The accounts-payable clerk has the primary responsibility for checking that invoice prices match the ones we were promised and quantities match the ones we received. That process is easily accomplished by simply matching up the documentation and putting them together for the posting and drawing of the accounts-payable checks. The documentation consists of a copy of the purchase order (price promised, quantity ordered), the receiving report and shipping invoice (quantity received, quality), and the formal invoice (quantity and price charged). All of the prices and quantities on the three pieces of documentation should match. If they do, the three attributes of price,

Case 4.2

Padding Potatoes for Petty Cash

The steward of a transient hotel of 200 rooms that did a large food business found it advantageous to purchase various food items from farmers and vendors who frequently offered potatoes, vegetables, and other produce at favorable prices to avoid having to haul the food items back to the farm.

To make the transaction, a storeroom clerk would make out a petty-cash purchase voucher, which he had the steward initial and for which the vendor would give a receipt. That paper work completed, the clerk would go upstairs to the cashier's office to get the cash while the vendor waited.

On the way, the clerk would alter the voucher. If, for instance, the purchase was for one bushel of potatoes, he would initially write the slip something like the following: 1 sack potatoes....365. Instead of specifying a bushel, he used the vague word "sack," and the original amount did not have the usual decimal point. Before he got to the cashier, he added a zero to the quantity, making it 10 instead of 1, inserted the decimal between the 6 and the 5, and added a zero to the end of the number. The resulting slip read: 10 sacks potatoes.......$36.50.

As the slip seemed to be genuine in all respects, the cashier would pay the inflated amount and the clerk would pocket the difference. When he couldn't make numerical changes, he would add an item or two to the slip, and collect that inflated total.

The receiving sheets were made out by the same clerk. It was a simple matter to alter the sheets as he had done on the invoice—thus eliminating any discrepancy between invoice and storeroom sheets when the auditor's office checked them. The alterations and additions to the receiving sheets were made, of course, after the steward had initialed them.

The storeroom clerk continued this practice for about three months—always using small amounts, but adding considerably to his income. Unfortunately for the clerk, the hotel hired a new auditor, who immediately questioned the practice of paying the money to the clerk. He arranged that vendors should be brought by the clerk to the cashier's office and paid directly.

At the close of the next month, the auditor noticed that the level of cash purchases was considerably lower than before. That change aroused suspicion, and the auditor reexamined all cash purchases handled by this receiving clerk. In several instances, the auditor checked directly with the vendors.

The auditor's investigation brought the clerk's scheme to light, and the clerk was terminated. But the exact amounts embezzled could not be determined, and since the clerk was not bonded, the hotel could not recover its lost funds.

Discussion

The failures in this case can be attributed to a poor petty-cash policy and improper voucher-control procedures. The clerk, in this case, had the advance approval of management to complete the sale. The frauds were committed after the manager signed the voucher.

Correct control procedures stipulate that petty-cash vouchers have numerical serial numbers, and are controlled, issued, and audited by the accounting department. The vouchers should have multiple copies, with one copy sent by authorized signers directly to the accounting department. That copy is compared in the audit process with the paid copy—to prevent the type of "change after authorization" fraud that occurred in this hotel.

Another violation that occurred was allowing an employee to pick up the cash for a vendor or another employee. Payees should be the only persons to pick up petty cash, and they should sign the voucher so the hotel has verification of the amount, and evidence that the payee was paid. Where applicable, a receipt or register tape should be obtained and attached to the voucher.

Finally, petty-cash disbursements should be continually scrutinized with the intent to minimize or even eliminate them. In the present case, the frequency with which farmers and others sold items to the hotel indicates a need to establish a more systematic and controlled approach—payment by check, or even requesting credit for repeat vendors.

---

quantity and quality have been verified, and the clerk can prepare a voucher to draw a check. If there are any discrepancies, an exception exists and the clerk needs to raise a "flag" by putting the documentation in an exception tray (some hotels prefer a more formal written exception form) so the controller can deal with them, usually by contacting the purchasing manager for action. This process is a form of "management by exception." A clerical employee does most of the work of checking prices and quantities by simply matching up the pieces of the paper trail. Management is involved only when exceptions occur.

The process has two interesting side benefits. First, we accomplish the verifications efficiently because we are using less costly clerks to do most of the work. Second, we get a full and effective division of duties. Even though we have been focusing on pieces of paper, those documents represent the work of several key players. The purchasing manager's work is represented by the purchase order, the receiving manager's work is represented by the receiving report, the outside supplier is represented by the invoice, and the accounting personnel are involved in the aggregation of the documentation and the posting. True to the basic principle of good control, we have three or more persons, excluding top management, involved in the transaction, making alterations or embezzlement quite difficult.

A final role of the accounting department is auditing transactions, which is accomplished monthly by reconciling the withdrawal side of the bank statement with the ledgers and journals that represent the purchase postings and paid accounts. That reconciliation and audit process should be kept separate from the accounts-payable clerk or persons drawing the payables checks. In larger organizations, it is easy to accomplish this division of duties. The accounts-payable clerk's chores can safely be combined with other subsidiary ledger jobs such as receivables or payroll. In small organizations where there may be only one bookkeeper, management or an external practitioner should handle the bank statement reconciliation.

The Role of Management

To ensure effective internal control in the areas of purchasing and expense control, top management must have an ongoing role. Rarely in this book do I suggest that top management be given continuous or ongoing tasks. Usually, top management plays an occasional or "oversight" role. Shopping around to check prices is an example of such spot verification. In the payment of the hotel's invoices, however, I make a firm exception. Top management—preferably the general manager himself or herself—must verify the documentation and sign all of the checks.

The accounting department delivers to the manager vouchers, documentation packets, checks, and ready-typed or window envelopes for those checks. The documentation packet consists of the purchase order, receiving report, and invoice. All exceptions should have been dealt with at this point, or a check would not be drawn. The manager checks the documentation to verify that the clerks and other employees have effectively done their jobs and that the prices, quantities, and quality of the goods and services are proper. He or she then cancels the supporting documentation,* signs the checks, personally supervises

---

*Cancellation is usually accomplished by signing or initialing the supporting invoice in permanent or indelible ink, although some managers prefer to punch or otherwise permanently mark the documentation. Cancellation of supporting documentation is important, since several frauds have been perpetrated whereby the same documentation was used more than once.

their mailing, and returns the documentation to the accounting office for filing.

The checks are delivered with envelopes so that the manager can personally supervise the mailing. The manager's secretary can put the checks in the mail, but they do not go back to the accounting department, although the cancelled documentation does. The key issue is that if a fraudulent payment is returned to the maker, he or she may find a way to cash it. If it is sent to the vendor, then only the vendor can benefit from it. The manager should also check the address on the check or envelope to see that it matches the one on the invoice. Duplicate and other fraudulent payments have been known to go to the address of an employee's or other person's fictitious "business."

Top management's ongoing role of verification and cancellation is a serious and important one in the invoice-payment process. In addition to the internal-control benefits, managers will be better informed about what the hotel's operations are buying, what the goods and services cost, and how often those items and services are being purchased. The role of the top manager is so critical that I strongly advocate the manager's setting aside three or four hours every month for the chore. If the manager is too busy or involved with solving a crisis at accounts-payable time, he or she should sign the checks, have his or her secretary compare them with the invoices, mail them, and hold the documentation for verification later. When the crisis passes or when more time is available, the manager can check the documentation in detail and cancel it. If he or she discovers a problem or discrepancy, it can always be dealt with after the fact. The key issue is that the top manager is personally involved in the process and is the final point of verification.

Recap: Division of Duties

The key ingredient for internal control in the areas of purchasing and expense control is division of the duties. In this case I am advocating separation of the accounting tasks, separation of custody from record keeping, and a division in the major managerial tasks of purchasing and receiving, capped by top-management overview of the entire process. The managers and the accounting department have the common goals of ascertaining the appropriateness of the price, quantity, and quality of the goods and services purchased by the hotel. Those attributes can be checked through a unique application of the concept of management by exception. The accounting department brings together all of the management people and tasks—represented by their paper trails—and matches them. If they match, all is well. If not, management investigates the discrepancies. The correct division of duties is an automatic by-product of the process.

Many hotels have monthly meetings of all of the key staff members associated with purchasing and bill payment. At those meetings, all invoices are discussed and approved for payment. The system being advocated here eliminates the need for such time-consuming meetings, yet still relies on the separate input of all the key players. The recap of the division of duties that follows demonstrates this point.

Division of Duties:

Purchasing and Paying for Goods and Services

- *Accounts-Payable Clerk*: Matches invoice with receiving record and purchase order; checks extensions and footings (math).
- *Purchasing Manager*: Approves price and authorizes payment.
- *Cashier*: Prepares checks and enters in check register.
- *Manager*: Compares checks with supporting documentation; signs; cancels supporting documentation; mails checks to payees.
- *Auditor*: Reconciles bank statement with ledger each month.

Appendix 4.1:

Petty-Cash Disbursements

Petty cash is a catch-phrase for funds of cash on hand—currency and coin—that are kept for minor, last-minute, or emergency purchases. That is, purchases outside of the careful system of checks and balances discussed throughout Chapter 4. The fact that these types of purchases fall out of the normal internal-control system causes them to be an area of special concern (e.g., there is no purchase order with a petty-cash purchase). The word "petty" probably evolved from the fact that the purchases made in this manner are usually small, or perhaps because the cash funds or cash boxes themselves are usually small.

The small relative size of the petty-cash funds in most operations sometimes affords them lax internal-control treatment. That is a mistake! Even though the amounts are small, frauds can take place, or the petty-cash fund can be the culmination of (or cover-up for) some unrelated fraud. For these reasons, and because ongoing analysis of the petty-cash expenditures yields important management information, a systematic approach to the control of petty cash is strongly recommended.

Minimize the use of petty cash. The most important internal-control principle regarding petty-cash disbursements is to minimize their use. Managers will find that they have to work hard and continuously to minimize these types of purchases. In most hotels, the use of petty-cash funds seems to grow constantly. It is easier for the staff to be lax in forecasting and planning when they know they can simply draw some cash and run down to the store to pick up supplies or food. Similarly, it may be easier to pay a local supplier for some items through petty cash, and thus avoid the cumbersome process of filling in purchase orders. The nature of most petty-cash purchases—an employee buys something and gets reimbursed—means that these purchases are also not in the receiving portion of the purchasing cycle. The bottom line with petty-cash purchasing is that the hotel cannot really ascertain the appropriateness of price, quantity, or quality.

Management should continuously scrutinize these purchases to glean information about whether operating procedures are lax and to attempt to eliminate as many of them as possible. With a goal of eliminating petty-cash purchases altogether, management may at least be able to minimize them! Any purchases that are systematic (i.e., appear in the petty-cash box consistently or frequently) are candidates for removal to the regular purchasing cycle. In some areas, certain goods and services (e.g., liquor, freight, advertising) are required by custom or even by law to be paid more quickly than the usual 30-day accounts-payable cycle. Sometimes, as a matter of convenience, these items end up being paid for with petty cash. That practice should be avoided! Even where tight credit or time restrictions apply, the vendors

EXHIBIT 4.5

Sample Petty-Cash Voucher

PETTY CASH VOUCHER	Date_____	**N⁰ 4978**	

Please pay to_____

_____ Dollars

For_____

Charge to_____

Reimbursed by Check No._____ | Received the above amount.

Dated_____

Courtesy: William Allen & Co. Form 7174

will extend some credit or, at minimum, allow payment by check. Hotels are urged to run a short cycle or mini-cycle of accounts payable, perhaps on a seven-day basis, to deal with these special situations. In that way, the same controls that apply to the 30-day cycle can be applied.

Separate Imprest Fund. The petty cash fund or "box" should be a separate or independent one. Petty-cash disbursements are not made from a regular-shift cashier's cash drawer. Instead, an independent imprest fund is set up, initially by drawing a check to "cash," and that currency is kept in a separate drawer or box. The term "imprest" refers to the fact that a fixed amount is advanced (or loaned), and the fund remains at that fixed amount. In other words, a set amount—say $100—is initially drawn and the currency put in the petty-cash fund. The fund will always be $100, even after several disbursements. After payouts, it consists of cash, plus vouchers representing the disbursements totalling the initial $100. The amount of cash in the imprest fund should be enough to last a normal accounting cycle—usually a month. In that way, cash replenishment can occur via the regular accounts-payable cycle.

Custody of the fund should be the responsibility of one individual, who is not an accounting or record-keeping employee. It is proper for a cash-handling employee to have custody of the petty cash, although the fund itself must be separate of any regular cashier's bank. Perhaps the ideal person to have custody of the petty cash is the head cashier. The manager's secretary or any clerical employee may also be responsible, provided the person has no accounting or bookkeeping tasks. The problem of off-hour access must also be addressed.

Petty-cash disbursements should be approved in advance by management. That advance approval is best accomplished by the voucher procedure.

Voucher procedure for disbursements. Vouchers for petty cash should be pre-numbered, multi-part forms like any other accounting document. Exhibit 4.5 is an example of such a voucher. Several management-level employees should be designated as authorized signers for petty-cash disbursements. These authorized signers will be issued a supply of vouchers by the accounting department. When a hotel employee needs to withdraw petty-cash funds, he or she can go to one of these managers, explain the necessity for and amount of the purchase, and receive permission for the withdrawal. The permission is evidenced by the signed voucher, which is then turned in to the fund custodian, with any original receipts or cash-register tapes affixed, to be placed in the box to replace the cash withdrawn. To maintain control of this system, it must be impermissible for one employee to pick up funds for another employee or for a vendor. Only the payee actually receiving the cash is allowed to pick up petty-cash funds.

The number of copies constituting the form will vary with the style of the operation and management, but a minimum of two copies is required (duplicate vouchers). The main copy (the back or "hard" copy) is the one that goes in the fund to replace the cash withdrawn and as evidence of the purchase. The second copy is retained by the authorized signer and sent directly and independently to the accounting office. The accounting department will collect those copies, keep track of the serial numbers, and compare the copies with the originals when it's time to replenish the fund. The purpose of having an independent copy go straight to accounting is to ensure against fraudulent changes being made to a voucher after management's approval, but before the cash is picked up. If the authorized signers prefer to keep copies for themselves to keep track of what and how much they sign for, then triplicate vouchers will be necessary.

The replenishment procedure involves roles for the accounting department and management that are similar to those in the regular disbursement process. Periodically, preferably monthly, the accounts-payable clerk picks up all of the paid-out petty-cash vouchers from the fund custodian. Those vouchers (along with any outside store or vendor receipts or register tapes affixed to the vouchers) are matched up with the copies sent directly by the authorized signers, checked for accuracy and discrepancies, and bound together to form the documentation for an accounts-payable check to be drawn, payable to "Cash—petty cash." That check, along with its supporting documentation, is sent to the general manager, along with all other payable checks.

The general manager's role is similar to that with other purchases—he or she checks the documentation for completeness, accuracy, and legitimacy; cancels the documentation; signs the check; and personally supervises the transport of the check to the head cashier, who cashes it at the bank and replenishes the petty-cash fund. By checking the petty-cash vouchers, the manager gleans information about any lack of continual planning, the number of emergency purchases, and which petty-cash purchases might be eliminated or transferred to the regular purchasing process.

The accounting department also is charged with periodic audit of the entire process, including verification of the petty-cash fund balances (along with the audit of all other fund balances) and numerical control of vouchers.

Appendix 4.2:

Merchandise and Inventory Control

Principles of Internal Control: Merchandise

Division of Duties. The three main functions involved with the purchase and handling of merchandise must be kept separate. They are

- Purchasing,

- Receiving and custody, and
- Record keeping.

I have discussed purchasing, receiving, and record keeping here in Chapter 4. The main thing to remember is that these functions must be kept separate. I will discuss custody in this appendix. For ideal internal control, the custody of the merchandise stores, usually referred to as the storeroom, should be separate from all of the other functions. If this isn't possible, the storeroom must be separated from purchasing and record keeping. The function of custody of stores incorporates physically storing the inventory of goods, protecting them, and issuing them to user departments via requisitions. In situations where cost or staffing levels is a major consideration, custody may be combined with receiving. In some larger hotels, the receiving manager supervises the storeroom clerks, a situation that usually provides adequate separation—provided purchasing and record keeping are separate.

Other Principles

If it is physically possible, limit employee access to the hotel to a single door and have a guard on that door. All parcels moving through that exit are subject to inspection. If there are steward's sales to employees, those parcels should be sealed with tamper-proof tape and signed by the relevant department head.

It is a good idea, if it's financially and structurally feasible, to have one central storeroom. It is certainly easier and cheaper to control stores with a single central storeroom, although in most hotels such space is just too valuable. That decision, like all others, should be made on a cost/benefit basis. Both quantities and access should be limited.

The storeroom(s) should be locked and the keys carefully distributed. The distribution of keys for storerooms represents a trade-off between control and policy. Hotels are open 24 hours a day but can rarely justify night storeroom clerks. Ideally, chefs, bar managers, and others should carefully plan their daily needs and requisition everything during daytime hours. That rarely happens, and there are always emergency requisitions at odd hours. If it is very difficult to gain access (i.e., if control is strong), guest service suffers. If access is too easy, control suffers. There is no ideal resolution, so make the storeroom reasonably secure but make provisions for management person-

EXHIBIT 4.6

Sample Storeroom Requisition

REQUISITION for ISSUES

NAME_____   OPERATION_____

DATE OF OPERATION:_____   PICK-UP TIME_____

CODE NO.	ITEM AND UNIT	REQ. UNITS	ISSUE	RETURN	CODE NO.	ITEM AND UNIT	REQ. UNITS	ISSUE	RETURN
	DAIRY – BREAD – CHEESE					**MEATS AND SEAFOOD**			
						B-4 STOREROOM (CANS & DRY GOODS)			
	FRESH PRODUCE, FRUIT & VEGETABLES								

nel (the manager on duty, for example) to gain access to storerooms, and to provide paper-audit trails of what they issue and to whom they issue it.

Requisitions are the accounting documents that provide the audit trail for the movement of goods from storerooms to user departments. They also play important roles in cost allocation and internal control. Requisitions should be serial-numbered accounting documents that are fully controlled by the accounting office. The storeroom clerks must fill out a requisition for everything that leaves the storeroom. The requisition, which looks like a PO or an invoice (see Exhibit 4.6), lists the items that were delivered, their cost, or price, and where they went. At the user department, a manager should sign the requisition indicating receipt of the merchandise and cost responsibility for it. The storeroom employees must send a copy of each requisition to the accounting department.

The system works just as well if the requisitions are first filled out by the users and then sent to the storeroom. The storeroom clerk still fills out the order, delivers it, and obtains the signature of the manager of the user department. Your hotel should use whichever variation works the best for your operation. Remember that if the paperwork makes someone's job easier, they will use and respect it. Storeroom requisitions should be designed and used in ways that make the chef's and other managers' jobs easier.

It's best if you keep perpetual inventory records for all items, but if that's too costly a policy, maintain perpetual inventories on high-value items only. Periodically, independent surprise counts should be made and compared with the perpetual-inventory records. The definition and concept of perpetual inventory, as well as its use in internal control, are discussed in the next section.

Finally, a physical inventory should be taken at least annually by the hotel's independent auditors.

Inventory Principles

Throughout the book, I have avoided discussing accounting details since the objectives of the book center on internal control. In the case of inventories, however, an understanding of their role in determining costs is essential to an understanding of their role in internal control. The concepts to focus on are periodic and perpetual inventories. Other details of inventory accounting such as flow assumptions (first in, first out; last in, first out) and the concepts of inventory management are beyond the scope of this book. References in the bibliography at the end of the chapter may be consulted for more information on those areas.

Periodic inventory. The concept of periodic inventory in accounting is, as it sounds, an approach to cost and valuation that relies on taking a physical inventory in each accounting period. A physical inventory simply means counting each and every item in inventory, recording it, and pricing it out. The resulting total is the inventory used on the balance sheet as the asset "inventory." The periodic physical inventory also plays an important role in determining expenses on the income statement. The cost of items that are sold, known in accounting as "cost of goods sold" (CGS), is calculated by figuring the difference between the current physical inventory and the prior count. The venerable formula for cost of goods sold for a period is:

$$CGS = I_1 + P - I_2$$

or

Cost of Goods Sold = Beginning Inventory + Purchases - Ending Inventory

The concept is quite simple. We try to assign costs to the appropriate revenues. Even if it's paid for, an item isn't a cost until it's used to produce revenue. Cost for any period is what you start with (beginning inventory) plus what you buy over the period (purchases).* Of course, if there is anything left at the end of the period (ending inventory), that is not cost, but an asset to be put on the balance sheet as well as to go into next period's cost. Hence, the ending inventory is subtracted.

Advantages of the periodic approach. Accountants like the periodic inventory concept because it is relatively simple and it yields the most accurate balance sheet and income statement. While an accurate physical inventory must be taken to use it, only one count needs to be taken per period. The ending inventory of one period will become the beginning inventory of the next. Additionally, it is less expensive to use than perpetual systems.

Disadvantages of the periodic approach. The main problem with the periodic-inventory approach is that it is virtually useless for internal control or any other managerial purposes. It is a simple but very accurate method of measuring balance-sheet inventory and CGS for the income statement. That advantage is also a disadvantage in that a physical inventory is required for each period for which an income statement is requested. If managers want monthly profit and loss statements, for example, then they must either accept estimates, or pay the cost of a monthly physical inventory.

Second, the periodic approach is a "default" approach to cost. In the formula, cost (CGS) is arrived at by placing everything into it, then subtracting what is left. In other words, everything except what is left is CGS, lumping true cost of sales together with waste, spoilage, and pilferage and other frauds. There is no separate listing of losses, and they are all aggregated in CGS!

Perhaps the most serious flaw, however, is that there is no theoretical or "book" inventory to use for the monthly inventory comparisons. It

---

*Cost is short for cost of goods sold, an expense on the income statement. Cost is used interchangeably here with expense.

makes absolutely no sense, for control purposes, to take periodic or surprise inventories when there is nothing to compare them to. The last period's inventory is just that—last period's inventory. It has nothing to do with this period or with what we should have been expecting or looking for this period. I have frequently heard hotel or restaurant operators where no perpetual systems are used respond to questions about merchandise control by saying: "We take inventory monthly." So what? What would they do with that inventory? There is nothing to compare it to. Of course, that monthly inventory allows them to make accurate monthly income statements, but does nothing for internal control.

Perpetual Inventory

The concept of perpetual inventory in accounting calculates cost using a direct approach. The requisitions for issues from the storeroom to user departments provide the information for both CGS posting and inventory reduction. Those postings, usually accomplished simultaneously, are performed by the accounting department from its copy of the requisition. Requisitions are usually triplicate, with one copy remaining with the storeroom, one held by the user department that received the issue, and the third sent directly to accounting for posting.

In simple operations, such as manufacturing or wholesale distribution, the total CGS can be obtained from the issue postings to the perpetual inventory. Hotels and restaurants are somewhat more complicated, and require a separate tracking of what is known as "direct purchases." Direct purchases are the perishable items—usually dairy, fresh fruits and vegetables, meats and seafood, and bread—that are sent directly from receiving to the various kitchens. We assume they are consumed the day they are received, so they are charged to cost each day.

The receiving report (see Exhibit 4.4) is the source document for those data. When perpetual-inventory systems or other cost-accounting systems are used, the receiving department and the receiving report play even larger roles than I discussed in Chapter 4. The receiving manager must flag all items on the receiving report as to where they go: the various preparation destinations for direct purchases, and the storerooms for all others. This is not difficult, however, because most hotels have only two or three destinations and a simple code can be developed. In the accounting department, the clerk known

Exhibit 4.7

Perpetual Inventory Card

RECEIVED							ISSUED					BALANCE	
DATE	RECEIVED FROM	QTY.	UNIT	PRICE	AMOUNT		DATE	ISSUED TO	REQ. No.	QTY.	AMOUNT	QTY.	AMT.

WILLIAM ALLEN & CO., N.Y. STOCK FORM 6170

as "cost accountant" or in smaller operations the accounts-payable clerk uses the receiving report to post simultaneously the inventory records for new receipts, and the CGS records for direct purchases.

Cost of goods sold, under a perpetual-inventory system, is calculated as frequently as is practical by the formula:

CGS = Storeroom Issues + Direct Purchases

The data for storeroom issues come from the requisitions and the data for direct purchases come from the receiving report. The cost of sales, then, can be accurately calculated as often as management wishes without the need for a physical inventory. A monthly calculation seems to be the most practical for both management decisions and financial statements, although some hotels like to calculate food and beverage cost weekly. The perpetual system even allows daily cost calculations, but they are not recommended as they are impractical and subject to too much error.

The perpetual inventory itself also must be posted, although most of that posting is done simultaneously with the other posting functions already discussed. The best way to understand a perpetual inventory is to look at a hand-prepared inventory card or record. I will explain handwritten examples to explain the flow, although perpetual-inventory systems are quite easily adapted to automation. Exhibit 4.7 is an example of an inventory card. A card (or record) is prepared and kept for each item in inventory. The individual inventory record is really a "subsidiary" accounting of the control balance sheet account called "inventory" (a direct analogy to the system used with accounts receivable as explained in Chapter 3). A summation of all the individual inventory records yields the total inventory for the balance sheet, known as the "book" inventory. The cards are a simple "T-account" type record with a debit and credit side. The debit balance represents the amount (recorded in units and dollars) in stock. Credits are posted from the requisitions to reduce inventory when issues are made to the users. Debits are posted from the receiving reports when shipments are received and sent to the storerooms.

The procedure is complicated by the fact that in most hotels there are a great many items. That is why maintaining a perpetual-inventory system is generally expensive. Today, and certainly in the near future—as labeling technology improves—automation will make perpetual-inventory systems more cost effective even for small properties.

A final issue in dealing with perpetual-inventory systems involves how to value or price the inventory. If the prices the hotel pays for its items remains constant, there is no pricing problem. That rarely happens, so the accounting department is faced with the issue of pricing, for example, ten cases of canned carrots being issued when five were purchased at one price and the other five at another, higher price. The conceptual issues of inventory-flow assumptions are beyond the scope of this book. However, it is possible to apply one flow assumption (LIFO, for example) to the hotel's official financial statements, while another (weighted average, for example) can be used for managerial purposes and operating statements. For perpetual-inventory systems, the weighted-average approach is recommended because it provides relevant information and is easy to automate.

Advantages of the perpetual approach. A perpetual-inventory system has advantages beyond its enabling of accurate periodic operating statements without the need for a physical inventory.

Perpetual inventories also are excellent for internal control because a theoretical or "book" inventory exists for all items. In other words, the hotel management knows how much of each item it should have on hand. When physical inventories are taken, the amount counted can be compared with the inventory records, and shortages noted. In fact those shortages are cumulated and eventually written off to cost. In contrast to the periodic approach, where the shortages were merely aggregated with CGS, we know and can deal with shortages separately. We can track them, watch for trends, and take appropriate action where necessary. We also know exactly which items are being pilfered—a fact that may more easily lead to solving the problem.

Because the perpetual records are "live"—always up-to-date and available for analysis—we can do our counting and checking either periodically or on a surprise basis. For high-value items, I strongly recommend that physical inventories be taken frequently—monthly or even weekly. Scientific sampling can also be used so that only few items need to be checked in order to infer some information about the condition of the entire inventory. Top management can also get involved. It is an excellent idea for the general manager, for example, to look up eight or ten high-value items in the inventory records and then go to the storeroom and count them. I guarantee that it will be a worthwhile experience!

Finally, perpetual-inventory systems are easy to automate, including tie-ins to purchasing systems. Automation will help reduce the expense that is the single disadvantage to the perpetual approach. Because it takes people to post the inventory—even in an automated environment—perpetual-inventory systems cost money to operate. That additional cost must be weighed against the internal-control benefits gained. Automation can really make a difference with inventory because so much of the posting can be simultaneously captured with other essential posting (payables, CGS, etc.).

Once again, I strongly recommend that all hotels use perpetual-inventory systems at least for their high-value items (wines and spirits, meats, etc.).

Glossary

Accounts Payable—Money owed by the hotel to its suppliers and vendors for goods and services received.

Accounts-Payable Clerk—An accounting department employee whose major responsibilities include compiling and checking the purchasing and receiving documentation, posting the accounts payable and appropriate inventory or expense accounts, and drawing the checks for payment of the accounts payable.

Blind Receiving—A description of the style of receiving of goods whereby the receiving clerk does not see a copy of the purchase order in advance.

Book (Theoretical) Inventory—The amounts, in dollars and units, of the goods that should be in inventory, based on the postings of the perpetual-inventory records; often compared with actually counted or physical inventory.

Competitive Bids—The solicitations used in a procedure for purchasing where suppliers formally reply to specified requests for goods; usually responses from two, three, or more suppliers are required to make the bids competitive.

Cost of Goods Sold (CGS)—An income-statement expense representing the cost of sales or dollar cost of the goods that have been sold.

Custody of Stores—The responsibility for goods in inventory in the storerooms; usually the function of the storeroom clerk.

Delivery Tickets—A shipping invoice or copy of the invoice that will accompany the actual shipment of goods; it usually contains the quantity shipped, the weights and counts, product descriptions, and sometimes the prices.

Direct Purchases—Items, usually perishable, that are received and sent directly to kitchens or other user areas rather than to stores.

Imprest—A fund, such as petty cash, where the amount is held constant.

Invoice—The official bill or notice from a supplier stating the items purchased by, shipped to, and received by the hotel, and the dollar amount for which the hotel is indebted; it is usually received in the mail, but occasionally may accompany the shipment.

Management by Exception—The process whereby key items, such as out-of-line numbers, are flagged for management's special attention; items not considered exceptional are assumed satisfactory and management's time is not spent on them.

Periodic Inventory—The inventory valuation and cost-of-sales system whereby an actual counted or physical inventory is taken each period, priced out, and used for the balance sheet and cost of goods sold.

Perpetual Inventory—The inventory valuation and cost-of-sales system whereby permanent records are kept for each item in inventory; such records are posted for each receipt of new goods, and each issue to users, with the latter yielding cost of goods sold, and the sum of the total inventory yielding the book or theoretical balance-sheet inventory.

Petty Cash—A fund (usually small) of cash on hand that is kept for odd-hour, last-minute, or emergency purchases.

Price—The exchange value of a unit of good or service, usually expressed in dollars; with quantity and quality, one of the three key attributes for purchase control.

Price Quotation—The process of soliciting prices from several suppliers, usually by telephone, to facilitate purchasing decisions.

Purchase Orders—Documents issued by the hotel to authorize a purchase and to bind the hotel to pay for it; purchase orders are numerically controlled accounting documents, limited in use to those with prior authorization.

Purchasing Department—A hotel department whose job is to purchase the best quality of needed goods and services at the lowest prices; serves as part of internal-control process.

Quality—A subjective judgment as to the degree of acceptability of goods and services received by the hotel; the degree to which goods and services match their specifications; with quantity and price, one of the three key attributes for purchase control.

Quantity—Refers to the counts, weights, or measures of the amount of goods and services; may refer to amounts ordered or received; with quality and price, one of the three key attributes for purchase control.

Receiving Report—A document sent by the receiving department to the accounting department itemizing the receipt of goods and services, and verifying their quantity and quality.

Replenishment—To refill or re-stock; used in the context of petty cash purchases for the process of turning in paid vouchers to draw a check to repay the fund for depleted cash.

Requisitions—A document sent by storeroom clerks to the accounting department to itemize the goods that were issued to user departments; a key document in the perpetual-inventory system for valuation and cost of goods sold.

Specifications—A formal list of attributes that fully describes goods and services; used by vendors to supply bids or price quotations.

Storeroom—A secure place where inventory is received, kept, and issued.

Storeroom Issues—The goods delivered from storerooms to users; evidenced by a document called a requisition.

Theoretical (Book) Inventory—The amounts, in dollars and units, of the goods that should be in inventory, based on the postings of the perpetual-inventory records; often compared with actually counted or physical inventory.

Selected References

Paul R. Dittmer and Gerald G. Griffin, *Principles of Food, Beverage, and Labor Cost Controls for Hotels and Restaurants (4th Edition)* (New York: Van Nostrand Reinhold, 1989).

Dennis H. Ferguson and Thomas Selling, "Probability Analysis: A System for Better Decisions," *The Cornell Hotel and Restaurant Administration Quarterly*, 26, No. 2 (August 1985), pp. 34-42.

A. Neal Geller and Raymond S. Schmidgall, "Cost Allocation Under the Uniform System of Accounts for Hotels," *The Cornell Hotel and Restaurant Administration Quarterly*, 21, No. 3 (November 1980), pp. 31-39.

Jarl G. Kallberg and Kenneth L. Parkinson, *Current Asset Management: Cash, Credit, and Inventory* (New York: John Wiley & Sons, 1984).

Eberhard E. Sheuing, *Purchasing Management* (Englewood Cliffs, NJ: Prentice-Hall, 1989).

John M. Stefanelli, *Purchasing: Selection and Procurement for the Hospitality Industry (2nd Edition)* (New York: John Wiley & Sons, 1985).

William B. Virts, *Purchasing for Hospitality Operations* (East Lansing, MI: Educational Institute of the American Hotel & Motel Association, 1987).

Glenn A. Welsch, Ronald W. Hilton, and Paul M. Gordon, *Budgeting, Profit Planning, and Control (5th Edition)* (Englewood Cliffs, NJ: Prentice-Hall, 1988).

Chapter 5

Payroll

Objectives

After completing this chapter, you should understand:

1. **The complex nature of operating a payroll.**
2. **The internal-control procedures for payroll.**
3. **The notion and importance of having a timekeeper.**
4. **Federal tip-reporting rules (Appendix 5.1).**

Legal Requirements

The critical internal-control tools of division of duties and documentation continue to be important when looking at payroll. With payroll, the most important variable (and sometimes the only factor) is the time worked by hourly employees each period. While there are other variables and other factors to check, the recording and verification of hours worked remains the single most important task in the control of this key expense. Verification of the correctness of hours worked also means automatic verification of the legitimacy of the payee's employment, and with careful document design, can also provide automatic verification of rate-of-pay, tips, and other benefits as well as simultaneous compliance with various official reporting requirements.

Payroll represents about one-third of the total expenses of most hotels. It is a significant area of management concern from the cost-control perspective, but is also important for internal control. This book, as it has in all sections, will concentrate on the internal-control aspects. The control principles and procedures that follow are designed to prevent embezzlement schemes (e.g., fictitious employees on the payroll; terminated or even deceased employees continued on the payroll with the embezzler cashing the check; or padding of hours with a kickback to the supervisor). They will also help to prevent the type of minor fraud so common in payroll: an employee working fewer hours than what's recorded as time worked, or an employee's having someone else (illegitimately) punch in or out for him or her.

The bookkeeping and reporting requirements for payroll and payroll accounting can be staggering. Taxes, benefits, and other deductions not only complicate the process, but each one adds its own reporting and record-keeping requirements and brings in myriads of governmental regulations affecting policing and information-gathering powers and reporting requirements. In addition to these externally generated pressures, hotels have internally generated information needs with respect to payroll, both for functional and managerial purposes: to provide accurate paychecks, to provide employees with accurate and relevant information about their pay, to analyze each department's operational performance, and to help control the hotel's payroll expense.

With such a complex and diverse set of objectives, payroll accounting has become a complicated process. The data need to be cumulated on at least three dimensions: by individual employee, currently and cumulatively (to date); by functional total (e.g., the sums of gross and net pay, each tax and other deductions withheld); and by operational segments (such as, rooms or F & B). The mechanics of payroll accounting are beyond the scope of this book, but I will cover those portions that affect or are critical for the internal control of payroll. It is sufficient to note here that the complex and diverse nature of the required data collection can be more easily accomplished by computerized payroll accounting, which allows for inexpensive simultaneous cumulation of data in several forms. Smaller hotels can accomplish the same results by having the payroll and check preparation done by an outside service. Many banks will do payroll inexpensively for their customers. Very small operations can also accomplish payroll accounting simply by using "One-Write"™ or "peg-board" payroll systems. These systems, by the use of carbons, quite ingeniously allow the simultaneous recording of data to several records (e.g., the paycheck itself, an employee record card, and journals to cumulate the legal and managerial information).

Physical and Structural Considerations

Since the control of hours worked is the most critical variable in payroll control, some consideration needs to be given to the physical layout of the hotel and to the house rules as they apply to employees' points of entry and exit, punch-in and punch-out procedures, dress codes, and shift-time specifications. It would be nice to design a hotel from scratch with unlimited resources to spend on control. Ideally, that hotel would have only one employee entrance, through which all employees would be required to enter and exit. Locker rooms for male and female employees would be just inside that one entrance so that employees could dress for work and lock up their personal property prior to punching in. On the way out they would punch out before changing to street clothes, and, of course, should be leaving with no parcels or bundles! With only one entrance, it would be easy to station a time-clock system, and to observe the employees' punching in and out (the role of a timekeeper).

Rarely will any hotelier have such a fantasy opportunity. Even if he or she did, custom or union pressures would intervene. Generally, employees are allowed time to dress for work on the hotel's payroll. Moreover, hotels are public buildings that depend on easy access to bring in business, an attribute that makes it difficult to control where employees enter and exit. As we will see, however, strict adherence to the internal-control principles will afford enough checks and balances to prevent most control problems. Also, new technology in automated timekeeping helps control even multi-entrance operations.

Internal-Control Principles for Payroll

Pay by Check Only. A requirement that all employee pay should be by check seems to be a reasonable policy that would entail little controversy. In practice, however, it is often violated. Tips are almost always in cash, and such temporary or occasional staff as banquet wait staff are sometimes paid in cash. In many operations, when a guest charges a meal to his or her room or credit card, the wait person is immediately given the tip in cash by the cashier. The employees may prefer it that way, but such a procedure is poor internal control. Such tipping should be recorded in the same manner that the revenue is recorded and collected in the same manner as the revenue. The employee would get his or her tip in the next paycheck.

There are some localities where the law requires a cash payroll, and some union contracts may even require it. Those rules can usually be satisfied by paying by check but making available paycheck cashing for the employees. Similarly, all employees, even temporary banquet staff, should be put on the payroll and paid in the normal cycle. There is no good reason why the rule of "pay by check only" should ever be violated.

Maintain a Separate Payroll Account. A separate checking account with special checks that have a different color and style from the hotel's regular checking account should be used for payroll. Functionally, payroll checks are usually different from regular checks in that they need a lot of "stub" space to report the pay and deduction information to the employee. The payroll account should be on an imprest basis—that is, it always has a theoretical zero balance. Money is deposited only when necessary and only in the exact amount needed to cover the payroll. A zero-balance account will be easier to reconcile and will cause such unusual items as unclaimed wages or uncashed payroll checks to stand out.

Payroll checks should also bear a legend such as, "void after 90 days," or "payable after 60 days only at the office of the payor." These practices will discourage employees from holding paychecks for long periods and thus make the auditing and reconciliation processes easier to accomplish. Unclaimed wages and uncashed payroll checks are sometimes symptomatic of fraud or other internal-control problems.

Pay Attention to Timekeeping. As I stated at the beginning of this chapter, the key variable in most payroll situations is time worked. Internal control for the time worked by employees implies verification of the accuracy of the reported hours (i.e., did the employee actually work the hours he or she is reporting as having worked?) That verification is similar to determining quantity of goods being purchased.

The best way to ascertain verification of hours worked is to install a clock or timekeeping system that requires employees to punch in when they begin work and punch out when they finish working or when they take major breaks. The clock unit in the more sophisticated systems cumulates the time worked over the period and either prints it out in report form, or sends it directly to the payroll-preparation system. Less sophisticated systems simply record the times in and times out on a card. These time cards are then turned in to the accounting department for mathematical summation and payroll preparation. In either case, the time worked is being recorded mechanically rather than by hand on the honor system.

Some hotels rely on supervisors to record the time worked by their employees. The hours are usually recorded in time books or on timesheets that are later turned in to the accounting department for payroll preparation. The use of supervisors to record time worked is an excellent check on the timekeeping system. Reliance on supervisor's time records as the sole source of the hours worked, however, is very poor internal control and should be avoided.

The use of a separate mechanical means of recording hours worked is the first step in good internal control of payroll. The employees can still be less than honest or careful in their punching in and out. Having the supervisors keep separate time records and checking those against the punch-clock totals makes good control sense. A higher level of control can be achieved by having an independent employee, a timekeeper, observe the punch-in and punch-out processes. With a timekeeper present it is more difficult for employees to report their time fraudulently or to have a friend punch in or out for them. The timekeeper, who reports to the accounting department, observes the punch-in process and confirms the identity of the individual employees. If the timekeeper is independent of the employees, their supervisors, and the payroll preparers, another level of division of duties is achieved. The time cards or clock records become an integral part of the source documentation that accounting and management must check each period.

The major drawback to having a separate timekeeper is cost. A timekeeper is an extra employee whose payroll cost must be evaluated against the added benefit of increased control in the payroll area. In larger hotels this cost is easily warranted, but in smaller properties it may be difficult to justify. The timekeeper's duties can be combined with others—for example, those of a security guard or receiving clerk. Another approach is to use part-time employees—particularly in hotels where the bulk of punch-in and punch-out activity takes place at uniform and predictable times. In either case, care should be taken to preserve the division of duties by not combining timekeeping duties with payroll preparation or paycheck distribution.

Division of Duties. The following functions should be kept separate for ideal internal control in payroll. While the list may look long and seem expensive, the only function added to the usual list is that of the timekeeper. All of the other functions are normal parts of most operations. The key is in knowing which ones should be kept separate and allocating duties accordingly:

- *Timekeeper*: Observes the punching in and out and verifies employee identity.
- *Supervisor*: Keeps own time records and approves time cards prior to payment.
- *Payroll Clerk*: Performs payroll preparation—assigns rates, computes wages and deductions, prepares individual and summary records, and prepares checks.
- *Manager*: Verifies documentation—tests the work of the payroll clerk against the time cards, cancels documentation, signs the checks, supervises distribution, and approves changes.
- *Paymaster (or cashier):* issues checks to employees.
- *Auditor*: Reconciles payroll bank account and statement.

Role of Accounting. The role of the accounting department in payroll is similar to that of purchasing and accounts payable. All documentation flows to accounting, where the paperwork is matched up and exceptions investigated. The division of duties and individual authorizations are ensured by verifying the paperwork and applying the same version of management by exception as was used for purchasing and payables. For example, the division of duties cited above requires that supervisors approve the time cards for hours worked before the payroll can be prepared. That approval can be achieved by proxy if the payroll clerk compares the supervisor's time records with the time-card totals. When they match, approval is automatic and the clerk can proceed with payroll preparation. If there are discrepancies, they must be investigated by the controller and the employee's supervisor.* Similarly, management is required to approve all payroll changes, including rates of pay. That approval can be represented by duly executed and signed change documents, described in more detail below.

The accounting department also has the responsibility for auditing all time records, change documents, and reconciliation of the payroll bank account. Additionally, in its management accounting and reporting functions, the accounting department must break down total payroll costs by operating unit or department, continually analyze those costs, and report discrepancies and trends to the appropriate managers.

Role of Management. The role of management in payroll is also similar to that in purchasing and payables. Payroll is a major expense for all hotels and is worthy of careful scrutiny by management. The general manager should sign all the payroll checks. The accounting department (payroll clerk) delivers the payroll checks to the manager accompanied by the supporting documentation. The documentation consists of the time cards, the supervisors' back-up time records, and where appropriate, change documents. The manager should look over all the documentation to test the work of the payroll clerk, as well as that of the timekeeper and all supervisors. Before the GM signs the checks, the documentation should be cancelled by indelible initial or a punch. The cancellation is to prevent a time card or change document from being used again fraudulently. In many of the newer automated systems, time-card cancellation is either automatic or unique enough by date and time to pose no threats. In the simpler or manual systems it is best to cancel the cards.

With respect to change documentation, the manager has to be especially attentive in his or her scrutiny. All changes in rates of pay, for example, are made by the payroll clerk only with management authorization evidenced by a duly signed change order. The manager

---

*Supervisor time records are usually kept by hand and are typically not as accurate as punch-clock records. You should expect minor discrepencies. Gain some experience with dual recordkeeping to establish policies for when differences are large enough to warrant your concern.

should see that these changes are accompanied by such a document approved by an authorized signer, and he or she should occasionally question the signer as to the advisability of making the pay-rate change. It is the payroll version of "shopping prices" to see whether purchasing is doing its job. With payroll, the "purchaser" is the management supervisor or, in larger hotels, a personnel or human-resource department. Finally, the manager should personally oversee the distribution of the paychecks.

Distribution of Paychecks. The distribution of paychecks also is subject to some specific internal-control rules. An important one is that paychecks, after they are signed, should not be returned to accounting and particularly not to the payroll clerk who prepared them. Thus, the division of duties between cash and accounting is maintained.* Another area of caution is in handing out paychecks to employees. Larger hotels have paymasters for this function. In smaller properties any cashier, for example the head cashier, will suffice. Accounting personnel involved in the preparation or audit of the payroll should not hand out the checks, and neither should the employees' immediate supervisor hand out paychecks—especially in smaller operations where the supervisor's time records may be the sole or key source of the hours worked. In practice, this prohibition will be difficult to enforce as supervisors like to hand out checks to their subordinates. However, many frauds have been perpetrated where a supervisor kept a terminated employee on the payroll for several weeks, or where completely fictitious employees have been "paid."

It is important in the distribution of paychecks to validate the identification of each employee, and occasionally to have the employees sign for their checks. Most outside audit firms will require that they (the auditors) be involved, on a surprise basis, with handing out paychecks. That idea is a good one, and should be repeated occasionally and randomly by management. In the author's opinion, it is worthwhile for the general manager to hand out paychecks occasionally. In addition to the internal-control aspects, the manager gains some valuable human-relations benefits from such an exercise!

Documentation of Changes. Changes in the payroll are made by the accounting department, but only with management authorization. Adding new hires, termination, or changes in rate-of-pay, tax status, and benefits are all considered payroll changes. Such changes need

---

*Once they are signed, paychecks are like cash and are easy to divert from the intended payee. Such diversion has happened many times.

documentation whether the payroll is prepared at the hotel or by an outside service. Some hotels prefer to have two sets of documents, one for new hires and terminations and another for changes to an existing employee's pay. There is nothing wrong with that approach, although it seems simpler to develop only one document and use it for all purposes. The form could have check boxes on the top to differentiate between new hires and other changes. Exhibit 5.1 is an example of such documentation.

In larger hotels there is a human-resource or personnel department that deals with all payroll changes and takes care of the documentation, including getting management authorization. The signed documentation then goes to the payroll clerk for processing. In smaller properties, management must fulfill this function themselves. In any event, top management must decide which managers are authorized to make payroll changes, and at what level. Stratified authority is common where a supervisor may have authority for small pay-rate changes or a certain number of new hires. Larger changes may require top management approval. Often these changes are linked to budgets developed earlier. All of these factors are policy concerns. The important internal-control issue is that no changes be made by the accounting department without the required documentation, thus ensuring both authorization and division of duties.

Unclaimed Wages. Unclaimed wages are paychecks that are never picked up or claimed by employees. Their existence should come to light in the distribution process when employees sign for their checks and the lists are audited for discrepancies. Unclaimed wages will also show up along with claimed but uncashed checks as outstanding checks in the bank reconciliation. The difference is that the hotel still has the custody of the checks yet unclaimed.

The internal-control significance of unclaimed wages is twofold. First, they may be unearned, and then the accounting department needs to determine why and how a paycheck was issued. Second, they are often symptomatic of frauds and other control weaknesses. All unclaimed wages should be vigorously and quickly investigated. If it is determined that the check in question is legitimate, every effort should be made to get it to the deserving employee. If that effort fails, all unclaimed checks should be re-deposited in the hotel's general bank account. The purpose is to move the funds out of the zero-balance payroll account and get them back into use. The accounting for that transaction is to debit cash and credit a liability account called

EXHIBIT 5.1

Payroll-Change Form

Payroll Data and Authorization Form

Check one	New employee	Salary adjust	Termina-tion	Data change	Date	Office name		Off no

Identification

Employee name and initials		Social Security No.	Employee code
Employee street address		Telephone no	
City and state			

Salary Information

Item		Present		Proposed					
		Monthly	Hourly	Increase			Monthly	Hourly	
1	Salary rate			Reason	Monthly amount	Hourly amount			
	Effective date of salary change			Promotion in classification					
2.	Classification and effective date if different from item 1			Merit without promotion					
3.	Charge time rate and effective date if different from item 1			Longevity, cost of living and other					
4.	Overtime payment method (check one)	No overtime	Straight time / Time and one-half	Conversion of overtime to base compensation			No overtime	Straight time / Time and one-half	
5.	Employee status (check one)	Full-time	Temporary full-time / Part-time	Total increase			Permanent full-time	Temporary full-time / Part-time	

Additional Payroll Information

Number of exemptions	Federal	State	City	Deductions (show dollars on monthly basis)	State disab	Hospitalization	Major medical	Bonds
Miscellaneous deductions	Type of deduction			Amount each month		For how many months?		

Separation Information

Pay through this date				Yes	No
	Separation check to include:	Pay accrued vacation		☐	☐
		Pay overtime bonus		☐	☐
	Firm materials returned			☐	☐

Separation remarks

Originated by	Date	Approved by managing partner	Date

Courtesy: AICPA.

INTERNAL CONTROL

5

Case 5.1

The Padded Paychecks

A 300-room resort hotel often employed local high-school students as part-time food-service and housekeeping workers. This practice benefited the resort, which often had short-notice needs for help, and it provided much-needed employment for the teenagers.

Department heads at the resort kept the time sheets for all hourly employees. Those time sheets were turned in to the accounting department weekly, and they were used as the sole source for determining time worked and calculating the payroll.

Millie, the housekeeper, saw a golden opportunity in the authority she had been given. Three high-school girls worked 10 to 15 hours per week as room attendants on the evening shift and in the linen room on weekends. Millie consistently entered on their time sheets seven or eight hours more than they actually worked, thereby padding their paychecks. Millie coerced the young women into kicking back to her the extra money from their paychecks. Since the employees were part-time, the extra hours were not sufficiently large to be noticeable in the housekeeping-department payroll ratios.

Unhappy with a situation they knew was illegal, the three girls complained to Millie. She silenced them by telling them they were now part of a criminal scheme and they would probably go to jail if they didn't stay quiet. The scheme survived for several months, until one of the girls confided in her aunt, a long-time employee of the resort. The aunt immediately informed the general manager, who dismissed Millie.

Discussion

The resort hotel should not have used the department head as the sole source of time worked. A punch-clock system, preferably with a timekeeper to observe the punch-ins and punch-outs, would have prevented the padding of hours. The department head time sheets can serve as an independent check of the time-clock data. Incidentally, in that type of manual, one-person payroll system, a department head could pad anyone's payroll—even if he or she weren't forcing kickbacks. Such systems are also more prone to honest mistakes.

Management also must shoulder some of the blame. Even though the frauds were only 7 to 8 hours, on a 15- or 20-hour part-time paycheck, they were substantial amounts. The manager signing the paychecks should have questioned teenagers who claimed to work over 20 hours per week. Also, independent checks on time sheets or cards, and occasional independent managerial handout of paychecks, would have made this fraud more difficult.

Finally, the hotel should have prosecuted Millie, and not simply dismissed her. If they had purchased fidelity bonds, there would have been no choice on the matter of prosecution.

"unclaimed wages." Thus, the hotel's bank account is restored and a liability is established to document the wages still owed—until it can be determined whether they were earned. If it is determined that the money was earned but is still unclaimed, the hotel will usually have to wait for a period of time before it can write off the liability and reverse the payroll expense. In some localities, the state or other government may have legal claim to these types of wages. Local laws should be checked for that fact and for the length of waiting periods.

Again, the internal-control significance of unclaimed wages is that they are usually a symptom of some control breakdown or weakness. Quick and vigorous investigation is the prescription, with changes to any internal-control weaknesses that may be found.

Glossary

One-Write™ System—A pen-and-ink hand bookkeeping system that uses carbons and inserts to allow a single writing of the numbers or data to be recorded simultaneously on several records. These systems are quite useful for repetitive tasks such as payroll, accounts payable, and accounts receivable.

Paymaster—A hotel employee whose responsibilities include the control of payroll, the analysis of payroll expense, and handing out paychecks; the paymaster should be separate from the payroll clerk, who prepares the payroll and the checks.

Stratified Authority—An approach to management authority whereby decisions are separated into levels, and lower-level decisions are permitted at lower levels of management; stratified authority allows for more efficient use of management time.

Time Cards—The documents upon which the time worked by employees is recorded, usually measured in hours; most time-recording systems are mechanical or electronic and thus use some type of card to record the time.

Timekeeper—An employee whose responsibility is to observe hourly employees as they punch in and out (record their time), to verify their identity and the veracity of the hours recorded.

Unclaimed Wages—Paychecks that are not picked up by the employees who are entitled to them; unclaimed wages are sometimes symptomatic of internal-control problems.

Appendix 5.1

Federal Tip-Reporting Law

by Allan I. Weiss, National Director, Tax Services

Pannell Kerr Forster

The Tax Equity and Fiscal Responsibility Act of 1982 contained a provision on tip-reporting compliance, and the Internal Revenue Service subsequently issued rules for large food or beverage establishments to follow for record keeping and tip-income reporting.

Starting in 1983, large food or beverage establishments were required to keep records of gross sales, charge sales, the tips shown on the charge sales, and tips reported by employees. Additionally, employers must file tip-reporting forms listing this information with the IRS. The tip-reporting rules did not change employers' responsibilities with regard to income tax, social-security tax, or federal unemployment tax, but failure to comply with the tip-reporting rules can result in substantial penalties.

This appendix explains the rules themselves, discusses how to file the tip-reporting forms, and, most important, suggests ways to explain the reporting requirements to tipped employees. Employers with questions are encouraged to contact any of Pannell Kerr Forster's offices.

What Is a Large Food or Beverage Establishment?

The regulations use two criteria to define a large food or beverage establishment. The first is that the operation normally employed more than ten employees on a typical business day during the preceding calendar year. The second is that tipping of the operation's employees is customary.

The rules state that a food or beverage operation is any business activity that provides food or beverages for consumption on the premises, other than fast-food operations. If an employer serves food or beverages at different locations, each location is treated as a separate food or beverage operation. Moreover, each food or beverage activity in a single building is considered a separate location if the customers, while provided food or beverages, occupy different areas for each activity and the gross receipts of the activities are recorded separately.

Example: A hotel's gourmet restaurant, coffee shop, and cocktail lounge, each in its own location, are treated as separate food or beverage operations if gross receipts from each activity are recorded separately.

An employer may also treat different activities conducted at different times, but in the same place, as separate food or beverage operations if the gross receipts of the activities at each time are recorded separately.

Example: A restaurant that records the gross receipts of its cafeteria-style lunch separately from the gross receipts for its full-service dinner may be treated as two separate food or beverage operations.

An employer can use the following formula to determine whether it normally employed more than ten employees on a typical business day during the preceding calendar year.

Average number of employee hours worked per business day during the **month of the operation's highest gross receipts**
plus
Average number of employee hours worked per business day during the **month of the operation's lowest gross receipts**
divided by two, equals
Average number of employee hours worked per business day.

The test is met if the average number of total employee hours worked per business day is more than 80. A new business with food or beverage operations will be considered a large food or beverage establishment if, after applying this calculation to any two consecutive months in the business's first calendar year, the average number of employee hours worked per business day is more than 80.

New businesses should constantly monitor their activity because a new business will immediately become responsible for tip reporting for the payroll period beginning after it meets the hours-worked requirement under this two-consecutive-month rule.

If an employer has more than one food or beverage operation, all of these operations are included to determine whether the employer is a large food or beverage establishment, each of the employer's food or beverage operations must keep its own tip-reporting records and complete its own report forms.

This applies not only to different operations under one employer, but also to members of a controlled group of corporations and other entities with more than one food or beverage operation.

Example: Employer A has three different food and beverage operations. The total gross receipts for all three operations were greatest in January and least in September. In January, the following statistics were obtained from the employer's records:
Average number of days worked in January (75/3) = 25.

	Days Open for Business	**Total Hours Worked**
Operation A	31	2,500
Operation B	20	1,000
Operation C	24	1,500
Total	**75**	**5,000**

Average number of employee hours worked per day (5,000/25) = 200.
If the average number of employee hours worked per day in September was 60, the employer would be a large food or beverage establishment because the number of hours worked on a typical business day was more than 80 (200 + 60 = 260/2 = 130).

Note that in determining who is an employee, the employer must include all employees are involved either directly or indirectly with the food or beverage operation, and not employees involved in the employer's other activities.

Example: A company operates a motel with a restaurant. The restaurant has six employees, each working an average of eight hours a day, and the motel has seven employees (housekeepers, manager, bookkeeper). The restaurant will not be considered a large food or beverage establishment because the company does not have more than ten employees who are either directly or indirectly involved with the food or beverage operation.

The second criterion, customary tipping of food or beverage employees, is not as technical as the first part of the definition. Generally, the decision on whether tipping is customary depends on the facts and customs of the particular eating or drinking establishment. However, the IRS rules say that tipping generally will not be considered customary for cafeterias.

Required Records

If you run a large food or beverage establishment, you are subject to specific record-keeping requirements. Among the items you must closely monitor for this record keeping are gross receipts, charge receipts, charged tips, and the hours directly tipped employees worked.

Large food or beverage establishments must record their gross receipts, charge sales, the tips shown on the charge sales, and the tips the employees report to the employer. Employers must keep detailed records of each tipped employee's hours worked and the sum of these hours or gross receipts attributed to each employee. Although only total amounts of these items will be needed to complete the IRS forms, the tips must be allocated on an employee-by-employee basis, by payroll period, and only to directly tipped employees, if the total tips reported for a payroll period are less than 8 percent of that period's qualified gross receipts.

The gross receipts, called "qualified gross receipts," to be reported are those from food or beverage operations, excluding:

- carry-out sales,
- sales on which a 10-percent or more service charge is added,
- tips reported on charge sales if the tips have been paid to the employee in cash and cash sales have not been reduced by the amount of these tips, and
- state and local taxes.

Included in gross receipts are the following:

- food or beverage charges to a hotel room (tips charged to a hotel room can be excluded if the employer's accounting procedures allow these tips to be segregated out),
- the retail value of complimentary food or beverages served to customers, and
- a good-faith estimate of the gross receipts apportioned to the food or beverages (cost of food or beverages, plus a reasonable profit) in situations where food or beverages are provided with other good or services (e.g., package deals).

Charge receipts are credit-card charges and charges under any other credit arrangement—for example, house charges, city ledger, and charge arrangements for country-club members. But charge receipts do not include food and beverage charges to a hotel room.

A charged tip is one included on a charge receipt. If the charged receipts are excluded, the related tips are excluded as well.

How to Allocate Tips

To allocate tips, employers must first compare the total amount of tips the employees report each payroll period with 8 percent of the large food or beverage establishment's gross receipts for that payroll period. No tip allocation is required if the total reported tips are at least eight percent of the establishment's gross receipts. This means that tip allocation will be required for any payroll period in which the reported tips are less than 8 percent of gross receipts, even though the reported tips equal or exceed 8 percent of the establishment's annual gross receipts.

If tips are not reported by payroll period, the employer must allocate the employees' reported tips to a given payroll period on the basis of hours worked in the payroll period or on the basis of gross receipts attributable to each employee for the payroll period. If an employee works in more than one of the employer's food or beverage establishments and does not separately report tips received in each establishment, the employer must allocate the employee's reported tips to a given food or beverage operation in a manner similar to that for allocating tips to a payroll period. Once an employer chooses an allocation method, it must be applied to all operations for that calendar year.

Good-Faith Allocation Agreements

Employers and their employees may agree in good faith on how the employer should allocate tips. To be binding, a good-faith agreement must be written and the employer and at least two-thirds of the members of each occupational category of tipped employees (e.g., wait staff, bus staff) employed at the time of the agreement must consent to it. The agreement must indicate how the employer should allocate the tips among the tipped employees in a manner that, in combination with tips the employees report, will approximately reflect in good faith the actual distributed tip income among the tipped employees.

Any agreement must begin with a payroll period that starts within 30 days after the agreement is made and terminates on the last day of the calendar year in which it became effective. Thus, an agreement must be renewed annually. An agreement can be adopted only if it will affect tipped employees in each occupational category and may be revoked by a written agreement that at least 50 percent of the affected tipped employees agree to at the time of the revocation. The employer must attach a copy of the agreement or agreements to the tip-reporting form that is filed with the IRS.

Required Allocation Formula

If a good-faith agreement is not in effect, the regulations require a standard allocation method to be used for each payroll period for which the reported tips are less than 8 percent of the establishment's gross receipts. No allocation is made to indirectly tipped employees (e.g., bus staff, service bartenders). Allocations are made only to each directly tipped employee who has a reporting shortfall for the payroll period. Calculating the allocation to each directly tipped employee not meeting the 8-percent amount is accomplished in seven steps, as follows:

(1) Multiply the establishment's gross receipts for the payroll period by 8 percent.

(2) Determine the total tips indirectly tipped employees report for the payroll period.

(3) Subtract the amount calculated in step two from the amount calculated in step one.

(4) Multiply the amount in step three by the percentage, expressed as a fraction, either of the number of hours each directly tipped employee works for the period over the total hours directly tipped employees work for the period, or the gross receipts for the period attributable to that employee over the total gross receipts for the period.

(5) For each directly tipped employee, compute the excess, if any, of the amount calculated in step 4 over the amount reported as tips for the period. The excess, if any, is the employee's shortfall for the payroll period.

(6) Subtract the total tips all directly and in-directly tipped employees report for the period from the 8 percent of gross receipts calculated in step 1. The result is the amount of tips to be allocated among

Hours-Worked Method

Directly Tipped Employees	Hours Worked in Payroll Period	Tips Reported
Employee A	180	$1,080
Employee B	172	880
Employee C	188	1,810
Employee D	176	800
Employee E	144	450
Employee F	160	680
	1,020	$5,700

The allocation computations would be as follows:

(1) $100,000 (gross receipts) x 0.08 = $8,000

(2) Tips reported by indirectly tipped employees = $500

(3) $8,000 - $500 = $7,500

(4)

Directly Tipped Employees	Directly Tipped Share of 8% Gross		Hours-Worked Ratio	Employee Share of 8% Gross
Employee A	$7,500	x	180/1,020	$1,324
Employee B	$7,500	x	172/1,020	1,265
Employee C	$7,500	x	188/1,020	1,382
Employee D	$7,500	x	176/1,020	1,294
Employee E	$7,500	x	144/1,020	1,059
Employee F	$7,500	x	160/1,020	1,176
				$7,500

(5)

Directly Tipped Employees	Employee Share of 8% Gross	Tips Reported	Employee Shortfall
Employee A	$1,324	$1,080	$244
Employee B	1,265	880	385
Employee C	1,382	1,810	—
Employee D	1,294	800	494
Employee E	1,059	450	609
Employee F	1,176	680	496
	$7,500	$5,700	$2,228

Since employee C has no reporting shortfall, there is no allocation to C.

(6) $8,000 - $6,200 (total tips reported = $1,800 (amount to be allocated among shortfall employees).

(7)

Shortfall Employees	Allocable Shortfall Amount		Amount of Ratio		Allocation
Employee A	$1,800	x	244/2,228	=	$197
Employee B	$1,800	x	385/2,228	=	311
Employee D	$1,800	x	494/2,228	=	399
Employee E	$1,800	x	609/2,228	=	492
Employee F	$1,800	x	496/2,228	=	401

Gross-Receipts Method

Directly Tipped Employees	Gross Receipts for Payroll Period	Tips Reported
Employee A	18,000	$1,080
Employee B	16,000	880
Employee C	23,000	1,810
Employee D	17,000	800
Employee E	12,000	450
Employee F	14,000	680
		$5,700

The allocation computations would be as follows:

(1) $100,000 (gross receipts) x 0.08 = $8,000

(2) Tips reported by indirectly tipped employees = $500

(3) $8,000 - $500 = $7,500

(4)

Directly Tipped Employees	Directly Tipped Share of 8% Gross		Gross-Receipts Ratio	Employee Share of 8% Gross
Employee A	$7,500	x	18,000/100,000	$1,350
Employee B	$7,500	x	16,000/100,000	1,200
Employee C	$7,500	x	23,000/100,000	1,750
Employee D	$7,500	x	17,000/100,000	1,275
Employee E	$7,500	x	12,000/100,000	900
Employee F	$7,500	x	14,000/100,000	1,050
				$7,500

(5)

Directly Tipped Employees	Employee Share of 8% Gross	Tips Reported	Employee Shortfall
Employee A	$1,350	$1,080	$270
Employee B	1,200	880	320
Employee C	1,750	1,810	—
Employee D	1,275	800	475
Employee E	900	450	450
Employee F	1,050	680	370
	$7,500	$5,700	$1,885

Since employee C has no reporting shortfall, there is no allocation to C.

(6) $8,000 - $6,200 (total tips reported = $1,800 (amount to be allocated among shortfall employees).

(7)

Shortfall Employees	Allocable Shortfall Amount		Amount of Ratio		Allocation
Employee A	$1,800	x	270/1,885	=	$258
Employee B	$1,800	x	320/1,885	=	306
Employee D	$1,800	x	475/1,885	=	454
Employee E	$1,800	x	450/1,885	=	430
Employee F	$1,800	x	370/1,885	=	353

directly tipped employees who had a shortfall for the payroll period.

(7) For each directly tipped employee who had a shortfall for the payroll period, multiply the amount of tips to be allocated among directly tipped employees by a fraction of each tipped employee's shortfall for the payroll period.

The result of these calculations is the employee's tip allocation for the payroll period. Here's an illustration of the calculations, using both the hours-worked and gross-receipt allocation methods. Employers must use one method or the other consistently throughout the year.

Example: Chef Company is a large food or beverage establishment with gross receipts for a payroll period of $100,000 and with tips reported for the payroll period of $6,200. Directly tipped employees reported $5,700, while indirectly tipped employees reported $500. The allocations under the hours-worked method and under the gross-receipts method are shown at left.

Employers may use their actual payroll periods to make these calculations or may use any time period that is not more than 31 days instead of their actual payroll periods. Note that in these illustrations and probably in most instances, there is and will be a difference in the tip amounts allocated to a particular employee depending on whether the gross-receipts or hours-worked ratio is used. Employers should use the ratio for which it's easiest to obtain required data.

Reducing the 8 Percent

Employers may request that the IRS lower the 8-percent amount (not to go below 5 percent) to a percentage that is the best estimate of the actual gross receipts constituting tips. Employers request this from the director of the IRS district in which the establishment is located and should document the request with additional information, such as menu prices, type of establishment, and location. The district director will then consider and act on the request.

Completing Form 8027

Employers will use Form 8027 to report tip income to the IRS. It must be filed by the last day of February following the year to which it applies. The employer must report the names and social security numbers of employees to whom a tip allocation was made by attaching photocopies of the employees' W-2 forms to the 8027 forms.

As the above paragraph implies, tip allocations will be reported to the employees on their W-2 forms. If a terminated employee receives a W-2 form before the year's end, the allocated tip amount may be estimated, and the word "estimated" should be clearly written on the W-2 form. If this is done, a revised W-2 form must be issued by January 31 of the following year. This form must show the actual tip allocation if the estimated tip amount differed by more than 5 percent from the actual tips allocated.

Every large food or beverage establishment is assigned its own 15 digit identification number. The first nine digits will be the employer's identification number, while the tenth digit will categorize the establishment as one that either:

(1) serves only dinner;
(2) serves dinner and other meals;
(3) serves meals other than dinner; or
(4) serves food, if at all, only as an incidental part of the business of service alcoholic beverages.

The last five digits will differentiate among multiple establishments reporting under the same employer-identification number, so that each establishment can have a unique number.

Telling Employees about the Tip-Reporting Rules

The key to reducing your paperwork and to avoid reporting employees' tip shortfalls to the IRS is to tell employees about the tip-reporting rules and possible IRS consequences. If tipped employees are cooperative and report their tips accurately, the 8-percent reporting requirement will, in all likelihood, be met, and the employer won't have to calculate allocated tip income and notify the IRS.

The Priority of Withholding Taxes

In some instances when employers calculate the taxes to be withheld from a tipped employee's wages, including amounts to be withheld because of the employee's reported tips, the employer will discover the total to be withheld exceed the cash wages due to the employee. The IRS has issued rules that state the order in which taxes should be deducted from cash wages (exclusive of tips that are under the employer's control). The priority is as follows:

(1) The employee's share of social-security tax the employer is required to withhold on cash wages (exclusive of tips).
(2) The federal income tax the employer is required to withhold on cash wages (exclusive of tips).
(3) The state and local withholding taxes the employer is required to withhold on cash wages (exclusive of tips).
(4) The employee's share of social-security tax required to be withheld as computed on the tips reported to the employer.
(5) The federal income tax required to be withheld as computed on the tips reported to the employer.
(6) Any other payroll deductions (e.g., union dues, wage garnishments) would be deducted from the balance of funds.

The following example illustrates the priority of withholding (amounts shown do not reflect currently effective rates or amounts):

Mr. Jones, a waiter employed in a dinner house, is remunerated principally through the tips he receives from the restaurant's customers, but he also receives wages totalling $40 per week. Mr. Jones is a member of a labor union, which has a contract with the employer in which the employer is to collect union dues by withholding $1 per week from the wages of each employee. Mr. Jones's wages are also subject to withholding of a state income tax imposed on both his regular wage and his tips received and reported to his employer. In addition, a state court also issued a garnishment notice requiring the employer to withhold $10 a week from Mr. Jones's wages for ten weeks.

On Monday of a given week, Mr. Jones furnished a written statement to his employer in which he reported receiving $160 in tips. The $40 wage to be paid to Mr. Jones on Friday of the same week is subject to the following withholding items: Mr. Jones does not turn over any funds to his employer, so his employer should

Taxes For	Regular Wages	Tips	Total
Social Security	$2.34	$9.36	$11.70
Federal Withholding	5.65	28.30	33.95
State Income Tax	1.20	4.80	6.00
Union Dues			1.00
Garnishment			10.00
Total Amount To Be Withheld			$62.65

apportion the $40 cash wage as follows:
The $6.85 balance of the federal withholding tax on tips ($28.30 less $21.45)

1.	Social security tax on regular wages	$2.34
2.	Federal withholding on regular wages	5.65
3.	State income tax on regular wages	1.20
4.	Social security on reported tips	9.36
5.	Federal withholding tax on reported tips	21.45
	Total amount withheld	$40.00

should be carried forward and deducted from the employee's wages in future weeks.

After reading this appendix, you may have reached the same conclusion that the author has: namely—the paperwork involved in these reporting rules may be time consuming and costly to employers. Tipped employees may have their own problems with the rules. The rules can not only highlight the under-reporting of tips to the IRS, but may also increase the chances of having tipped employees' income-tax returns examined. Additionally, the withholding priorities will also affect tipped employees whose cash wages are insufficient to cover their withholding requirements.

PKF believes that if employers and employees understand the ramifications of these rules and communicate with each other, the rules can be satisfied with minimal cost and exposure to everyone.

Selected References

Paul R. Dittmer and Gerald G. Griffin, *Principles of Food, Beverage, and Labor Cost Controls for Hotels and Restaurants (4th Edition)* (New York: Van Nostrand Reinhold, 1989).

Dennis H. Ferguson and Florence Berger, "Employees as Assets: A Fresh Approach to Human-Resources Accounting," *The Cornell Hotel and Restaurant Administration Quarterly,* 25, No. 4 (February 1985), pp. 24-29.

Dennis H. Ferguson and Florence Berger, "The Human Side of Budgeting," *The Cornell Hotel and Restaurant Administration Quarterly,* 27, No. 2 (August 1986), pp. 86-90.

Dennis H. Ferguson and Thomas Selling, "Analyzing Food and Labor Costs," *The Cornell Hotel and Restaurant Administration Quarterly,* 24, No. 3 (November 1983), pp. 31-39.

Chapter 6

Rooms-Income Control

Objectives

After completing this chapter, you should understand:

1. The basic flow of and documentation for front-office (guest) accounting.
2. Internal-control procedures for rooms revenue.
3. The role of such independent sources of data as housekeeping.
4. The audit procedures for rooms revenue.
5. The implications of technology on front-office control.

In the hotel industry, rooms revenue is approximately 60 percent of all revenues. Many hotels have no food and beverage or other income, and their rooms generate all of their revenue! The rooms business tends to be more profitable than other sources of hotel revenue, so the rooms-revenue portion of hotel income is a critical area for which sound internal controls are essential.[1]

The complexity of guest accounting in hotels is often misunderstood. The processes by which we check in guests, keep track of all of the charges they incur, and settle their bills are far more complicated and time-consuming than they appear to non-hoteliers. Their complexity and the lack of general understanding about the flow of data and the documents required in guest accounting are factors that helped cause the hotel industry to delay automating for perhaps 20 years.[2] That complexity was first summed up so well in the classic book *Hotel Accounting:*

> There is hardly any other business in which the amount involved in each individual transaction is so small and where these transactions, cash or credit, follow each other with such rapidity. A guest may arrive and take a room, have his baggage delivered, use the telephone and valet service, have his meal in his room or in the dining room, send a telegram, purchase cigars, and dictate a few letters to the public stenographer, all within little more than an hour. During the same time he must be registered; his name must be listed so that mail and telephone calls can reach him; an account must be opened for him; the baggage porter, telephone operator, valet, restaurant cashier, telegraph office, cigar stand, and the public stenographer must all record the charges for their services, and must report the charges to the bill clerk, who, in turn, must post them to the guest's account. All this must be done with such rapidity that the account is up to the minute, day or night, for the guest may ask for his bill at any moment and leave the hotel.[3]

Unless this complex process of guest accounting is understood, it is difficult to comprehend the internal-control procedures required for rooms revenue. For that reason, we will present a brief overview of the guest-accounting cycle. I assume most readers are at least familiar with the process.[4]

---

[1]See: Pannell Kerr Forster, *Trends in the Hotel Industry* (Houston, TX: PKF, 1989).

[2]See: A. Neal Geller, *Executive Information Needs in Hotel Companies* (New York: Peat Marwick & Mitchell, 1984), Chapter 2.

[3]Ernest B. Horwath, Louis Toth, and John D. Lesure, *Hotel Accounting (Third Edition)* (New York: Ronald Press Company, 1963), p. 9.

[4]For more detailed discussions, see: Jerome J. Vallen and Gary K. Vallen, *Check In • Check Out (Fourth Edition)* (Dubuque, IA: William C. Brown, 1991); and Michael L. Kasavana, *Effective Front-Office Operations* (Boston, CBI, 1981).

Guest Accounting and Documents

Guest accounting is also known as "front-office accounting" as it involves the front office and front-desk staff of the hotel. The process includes all guest financial contact from check-in to check-out. In the following presentation the documents and flow of data are presented as if all forms were completed by hand in pen and ink. To find a hotel today where guest documents are actually filled in by hand would indeed be difficult. In the next five or six years, I foresee even very small hotels of fewer than 50 rooms having fully automated front offices. The cost of automation equipment is coming down and the ease of using it is increasing at such rapid rates that fully automated solutions will soon be the most affordable ones.

I have chosen to present the accounting flow in a manual environment for several reasons. First, it is easier to understand and follow in that form, and second, automated systems use the same flow and essentially the same documents as the manual systems. Readers will find it much easier to understand automated front-office systems if they view those systems in the same manner as the manual ones. Also, it is a good approach to use hand-completed documents to train staff and to communicate with programmers and other support staff affiliated with the automated systems. An understanding of the flow of information in a manual environment is also essential to analyze an automated system's internal-control features. Many of the modern automated front-office systems are excellent from the control perspective, but some are remarkably poor. Imparting the ability to recognize the difference and to isolate and correct weaknesses are important objectives of this book.

The best way to view and understand guest accounting is through the documents. The first document is the registration card. Registration cards are serially numbered accounting documents and are the first point of formal contact with the guest. They are used in the registration process to capture biographical, geographical, and credit information about the guest, and to record data about his or her stay at the hotel. Exhibit 6.1 is an example of a typical registration card.

When a guest has an advance reservation, registration cards are "pre-prepared" and the guest only has to verify the information and sign the card. It is at the registration process where credit is established for the guest—in modern times usually by taking an imprint of a major credit card (and later obtaining authorization from the credit

EXHIBIT 6.1

Guest-Registration Card

| RECEPTIONIST | | | | | | GUEST REGISTRATION |

ACCOUNT NUMBER	ARRIVAL DATE	DEPARTURE DATE	ARRIVAL TIME	NO. ROOMS	ROOM TYPE

DAILY RATE	NO. OF GUESTS	ADVANCE DEPOSIT	ROOM NO.	PACKAGE PLAN

Name (please print)

Address

City   State   Zip

Company / Convention

CU Dept #   Lic. Plate #   State

METHOD OF PAYMENT:
☐ CASH/CHECK   ☐ MASTERCARD   ☐ DINERS CLUB   ☐ VISA   ☐ AMERICAN EXPRESS   ☐ CARTE BLANCHE

☐ STATLER CLUB   ☐ OTHER   ☐ DIRECT BILL TO: _____

GUEST SIGNATURE **X**

SAFETY DEPOSIT BOXES ARE AVAILABLE FOR THE SECURITY OF YOUR VALUABLES.
The hotel assumes no responsibility for loss of money, jewels or other valuables unless placed in our safety deposit boxes located at the front desk. We are not responsible for articles left in room or automobile.

I agree that my liability for this bill is not waived, and I agree to be held personally liable in the event that the indicated person, company or association fails to pay for the full amount of the charges.

EXHIBIT 6.2

Guest Folios

ROOM				RATE		

FOLIO NUMBER **55022** Ⓢ

STREET		IN DATE	OUT DATE

CITY	STATE	CLERK

Sheraton—Syracuse Motor Inn
7TH NORTH & ELECTRONICS PARKWAY
SYRACUSE, NEW YORK 13088
SHERATON HOTELS AND MOTOR INNS,
A WORLDWIDE SERVICE OF ITT

FIRM		

	STARTING READING	CLOSING READING	TOTAL CALLS

DATE	REFERENCE	CHARGES	CREDITS	BALANCE	PREVIOUS BALANCE PICK-UP

REMARKS

GUEST SIGNATURE

CHARGE TO

STREET

CITY STATE

L C NO   CK BY

Statler
Cornell University
Ithaca, N.Y. 14853-7001
(607) 257-2500 • (800) 541-2501
Telex: WUI 6713054 • Fax: (607) 257-6432

ARRIVAL
DEPARTURE
NO. IN PARTY
RATE

ACCT. NO.		ROOM NO.		
#	DATE	DESCRIPTION		AMOUNT

DIRECT
BILL
TO:

COMPANY   STREET

I agree that my liability for this bill is not waived and agree to be held personally liable in the event that the indicated person, company or association fails to pay for any part or the full amount of these charges.

CITY   STATE   POSTAL CODE

SIGNATURE

Exhibit 6.3

Daily Accounts-Receivable Transcript

DAILY TRANSCRIPT OF
ACCOUNTS RECEIVABLE

DATE _____ 19_____

Hotel Register Co., 226 W. Ontario St., Chicago, Ill. 60610 Form 75

1 ACCOUNT NO.	2 ROOM NO.	3 NUMBER OF GUESTS	OPENING BALANCE		DEBITS													CREDITS				CLOSING BALANCE	
			4 DEBIT	5 CREDIT	6 ROOMS	7 RESTAURANT	8 BEVER-AGES	9 TELEPHONE LOCAL CALLS	10 TELEPHONE LONG DISTANCE	11 LAUNDRY	12 VALET	13 CASH DISBURSE-MENTS	14 TRANS-FERS	15	16 TOTAL DEBITS	17 CASH RECEIPTS	18 ALLOW-ANCES	19 TRANS-FERS	20	21 DEBIT	22 CREDIT

TOTALS

Courtesy: American Hotel Register Co. Form 75

EXHIBIT 6.4

Housekeeper's Report

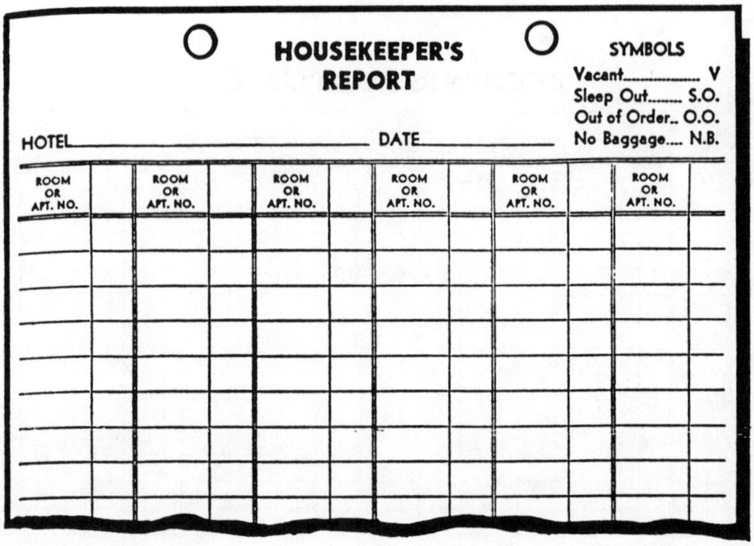
HOUSEKEEPER'S REPORT

SYMBOLS
Vacent.............. V
Sleep Out....... S.O.
Out of Order.. O.O.
No Baggage.... N.B.

HOTEL________________ DATE________

ROOM OR APT. NO.		ROOM OR APT. NO.		ROOM OR APT. NO.		ROOM OR APT. NO.		ROOM OR APT. NO.		ROOM OR APT. NO.	

Courtesy: American Hotel Register Co.

card company). Registration cards can also play other information-providing roles such as becoming the data source for guest history files, a tracking and recording device for check cashing, or a telephone list. Finally, registration cards are used to make up the document that is used to record the guest's charges and prepare his or her bill: the guest folio. Registration cards will be permanently filed alphabetically and chronologically.

The guest folio is also a serially numbered accounting document. It is a principal revenue document—the primary source document used to record rooms revenue in the journals—and thus must be constantly and accurately verified as to numerical sequence. Exhibit 6.2 shows examples of typical guest folios.

Like all accounting documents, folios are controlled by the accounting department and issued to the front office in blocks. Accounting must verify the existence of all folios each month by serial number. That type of ongoing inventory and audit requires that no folio ever be destroyed. Your employees must be trained so that when they make a mistake on a folio, they void it but do not destroy it. The voided folio is turned in along with the paid folios in their normal bank turn-in. When the accounting department performs its monthly audit of folios it must check those in storage, those issued to the front desk but still unused, those used but still on file at the front office (guests still in-house), and those turned in as settled (either paid or transferred to city ledger). Used or "paid" folios will be permanently filed by serial number.

From the discussion of accounts receivable, you will recall that hotels have two types of accounts receivable. There is the direct billing sent to customers, the city ledger, and there are all the charges incurred by guests during their stay, the guest-accounts receivable. The guest folio represents the individual or subsidiary form of the guest-accounts receivable. Another way to view it is that the guest-accounts receivable are a sum of all of the folios of the guests currently in the house. Whenever a charge of any type is incurred by a guest that charge is posted to the guest's account. That posting is physically accomplished by writing it down on the guest's folio. The charge for the room rental (plus applicable taxes) is also recorded on the folios—usually all at the same time during a process called the "night audit."

The sum of all of the guest folios is the total or controlling guest accounts receivable. It is also a convenient way to sum and view the total daily revenue of the hotel and its various components (e.g., rooms, F&B, valet, garage). A summary document is usually prepared to list and show all of these components and their totals. Such a document goes by several names, but I will simply call it the summary document. The example that is shown is called the Daily Transcript of Accounts Receivable, and can be seen in Exhibit 6.3.

When looking over Exhibit 6.3, one can see a series of columns with headings across the top. From right to left, those columns represent the guest information (name, room number, the opening or starting balance for the guest that day), a series of debits (for charges incurred by the guest that day such as room, F&B), a series of credits (for payments or other reductions), and the closing or ending balance for the day. Each horizontal line would be used for another guest (i.e., for another folio).

Another way to look at this process is that the folios represent the individual guest's beginning balance, charges for the day, payments or other reductions for the day, and ending balance. The folio depicts these transactions vertically. The transcript of accounts receivable depicts the same transactions and information horizontally, and it lists all the guest charges. The folio shows all charges, payments and balances for the guest's entire stay, while the transcript shows only one day at a time. A guest who stayed at the hotel for three days, for example, would have charges and payments for all three days on one folio; the same information would be found on three different accounts-receivable transcripts, one for each day. As the summary document, the transcript is also a good way to sum and audit the individual components of the total revenue. For example, all rooms revenue posted to guest accounts for the day can be totalled on the transcript. Similarly, the day's restaurant, telephone, or any other departmental charges can be totalled on the transcript. It must be remembered that the folios and transcript contain only the revenue charged to guests' accounts, which typically is only part of the revenue generated by those departments. The rest is cash or credit-card sales. Nonetheless, the transcript (or other summary document) plays important audit and internal-control roles that will be defined in more detail below. The housekeeper's report entails some important internal-control roles. Exhibit 6.4 depicts a typical, although simplified, housekeeper's report.

In hotels today one will find a wide variety of documents referred to as either "housekeeper's reports" or "housekeeping reports." They play a myriad of functional roles for the housekeeping department and for other areas of the hotel, particularly the front desk. They also originate at different points: some begin in housekeeping and end at the front office, while others move in the opposite direction. If it seems confusing as described here, it is often confusing in practice. In this book I will avoid the confusion by dealing only with the internal-control role of this vital document. The internal-control aspect of the house-keeper's report is very specific in its requirements and in the direction of its movement. It originates at housekeeping and flows eventually to accounting. I will cover the internal-control role of the housekeeper's report after I conclude this discussion of accounting documents.

The final guest-accounting document with a critical internal-control role is the allowance voucher. Exhibit 6.5 depicts a typical hotel allowance voucher. Allowance vouchers are also multi-part, serially numbered accounting documents. Hence they are controlled by the accounting department, issued in blocks to user departments, and audited periodically for content and the integrity of the numerical sequence.

Allowance is the term used here to indicate a credit or other reduction in rate or charges incurred by a guest. Some hotels refer to that process as a credit or a rebate. Allowances arise for a variety of reasons ranging from minor complaints or disputes, such as a guest's claiming he or she did not make a local phone call, to major complaints or even complimentary (no charge) rooms.

Exhibit 6.5

Allowance Voucher

No.: 3629

ALLOWANCE VOUCHER

Name of guest: _____ Room #: _____

Amount: _____

Reason:

Disputed Phone Call:	_____	Public Relations:	_____
Disputed Spectradyne Movie:	_____	Complimentary Room:	_____
Disputed Minibar:	_____	Complimentary Food & Berverage:	_____
Disputed Parking:	_____	Exchange/Refund at Cafeteria:	_____

Complaint (explain): _____

_____

Other (explain): _____

_____

Cashier: _____   Authorized Signature: _____

   The important internal-control issues for allowances are to ensure that the reduction being given to the guest is a legitimate one, and that the correct party gets the credit. It is easy to see that if there is no system of checks and balances on credits or reductions, a dishonest employee could use the process to perpetrate a fraud. For example, a clerk could post an "allowance" after the guest pays his or her bill (although the guest is not entitled to the rebate and has no idea the credit is posted) and then simply pocket the amount of the credit! The system of checks and balances necessary to prevent this type of fraud and other peculations in the allowance and credit areas are fairly complicated and quite precise. They are covered in detail below in the section titled "allowance-voucher procedure."

Guest Accounting: A Schematic View

Exhibit 6.6 (on the next page) depicts the flow of information and documents necessary for good internal control of the rooms revenue. It also serves as a good review and recap of the guest-accounting cycle.

Exhibit 6.6

Flow of Hotel Revenue

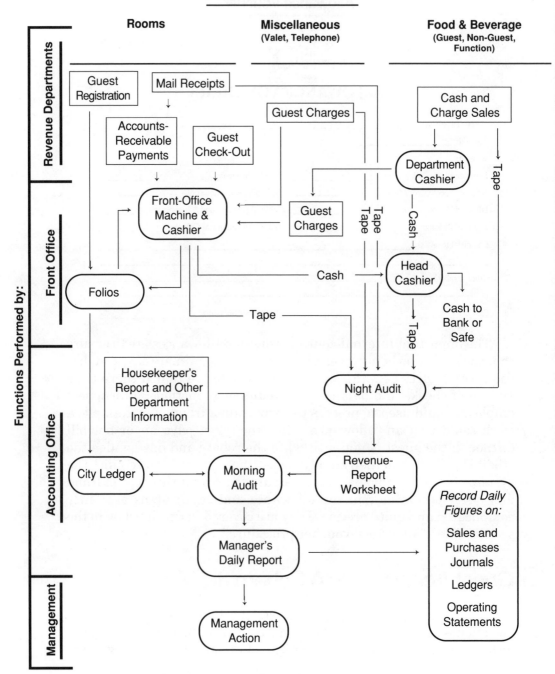

Modified from: James J. Eyster, Cornell University, 1975. Used by permission.

As Exhibit 6.6 depicts, the guest checks in by registering at the front desk. He or she fills in and signs a registration card, establishes credit, and is taken to his or her room. The front-office staff prepares a folio from the data on the registration card (as well as from advance reservations information, where applicable). When the guest wishes a meal or other service charged to his or her room, the revenue-center employees prepare a charge and send it to the front office for posting. The front-office staff continually (and rapidly) posts all charges that guests incur to their folios. The charge for the nightly room rental is either posted automatically (in the newer automated systems) or posted by hand, usually at night in a process called the "night audit." When the guest wishes to check out, he or she comes to the front office and settles his or her bill. The front-office cashiers turn in their banks, cash, checks, and credit-card vouchers to the head cashier and the paid folios to the accounting department.

The accounting department prepares summary documents (such as the summary transcript) and audits all of the revenue and daily postings, including any allowances. A copy of the housekeeper's report also goes to the accounting department and plays a role in the daily audit. Reports and documents from the head cashier and from the hotel's bank also play important roles in this audit process. In a moment, I'll discuss the rooms-revenue audit process in detail in a section called "daily audit process."

I have discussed all of the schematic pictures and processes as if they were in a manual environment. Many hotels have automated their front offices today, and most others will do so in the future. The key issue in automation is that the flow of information, the processing of data, and the documents themselves are exactly the same when one moves from manual processing to automatic electronic processing. Some documents and even some portions of the audit trail may change or even seem to disappear. They do not disappear, however. They may become "invisible" to the eye, but they are there in electronic storage, and can be and should be checked and audited in the same way they were in the manual environment. This concept is explored in more detail in Chapter 9.

Internal-Control Procedures for Rooms Revenue

The central theme in the control of revenue from rooms is that all of the

Case 6.1

The Phantom Guests

The night clerk at the front desk and the assistant manager at a motel had developed a scheme of selling rooms to guests without having them register, provided the guests paid in advance. The money, of course, was split by the clerk and the assistant manager. They were aided in their scheme by the lax behavior of the bookkeeper, who failed to check the housekeeper's report for six months.

The bookkeeper eventually did read the housekeeper's report and found that a number of rooms were reported as being occupied, although no registration or revenue was found for those rooms on the front-office records.

The hotel's management laid a trap for the two, into which they quickly fell. Having been caught, they confessed.

Discussion

In this case, the major weakness is obvious—the housekeeper's report was not checked regularly. The housekeeper's report should be an independent source of estimating rooms revenues. It should originate in the housekeeping department, list the rooms occupied each day, and be sent to the accounting department (or, at least a copy should go directly to accounting). As part of its daily audit process, the accounting department should check that all rooms shown as occupied on the housekeeping report are charged to guest accounts. In that way, the entire housekeeping department would have to be in on the collusion, adding an additional measure of division of duties to rooms income.

Also, rules on guest registration, credit checks, and numerical control of folios all should be adhered to. If automated key systems are feasible, they should be installed, and the daily key-cut reports audited each day by the accounting department.

---

rooms income should come to the hotel! We are trying to prevent a clerk or other employee from "selling" a room and pocketing the cash. We are also trying to ensure that the rooms are sold at the correct rate, and where changes or differences are warranted, that they go to the deserving recipient and not to an embezzling employee. To accomplish effective internal control in rooms revenue, four key areas must be verified:

- Document control,
- Rooms inventory,

- Independent revenue sources, and

- Auditing.

Each of the four areas involves an important internal-control principle in and of itself. To ensure tight control of rooms revenue, however, you should see to it that all four are practiced simultaneously.

Document Control. The concept of document control has been stressed repeatedly throughout the book. To reiterate, the notion of "accounting documents" has as a primary characteristic the use of serial numbers so that individual documents can be controlled and traced, if necessary. With revenue documents, strict numerical control is critical.

The simplest and, perhaps, one of the crudest embezzlement examples would be the case where a clerk, after receiving payment in cash from a room guest, destroys the folio and simply pockets the cash. For such a crude embezzlement to go undetected, several components of division of duties would have to break down, because the room clerk is not the only person involved in a guest's staying a night in the hotel. The success of such an embezzlement would also imply that the folio was the only source of information about that guest's stay, and that when the folio was destroyed, all evidence of the stay vanished. If we assume for a moment that such a breakdown could happen, the theft would be possible. But if there were strict control of the revenue documents, subsequent audits would reveal the missing folio number. We would not know the amount of the transaction, but at least we would know that a folio was missing. By itself, that level of document control can be a strong deterrent. As part of a combination of all the elements of revenue control, accurate and detailed document control becomes a powerful part of the internal-control process.

Employees must be trained and subsequently reminded that documents are sacrosanct. Your employees must come to value the importance of keeping track of each and every document, and learn to turn in voided documents when errors are made. Just the knowledge that revenue documents are carefully accounted for will act as a deterrent to embezzlement of the type alluded to above.

Rooms Inventory. In most well-run retail sales establishments, inventories are kept for all merchandise. Those inventories are adjusted upward when new merchandise is delivered, and adjusted downward for sales. When a physical count is taken, it can be compared to the theoretical or "book" inventory to calculate losses. Similarly, if inventories are taken at the beginning and end of a sales period (and no new deliveries have come in), the difference would represent the theoretical sales level. That "expected sales level" can be compared to actual sales, with any differences presumed to be thefts or other losses. Indeed, some hotels and restaurants operate such inventories and sales-value checks for food and beverage sales, as discussed in the next chapter.

It would be quite effective if a similar inventory approach existed for rooms sales. In addition to the crude "folio destroying" embezzlement discussed above, hotels are vulnerable to having employees "sell a key" to a friend or any late-night arrival. It is not so unusual for certain types of guests, particularly very late at night, to approach a room clerk and say something like, "I'll give you 50 bucks. Let me have a room key, and I'll be out by 5:00 AM!" A room clerk can be quite tempted to oblige such a request. The control of revenue documents does no good in that case since a folio is never prepared! An inventory of rooms sold would be effective, however.

How can hotels achieve such a rooms-sold inventory? Here's how: Hotels have a fixed number of rooms, each for sale every night. Hotel rooms are inspected, cleaned, and re-inspected daily by the housekeeping department. It is a fairly simple matter for the housekeeper to record, as each room is inspected, whether the room had been occupied or vacant the previous night. In fact, those data are typically recorded along with considerable functional information on the housekeeper's report (Exhibit 6.5 is an example of a simplified version of such a document). For internal-control purposes, we are not interested in all of the functional aspects of the housekeeper's report. When the paperwork makes employees' jobs easier (as do the functional aspects of the housekeeper's report), they are more likely to take meticulous care of the forms. For internal control, it is sufficient to know whether or not the room was occupied. It also helps to have an estimate of whether or not the room was occupied by one or two guests—an estimate that may be difficult to make from the housekeeper's perspective.

The housekeeper's report is a good surrogate for an inventory of product sold. The rooms listed as occupied on the housekeeper's report can be compared with those actually sold, with any discrepancies noted and investigated. A hotel can even obtain a crude but sometimes useful estimate of daily rooms revenue by "pricing out" the housekeeper's report with the average room rate. Some hotels even try to price the rooms occupied with their likely actual rates.

Now, for a room clerk to perpetrate the sell-a-key fraud, the housekeeper and, perhaps, some maids will have to collude and purposefully mark an occupied room as vacant. The division of duties in the rooms-sales area makes the fraud difficult to pull off. The details of how the accounting department conducts the check of the housekeeper's report is discussed more fully in the section on the daily audit process below. Suffice it for now to point out that an independent copy of the housekeeper's report should go directly from housekeeper to the accounting department as early as is feasible each day. I have no major objection to copies of the housekeeper's report or other communications used for functional purposes going from the housekeeper to the front office, as long as an independent copy goes directly to accounting.

Independent Revenue-Information Sources. The notion of independent sources of revenue information means that estimates of sales should be made from sources that are not part of the normal audit trail—that is, not in the transaction process or not from regular source documents. In the rooms area, this principle implies that you find estimates of sales without looking at room clerks, cashiers, the head cashier, income auditors, or any of the documents they produce. Borrowing from computer jargon, some people refer to that idea as "off-line," because the normal transactions and their documentation are considered "on-line." A general problem with independent sources of revenue information is that they are often less accurate than the on-line measures. Their independence, however, allows them to be useful. Always remember that they are estimates to be used as checks and balances and not as documents to record sales.

While the best example of such a source for rooms is the housekeeping department and the housekeeper's report, the following are some other possible sources.

Some hotels require that all guests be shown to their room at check-in by a member of the bellstaff. The bell captain usually keeps a log or report of which bell persons are sent, where they go, and when they go there. Such a bellstaff report would make a good additional estimate of rooms sold that should be turned in daily to the accounting department. It must be remembered, though, that such a report would only list rooms checked-in. Those already in the house would not be on the daily report.

The room-key systems in many hotels have been improving in recent years. In an effort to afford guests better security, hotels have begun to use automated electronic key systems. These various systems produce a unique key at each check-in, good for that guest's particular stay. The "key" is usually punched out of an index card or plastic card with a computer-generated numerical sequence that is recognized by the room's door lock. These new systems afford perhaps the best new internal-control hope in years. Since the systems rely on a computer—usually a PC—to generate the punches, a permanent audit trail is created. The daily key report that is produced should be audited by the accounting department and can serve as an effective independent source of rooms sold. The system operates on the premise that keys are cut only when a check-in occurs. Thus, the report of keys cut and the room numbers they are cut for should be comparable with the list of actual rooms sold.

In my opinion, future development of automated keys, particularly when the key systems have full interface with the property-management systems, offers great promise for excellent internal control. The next step should be an automatic comparison of the key report and the tally of rooms sold, with exceptions printed out. Future steps can include automatic comparisons with an automated housekeeping report, and even automatic billing whenever a key is cut!

Auditing. The final step in the complete control of rooms income involves the role of the accounting department in auditing sales. Such an audit is performed daily (ongoing) as well as periodically. The process is fairly complex and varies greatly from hotel to hotel. Periodic auditing is performed, usually monthly, to verify the integrity of the numerical sequence of documents, to check the revenue (settlement) sources against the bank and credit card deposits (usually in combination with the bank-statement reconciliation), and to match the rooms revenue with other departmental revenues, statistics, and budgets.

From the internal-control perspective, the most important audit functions occur daily. The night audit is an excellent example. Almost all hotels have a night-audit process and most have a person or position called the "night auditor." In many hotels this person plays a variety of roles including auditor, desk clerk, cashier, and even night manager. For internal-control purposes, particularly the division of duties between cash handling and bookkeeping, the night auditor should not act as a cashier. Not surprisingly, the night auditor usually works the "third shift" from midnight to early morning. He or she posts any guest charges that may come in after the evening clerks leave; verifies arrivals, departures, and the list of active guest-accounts receivable; verifies other departmental income and charges; posts the room charges to all guest's accounts; prepares the summary document; and begins many of the daily audit functions listed below.

Many hotels also have a morning-audit process during which the daily-audit functions remaining from the night audit are completed. The person performing the morning audit, usually called "income auditor," also works on periodic audit tasks and may have other accounting or auditing tasks such as food and beverage auditing. Increasing front-office automation is changing the role of the night auditor and other parts of the auditing process. In many cases, it is no longer critical to have someone there in the middle of the night to post room charges, since the system can post them automatically. For internal-control purposes, it is not important whether the key elements of the daily audit process are performed at night or the next morning, as long as they are performed daily! For that reason I won't refer to the time of day, but I'll simply call it the seven-step daily-audit process.

Seven-Step Daily Audit Process

The daily-audit process assumes that a summary document exists or is produced that includes the names, room numbers, room rates, account balances, new charges, and payments, allowances, or other reductions for all guests in the house for the day. The transcript, depicted in Exhibit 6.3 is such a summary document. The summary document, either by electronic totalling or its own mathematical make-up, should also include column totals for all of its elements. With a verified summary document in hand, the accounting department people can begin the seven-step daily audit process:

1. Check math,
2. Match folios with summary document,
3. Check housekeeper's report,
4. Check room rates,
5. Check departmental totals,
6. Check turn-ins, and
7. File documents.

Checking the math in the summary document is an important first step. It is critical that there be no errors in the summary, as it will be the surrogate for all the folios in the audit process. Checking the math is often known as checking the footings and extensions. The extensions are the horizontal mathematics, and the footings are the column summations. In most electronically prepared summary documents, it is not necessary to check the mathematics daily because computers usually do not make mathematical errors. People, however, do make mistakes, so it is a good idea to audit occasionally for math and other errors or omissions (perhaps once or twice per month).

Matching the folios with the summary document is the next logical step in assuring that we have accurate surrogate representation of all live guest accounts. In physical situations where an actual file (tub, bucket, bin) of folio documents is kept at the front desk, the summary document, once it is checked for both mathematical accuracy and representational accuracy with respect to all of the folios, becomes the key subject of the rest of the audit efforts. In that way, the file of live folios is immediately available to the desk clerks for check-in, check-out, and posting. In fully automated front offices, an analogous situation exists where it is difficult (in some software packages, impossible) for auditors to gain access to the folio files and manipulate or check them, while allowing simultaneous access to the desk clerks. Additionally, it is better for the auditors to complete their work carefully and without time or operational pressure—a feat far more easily accomplished with a printed summary than with the live accounts, paper or electronic.

Checking the housekeeper's report is perhaps the single most important step for internal control of rooms revenue. As was discussed earlier, the housekeeper's report is the closest thing we have to a daily inventory of rooms—both sold (occupied) and unsold. Checking the housekeeper's report is conceptually quite simple and direct: all rooms marked as occupied that day on the housekeeper's report should be on that day's summary document as having been charged to someone's account. Conversely, if a room is marked occupied by the housekeeping department and does not appear on the summary of accounts, we have a serious discrepancy that warrants immediate investigation!

For the housekeeper's report to be useful in this manner, it must come independently and directly from housekeeping to accounting. If the report first stops at the front desk for checking or correcting, it might just as well not be used. Incorporating housekeeping in the audit of rooms revenue adds an ideal step in the division of duties. Since housekeeping personnel inspect the rooms anyway, there is no additional payroll cost to this excellent auditing and control measure. In most hotels, the housekeeping inspection documents will be far more complicated than the one depicted in Exhibit 6.4. They typically include many functional items for room inspection and other use by the housekeepers. There is no problem with the added information, but the accounting department does not need any more information than which rooms were occupied the previous night and, perhaps, whether they were occupied by singles or doubles.

Many fully automated front-office or property-management systems include an automatic housekeeper's report. Some even check the housekeeping input against the folios and produce exception reports for the audit process. Those added electronic amenities are fine, but I believe the process of having the housekeeper independently produce a simple daily inventory is invaluable. By having it separately produced, we gain the off-line independence so critical to internal-control checks and balances.

Checking the room rates involves checking each rate charged for each room on the summary document against an established schedule of rates. More will be said about fixed room-rate schedules below. What is important here is that every rate charged to guest folios must conform to the schedule or there should be a properly executed allowance voucher authorizing the rate change attached to the folio. Room-rate checks of this type can also be built into the routines of fully automated electronic systems, but a separate allowance-voucher document must exist, a procedure that I will discuss more fully on the next page.

For control purposes, the hotel must never allow room clerks or for that matter any one individual to change the rate charged from that prescribed for the room on the particular night without management's authorization and proper audit trail and division of duties—all of which come with proper allowance-voucher procedure. Without such safeguards, as I already pointed out, a dishonest clerk could reduce a guest's room rate after the guest paid, or otherwise without the guest's knowledge, and pocket the difference. Incidentally, a complimentary room should be considered as the same type of rate-change transaction, with the rate changed to zero. While the type of fraud I describe here may be rare and somewhat crude, mistakes and errors often happen in assigning room rates. The daily room-rate check helps catch and correct mistakes as well as frauds.

Checking the departmental totals involves matching the totals on the summary document for each type of revenue with the totals reported on the summary documents and reports produced by each of those revenue generating departments. Most operating departments, for example the various restaurants and other food and beverage outlets, operate with separate systems from those of the front office, and they produce their own summary documentation.

In some of the automated systems, interface is possible between the components that operate the front office and those that operate the other outlets. That type of interface means that the outlets can post charges directly to the guest's folios. While that function is important and convenient, the summaries produced in the outlets will still have to be audited on their own, and, with respect to the daily audit of rooms income, have to be checked with the rooms-summary document to ascertain the correctness of the charges to guests' accounts.

Check turn-ins means checking the totals on the summary document for each type of settlement (e.g., cash, various credit cards, transfer to city ledger) against the documentation produced by the head cashier. That documentation should summarize the total actual turn-in as received from the various shift cashiers, the types of settlements, and the banking activity. The bank deposits should also be checked against the totals of cash (cash and check) as reported on the summary document. As I pointed out in the chapter on cash receipts, it is also a good idea to have the hotel's bank send back duplicate deposit slips. Since there will be a time delay in that process, these slips will have to be checked in the periodic audit rather than each day. This point in the daily audit is also a good time to check the cashiers for cash over and cash short and send major deviations to the controller for investigation or possible action.

The only cashier and revenue-receipt activity not audited at this point is accounts receivable (city ledger), which is usually audited monthly. The daily transfers to city ledger are audited, however, as part of the daily audit process.

Filing is the last step in the daily process. The files of documents will be more easily accessible, much more useful, and have greater accuracy for auditing if filing is done daily—easiest to do as the final step in the daily audit process after the guest checks out. Registration cards are best filed alphabetically and chronologically, say, by the month or quarter depending on the volume.

Registration cards should be cross-referenced to the folios. The serial number of the folio should appear on the registration card and vice versa. In electronic systems, or with modern "one-shot" multi-part folios, the registration card and the folio often have the same serial number. Used folios are filed numerically—that is, by serial number. (Most auditors generally prefer that revenue documents be filed numerically.) If a particular guest's folio needs to be retrieved in the future, his or her name and date of stay will quickly yield the registration card and thus the folio serial number. The folio can then be retrieved by number and referred to or copied.

Allowance vouchers will also be **filed numerically**. The summary documents and housekeeper's reports will obviously be bound by their calendar dates. Other rooms-revenue documentation can be filed according to almost any method, at the controller's discretion.

Allowance Procedure

As I pointed out earlier in the chapter, allowances involve giving reductions in rate or revenue to guests for a variety of reasons. In other sections of the book, for example in credit and collections, where write-offs were discussed, I pointed out the dangers inherent in such a process. The main concerns are **(1)** the allowances to be granted should be legitimate, and **(2)** they should be given to the correct, deserving party. To verify those concerns, two key issues should be maintained when granting reductions in revenue: management authorization (the permission aspect) and division of duties (the audit-trail aspect). It is critical that all allowances be made with a duly authorized voucher, and always signed by someone other than the clerk who will post the voucher. The voucher will then serve the roles of permission, division of duties, and audit trail (since a copy is sent to accounting).

To avoid top management's having to be involved with all allowances, I recommend a stratified level of authority. Most hotels use dollar amounts to accomplish such stratification. Allowances for disputed local calls, for example, should be left for the desk clerks to resolve. Higher levels of allowances may require a supervisor's signature, and some, such as comps, may require the general manager's signature. The exact stratification of who is given what level of authority is a policy issue that must be decided by management. The important concerns are that division of duties and a proper audit trail be maintained. In the cases of minor disputes, where the desk clerks have authority, the clerk settling the dispute and posting the credit must get another clerk to sign the voucher. The other clerk, in that case, is acting as authorized signer and turns a copy into the accounting office. While

Case 6.2

Fake Allowance Vouchers

An annual audit found that a large proportion of allowance vouchers for a 300-room transient hotel had not been approved. When the manager received the large stack of unsigned vouchers for approval, he at once doubted whether many of them were genuine, particularly the large number that involved rate adjustments and allowances for days charged in error.

The positions of bill clerk and cashier were held by the same person, who was allowed to make out and sign all allowance vouchers. Every so often, usually once a day, the manager would stop by this clerk's station and ask to see the vouchers. After a casual inspection, the manager would hand them back, sometimes initialing them. The vouchers were not kept in numerical order and the bookkeeper accepted them on the strength of the cashier's signature alone.

The manager's investigation revealed the following scheme:

One of the cashiers in the combined position was holding out a few dollars from the guests' payments made in cash where the guest did not ask for a receipt. The cashier then made out an allowance voucher for the money subtracted. These vouchers were kept separate from the legitimate vouchers and were, of course, not submitted to the manager. To avoid suspicion, this cashier also left several of the legitimate allowance vouchers for the other cashier to make out, so that there was no great difference between the number of vouchers made out by the two cashiers. Most of the fictitious vouchers were ostensibly for allowances on room rates.

Discussion

The 300-room hotel made the typical mistake of obtaining allowance vouchers without implementing the procedures necessary to make them an effective control device.

The concepts behind an allowance-voucher system are twofold: permission and audit trail. We do not want to reduce a guest's rate or charges without proper reason and managerial authority—which is the permission aspect. We must also ensure that correct allowances are posted to the deserving account—the audit-trail function.

A well-designed voucher system will accomplish both. The vouchers should be multi-copy, have serial numbers, and be controlled by the accounting department. When an employee is confronted with a problem requiring a rebate or credit, he or she should fill out an allowance voucher, have it signed by an authorized signor, and then post the allowance to the guest's account. The signor must send a copy directly to the accounting department. The accounting copy serves as a "flag" that an allowance has been posted and prevents alterations to the allowance from being made after authorization.

To ensure that the hotel's guests receive the full allowances that they are entitled to, policy should require that the guest also sign the voucher, indicating that they are aware of the credit and have received it.

Finally, the accounting department must fully audit all vouchers—the function blatantly missing in this 300-room hotel. They must be accounted for by serial number and the copies matched up to check for unauthorized changes. The income audit also verifies allowances. For example, the room-rate review requires that any rate below posted rates be accompanied by a duly authorized allowance voucher.

The audit-trail aspect of the voucher system also ensures division of duties between the employee initiating the allowance and the one authorizing it—allowing stratified levels of allowance authority to be implemented without any loss of control.

---

establishing strata for authority is a management-policy issue, verification of that authority is a control issue and thus is the concern of the accounting department. Both dimensions can be verified through the allowance-voucher procedure.

Allowance vouchers (see the example in Exhibit 6.5) should be individually designed to fit your hotel. A single, well-designed voucher should serve all of a hotel's credit and rebate needs, from a minor mini-bar dispute to a complimentary room. The vouchers should be accounting documents—multiple-part, serially numbered, and controlled and issued by the accounting department. Blank vouchers should be issued to the front office, to other outlets where guest settlement is apt to take place, and to the various authorized signers. The vouchers should be at least in duplicate so that one copy can be sent independently to the accounting department. If the authorized signers wish to keep copies, then the vouchers need to be in triplicate.

The original or front copy of the voucher is attached to the folio when the allowance is posted (or to the guest check in the case of food and beverage allowances). The second copy is sent independently to the accounting office and serves several important purposes. First, its existence prevents a clerk or other employee from making changes to the voucher after it has been signed. It also prevents clerks from posting different amounts since all posted allowances will be audited. The easiest way to audit vouchers is to match the independent copies with the originals, and "flag" discrepancies. Finally, the accounting copy also serves as a reference for the income auditors whenever they find a rate discrepancy in the daily audit process. Any rate deviations, including complimentary rooms, should be accompanied by a properly executed voucher, and the accounting copy is easiest and fastest to

Case 6.3

License to Steal

Guests of a certain medium-size transient hotel were supposed to be charged for an extra day if they retained their rooms after 9:00 PM on the day of departure. The front-office cashiers, however, did not make an entry for the charge on the guest bill until the money was actually collected. The usual procedure was to collect the cash from any guest who paid without questioning the charge, and then enter the amount on the bill. The extra charge was routinely omitted if the guest objected.

One of the cashiers realized that this loose method of charging presented the opportunity for personal gain. He would occasionally hold out the extra money, making no charge or credit for it on the guest bill. This was done only in cases where the guest did not take the receipted bill. Otherwise, the cashier did not take chances, put the money in the drawer, and made the correct entries.

Although most of the guests objected to the hotel's attempt to levy an extra charge and were not compelled to pay, the cashier was still able to add a substantial sum to his monthly salary before he was caught.

Discussion

In this case the hotel's policy really gave the clerks the license to steal. "Go out, Mr. Clerk, and collect from whomever you can. If guests resist, don't pressure them." What an opportunity! Why tell the hotel if a guest did pay (especially a cash-paying customer)?

The correct way to handle situations like the extra-day charge in this case is to charge everyone (the time and amounts are management-policy issues and do not affect internal control), and credit back those that resist with a properly executed and authorized allowance voucher, as discussed in this chapter.

The important internal control point is that the clerk's complete control over the allowance transaction had to be removed, and replaced by an audit trail and division of duties through the voucher system. The management-policy issue of when to allow credit for those guests who resist would not be affected by the control procedures.

---

check that this policy has been followed.

The accounting copies should be periodically reviewed by all members of top management for information purposes. Since allowances are usually granted in response to guest dissatisfaction or complaint, they are a valuable source of management information about where complaints are originating, and the nature of the problems.

To prevent the type of fraud where clerks intentionally fail to inform the guest of the existence of a credit (and, hence, can pocket the credit themselves), guests should be asked to sign the original allowance voucher when they are settling their bill. The hotel has the guests' signatures on file (on the registration cards) and can always verify them. The clerk is inhibited from posting a different, fraudulent amount of credit to a guest's account because a separate copy of the voucher is sent to the accounting office.

In hotels where allowance fraud is suspected, it is also a good idea for the accounting department periodically to check some of the allowances by mailing confirmation letters to a sample of former guests, and asking them to verify both the fact that they actually received the credit and the credit's amount. That letter is also a good public-relations opportunity to apologize again for the incident that caused the guest to seek the allowance.

Other Issues

Room Rates. From the perspective of internal control, the single most important issue is that room rates be fixed and published on a management-approved room-rate or tariff list. All rates that are charged to guests must conform exactly to the fixed schedule or be accompanied by a duly-executed allowance voucher authorizing the variation. The issue is not that rates should never vary or change, but rather that they must not be changed without authorization and a proper audit trail, as already discussed above. The weakness that is created if that rigid policy is not enforced is that a clerk can change rates without authorization or without the guest's even being aware of it. The guest would pay the incorrect rate and the clerk would pocket the difference! In addition to fraud protection, good rate-changing policy helps prevent mistakes in rate assignment.

The modern theories of yield management and other creative selling and price-management programs complicate the process of fixing rates and vouchering changes. The fact that those concepts are becoming more common, however, makes it even more imperative that hotels set up formal systems to ensure that all rate changes have management's approval, are traceable through a solid audit trail, and are easy to audit. The allowance-voucher procedure described above is the best way to meet all of those goals.

Hotels will find it easier to implement rate-management programs if they minimize the number of different rates charged by the hotel. That feat is easier to accomplish in newer properties where the rooms are standardized. In older properties, it may be more difficult to limit the number of rate classes. Either way, differences in seasons, day of the week, view, altitude, configuration, furnishings, and affiliation all contribute to the complexity of room rates. These complexities only make it more imperative to implement the recommended controls.

Transfers and Errors. If you look back at the transcript (Exhibit 6.3), you'll see columns for transfers and miscellaneous items. Clerks posting accounts and preparing guest bills, whether by hand or in fully automated systems, will make errors that need correcting. Similarly, charges will be posted to one guest's room when they should have been posted to another guest's room. Those errors will happen, even in fully automated systems, often because the guests fail to make it clear which room account should get the charge for a drink or meal. Since we are in the business of accommodating guests, we need to make such changes smoothly and easily.

The control issues involved in transfers and errors are the same as those with rate changes or allowances. Specifically, if solid audit trails and authorization plans are not in place, a clerk could post a false error and pocket the difference. The solution is straightforward: it is the same procedure as for allowances described in the previous section. In fact, I prefer that errors be treated like any other allowance. Similar vouchers (preferably the same ones) can be used with a section or column added for errors. Stratified levels can be set up so that small errors can be corrected with a supervisory signature, while larger ones require a manager's signature. In that way, large or repetitive errors are brought to management's attention.

As for simple transfers of charges from one folio to another (called "debit-credit transfer" in hotel parlance), it is probably easier to develop and use a simpler form just for that purpose. Generally, those transfers can be accomplished with a supervisor's signature, or even with one clerk signing for another—as long as the signer sends a separate copy to accounting to ensure the audit trail and division of duties. Again, the key issue is not to make it difficult to accomplish the transfers, but to be able to verify that the transfers are legitimate, and to leave an audit trail for future auditing and checking.

Externally Generated Guest Services. Hotel guests often desire or request goods and services that are not produced by the hotel. Examples are flowers, special printing, delivery charges, and theater tickets. It is as important to create a solid audit trail for these externally generated items as it is for hotel generated ones. Separate charge vouchers controlled with serial numbers should be used for each type of charge, and monthly summaries should be audited.

The hotel should develop specifications for each item, evaluate suppliers, negotiate prices, and designate official suppliers. Those suppliers should supply the products as needed, leave invoices that can be posted to the guest's folios, and mail monthly statements to the hotel summarizing all guest deliveries over the month. The hotel should pay the vendors monthly through the regular accounts-payable process described in Chapter 4. The hotel collects for the outside items from the guests along with regular revenue and pays for the items through normal channels. Many of the extras, in fact, can become legitimate profit sources for the hotel—sold to the guest at a fair retail price, with the hotel paying a discounted or wholesale price.

Travel-Agency Commissions. Travel-agency commissions can often pose problems for hotels—particularly in verifying the commissions prior to payment. Payment of travel-agency commissions should be treated in exactly the same manner as any other payable. They should be paid once per month along with the other bills in the monthly cycle. They should be prepared by the accounts-payable clerk with a check and accompanying documentation for the general manager's verification, signature, cancellation, and mailing. With proper documentation, the possibility of fraudulent payments diminishes.

The major difference between travel-agency commissions and other accounts payable is in the documentation. With travel-agency commissions, there are no purchase orders or receiving reports. The analogous documents for travel-agency commissions are the vouchers that accompany the reservation or check-in and a copy of the guest's folio. The folio is most important as it is evidence that the guest actually stayed at the hotel and records the length of stay and the rate charged. It is a good idea to send an extra copy of the folio with the payment so the travel agent knows how the commission was calculated. Often a client cuts a stay short or changes rates, and the agent may think the hotel calculated the commission incorrectly.

Note that the accounting department, prior to presenting the check and documentation to the manager for approval, should verify the travel agency's authenticity by looking it up in industry guides and verifying its number.* With many of the fully automated front-office

---

*For example: American Society of Travel Agents, *A.S.T.A. Membership Directory* (Alexandria, VA: A.S.T.A., 1990); Association of Retail Travel Agents, *Membership Listing* (Washington, D.C.: A.R.T.A., 1989).

systems and even in manual environments, such verification and agency-number entry can be accomplished ahead of time by the reservationist or front-office clerks.

Advance Deposits. Advance deposits are payments made in advance by guests to guarantee or hold reservations. They play a very important role in banquets and conferences, and will be discussed more completely in the chapter on banquets and contractual business. The key control issues for deposits are keeping track of them and ensuring that they are credited to the proper account at the proper time. As for the actual receipt of the cash payment (or check or credit card), advance deposits are no different from any other cash receipts (see Chapter 2). The hotel receives cash only at *bona fide* cashier stations—usually the front desk—and through the mail.

Keeping track of the credits to the guests' accounts is best accomplished by setting up a city-ledger account (accounts-receivable account) for the guest or group at the time the reservation is made or the function is booked. When the payment is received, it is simply posted as a normal city-ledger payment, and thus is credited to the guest's account. Since the guest has yet to accumulate charges, the account will carry a credit balance for the amount of the payment. In fully automated systems, that process should result in the creation of a folio that reflects the credit balance. This desirable procedure should also occur in manual front offices. When the guest checks in, it works very well to have a folio already showing the guest's advance payment.* In manual environments, some sort of chronological or "tickler" file must be created for those advance folios.

From the internal-control perspective, the division of duties already present in the cash-receipts program is merely implemented here.

---

*The credit is to a liability account at this point, instead of to revenue. It represents unearned revenue that will be recorded when earned by an adjusting entry that will simultaneously reduce the liability.

Glossary

Advance Deposits—Payments made by guests to the hotel in advance of their stay to hold specific space; advance deposits are recorded as a liability until they are earned by having the guest actually use the hotel's services.

Allowance—A credit, rebate, or discount given to a guest that lowers the rate, price, or revenue to the hotel; allowances are often issued in response to a guest complaint.

Allowance Voucher—A pre-numbered accounting document used to post and record allowances; allowance vouchers have both permission and audit-trail roles.

Automated Front-Office System—The generic term for computerized guest-accounting or front-office systems; also used to describe the broader property-management systems.

Check-in—The process of registering a guest and issuing him or her a room.

Check-out—The process of settling the bill (folio) with the guest.

Complimentary Room—A guest stay where the price for a room-night is zero, usually for reasons such as public relations or sales.

Daily Audit Process—The accounting process of checking and verifying all of the documentation and audit trails for rooms revenue; may include portions of what were traditionally called the night audit and the morning audit.

Daily Transcript (of accounts receivable)—A summary document of all live or active guest folios, ranging from the older hand-prepared versions to computerized spreadsheets.

Front Office—The front desk and all guest-accounting operations of a hotel.

Front-Office Accounting—Guest accounting, or all of the processes involved in checking a guest in, accumulating his or her charges, and settling the bill upon check-out.

Guest Accounting—Front-office accounting.

Guest Folio—An individual guest's account with the hotel, or the amount the guest owes the hotel at any point in time, usually evidenced by a written document or computer file.

Housekeeper's Report—A document prepared daily by the house-keeping staff that lists the rooms status for the previous night; an inventory of rooms occupied.

Independent Sources of Revenue—Data sources that are not part of the revenue-recording documents but that allow estimation of the revenue; examples are the housekeeper's report for rooms, or cover counts in restaurants.

Interface—A mechanical process whereby one system is connected to or able to communicate with another.

Manual Environment—In the rooms-revenue context, a front-office or guest accounting system that is posted and prepared by hand.

Mini-bar—In-room vending of food and beverage items.

Morning Audit—The portion of the daily audit of rooms revenue that is traditionally performed during the morning following the transactions.

Night Audit—The portion of the daily audit of rooms revenue that is traditionally performed during the night following the transactions.

Off-line—In the context of revenue, an item of data that is not part of the revenue-recording cycle or documentation.

On-line—In the context of revenue, those items that are part of the official revenue-recording cycle or documentation.

Rebate—A discount or allowance given to a guest.

Registration Cards—Documents that are used at check-in to capture information about the guest, his or her credit worthiness, and his or her stay.

Room-Rate (Tariff) Schedule—A fixed and published listing of the various room rates charged by the hotel.

Rooms Revenue—Sales, in dollars, by the rooms department.

Rooms-Sold Inventory—A daily listing of rooms occupied.

Tariff—See Room-Rate Schedule

Travel-Agency Commissions—The fees paid to travel agents for sending business to the hotel; usually a percentage of room sales generated by the travel agent's client.

Yield Management—A systematic approach to managing room rates so as to maximize total revenue.

Selected References

Roy Alvarez, Dennis Ferguson, and Jerry Dunn, "How *Not* to Automate Your Front Office," *The Cornell Hotel and Restaurant Administration Quarterly*, 24, No. 3 (November 1983), pp. 56-62.

American Society of Travel Agents, *A.S.T.A. Membership Directory, 1990*, (Alexandria, VA: American Society of Travel Agents, 1990).

Association of Retail Travel Agents, *A.R.T.A. Membership Listing, 1989* Washington, DC: Association of Retail Travel Agents, 1989).

Peter Dukas, *Hotel Front Office Management and Operation (3rd Edition)* (Dubuque, IA: William C. Brown Company, 1970).

Ernest B. Horwath, Louis Toth, and John D. Lesure, *Hotel Accounting (3rd Edition)* (New York, Ronald Press Company, 1963).

A. Neal Geller, *Executive Information Needs in Hotel Companies* (New York: Peat Marwick & Mitchell, 1984).

Michael L. Kasavana, *Effective Front Office Operations* (Boston: CBI Publishing, 1981).

Joseph A. Marko, "A Practical Guide to Automated Property Management Systems for the Lodging Industry," (Ithaca, NY: Cornell University, 1980).

Pannell Kerr Forster, *Trends in the Hotel Industry* (Houston, TX: Pannell Kerr Forster, 1989).

Jerome J. Vallen and Gary K. Vallen, *Check In • Check Out (Fourth Edition)* (Dubuque, IA: William C. Brown, 1991).

Chapter 7

Food & Beverage Control

Objectives

After completing this chapter, you should understand:

1. The nature of the internal-control problems encountered in food and beverage operations.
2. The procedures for internal control of food and beverage revenue.
3. The concepts of duplicate checking and pre-checking.
4. The auditing procedures for food and beverage revenue.
5. The effects of automation on food and beverage operations.

The restaurant business is noted for being a difficult one. Running a food and beverage operation is far more complicated than it seems to people outside the business (unfortunately, also to some people inside the business). Effective internal control in food and beverage operations is also complicated and difficult to achieve. While internal-control failure is only one of the complex issues that makes operating restaurants difficult, it is a critical one. This chapter will help you construct a program that makes good internal control achievable for food and beverage operations—from small restaurants to large hotel food and beverage departments. Some additional complexities arise with banquets and other contractual types of business. I will deal with those issues separately in the next chapter.

Poor Natural Division of Duties. In most restaurant situations, there is a poor natural division of duties, because the wait staff is involved with or controls virtually every aspect of the transaction of selling food or beverages to the guest. Before discussing that problem in detail, it is useful to view contrasting situations by looking at similar processes in other industries.

In a manufacturing concern, automobiles for example, there are literally dozens of different people in several departments who are involved with production, inventory, sale, shipment, billing, collection, and accounting for the sale of units to a dealer. All that activity takes care of just the wholesale level. At retail, the dealer sells the car to the customer with at minimum a sales person, a sales manager, and a credit manager involved, plus the preparation staff.

Contrasting a similar situation in food and beverage—the sale of a manufactured product to the customer—there are very few players and almost no division of duties. The wait person handles sales, delivery and shipment, billing, and, in most instances, settling the bill. Often, he or she is even involved in some of the manufacture! If you look back at the first chapter where I discussed division of duties, you'll see that splitting up pieces of a transaction over several different persons makes fraud and embezzlement far more difficult. Division of duties is rarely present in food and beverage operations. To make matters worse, incidents of collusion appear to occur more frequently in restaurant operations.

Historically, the kind of detailed duplicate-check systems that ensure better division of duties were prevalent in hotels and free-standing restaurants in the '30s and '40s. After World War II, and throughout the '50s and '60s, labor costs in the hotel and restaurant industries began to escalate. In an attempt to regain previous profits, full duplicate-checking systems and other internal-control measures became casualties. In the '70s, new electronic cash registers (ECRs) were developed. That development continued through the '80s so that there now exists inexpensive, sophisticated, yet simple-to-operate, point-of-sale (POS) systems that allow an easy and beneficial return to the level of control that most hotels and restaurants routinely enjoyed 50 years ago. Furthermore, these new devices provide features that make the jobs of chefs and other food-service workers far more easy. These points are discussed in the next section.

First, the following are the key ingredients for internal control of food and beverage revenue:

- Checking,
- Document control,
- Division of duties,
- Independent revenue sources, and
- Auditing.

Food and Beverage Checking

Checking serves as a foundation and is important to the overall program of food and beverage internal control. A theoretical definition of checking is a comparison of the recorded cash receipts and charges of food and beverage sales against a separately created record of the food and beverages actually served. That theoretical definition translates in practice to comparing the products that leave the preparation areas with the bills that will be presented to the customers (guest checks). In simple terms, if it leaves the kitchen or service bar, it must be charged to someone's account.

This concept is reminiscent of the policy proposed in the last chapter on rooms: if a room is determined to be occupied by housekeeping, it should be billed. The food and beverage area has a direct analogy: if a product has been sent to the dining rooms, it should be billed. There are some key differences, however. The housekeeping information used in rooms was an independent source (i.e., it was "off-line" and not part of the regular revenue audit trail). The records of product served that will be compared to billings in the food and beverage operations are part of on-line documentation, not an independent source. In fact, the checking system, by making cooks and preparers part of the actual revenue-audit trail, plays an important role in a deliberate attempt to increase the division of duties in these operations. In a moment, I'll explain some other independent revenue sources.

First, I will discuss the duplicate-check system as it operates in a manual environment with the full number of employees, including a separate checker and a cashier. Later, I will explore other variations, and discuss the implications of electronic systems.

With the full duplicate-checking system, the wait person takes the guests' orders on a duplicate check or voucher. The duplicates can be produced in one of two ways. First, the guest checks themselves can be multi-part documents. This approach is preferred in manual systems, since it ensures that all orders written on the check will appear on the final copy, the guest's bill. Its drawbacks are that these forms are expensive, and the process takes as many copies as there are orders taken. In other words, in a fine-dining establishment, where there are apt to be five or more courses plus beverages, the documents would have to be six or seven copies deep. It is difficult to get that many copies to print through to the last one. The second way to produce duplicates is to have a separate "book" or voucher pad for the duplicates. This approach has the advantage of being less expensive and of allowing as many separate orders as are necessary for each party. Its drawback is that there is no guarantee that when a duplicate is filled out it will appear on the guest check. Although some very clever duplicate books have been developed—where the "dupes" fold over a piece of carbon that is on top of the guest check so that all entries on dupes also appear on the check—the best way to guarantee that duplicate entries appear on the guest check is by employing a separate checker.

The way it works is that after the wait person takes the guest's order on the duplicate, he or she stops at the checker's station where the checker quickly verifies that the dupe and the guest check are the same (unnecessary with multi-part forms or with well-designed carbons), hands the dupe back to the wait person, and then proceeds to enter the items, by price, in the checking machine with concurrent indelible printing on the guest check. The wait person, meanwhile, takes the dupe to the preparers in the kitchen or bar.

The preparers take the dupes from the wait staff and use them to produce the orders. This part of the process is the key to food and beverage revenue control. The preparers must be trained to produce no orders without a dupe. Thus, the preparer becomes part of the revenue recording cycle—part of the audit trail—and an integral part of the transaction. That is the essence of division of duties! It is also a good idea to have the preparers put the dupes in a lock-box when they are finished. The accounting department should collect the dupes from the boxes after each shift.

When the guest's meal is complete, the wait person retrieves the guest check from the checker and takes it to the cashier. The cashier totals the check in his or her ECR, and gives it back to the wait person to present to the guest. The guest then settles the check with the cashier. It is customary in "fine dining" for the guest to settle the check with the wait person. It is far better for division of duties, and internal control, however, if the customers pay the cashier directly.

Recapping the food and beverage sales cycle, you'll see a four-way division of duties, with four separate sets of documents, each recording the same food and beverage items:

Person	Document
Waitstaff	Guest check
Checker	Checking-Machine Tape
Preparer	Duplicates
Cashier	Cash-Register Tape

As we shall see in the section on auditing, the four sets of documents can be separately audited to verify the food and beverage sales. In fact, summing each of the four should yield the same totals. The more important issue for operational control is that we have changed a situation with poor natural division of duties into one with a four-way separation. And we have brought the preparation people into the process, making them an integral part of what is essentially a management function.

Several variations should be discussed. Many operations would prefer to save both an employee and a machine by combining the checker and cashier. The weaknesses of this combination are that one audit trail is eliminated and the customer must pay the wait person. With the modern electronic systems, however, that combination is more feasible than, say, 20 years ago. Implications of the machines will be discussed later, but for now it is sufficient to point out that electronic point-of-sale devices create better audit trails and greatly simplify the process of producing duplicates.

Another variation is to eliminate duplicates and rely on the checker to verify that all food and beverages that leave the kitchen or service bar are actually on the guest checks. In that variation, the waitpersons take orders directly on the guest checks, leave the guest checks with the checker, and orally order items from the preparers. The checker, meanwhile, enters the items in the checking machine and prints the prices on the guest check. When the waitpersons deliver the food items to the dining room, they stop at the checker station and the checker "checks" what is on the tray against the guest check and returns the guest check to the wait person. The waitpersons total the checks or, preferably, present them to a separate cashier to total and then present them to the customers. The customers pay the cashier.

While this variation seems elegant, I cannot recommend it, for several reasons. First, the whole process of comparison of record with product relies solely on the visual skills of the checker. The job would become a super-human task in a busy operation. Second, the preparers simply fill oral orders. They are not part of the audit trail and do not contribute to division of duties. Finally, there are fewer documented parts of the audit trail—only the guest checks and the checking or cash-register tapes.

The procedures without dupes came into favor in the '60s when costs of labor and cash registers skyrocketed. Today's point-of-sale devices have negated the cost issue and permit a return to a full duplicate-checking system and even beyond.

Document Control

The poor division of duties I mentioned earlier, particularly the notion of the customers' settling bills with the wait staff, makes precise control of the revenue documents—the guest checks—even more imperative. Even in commercial hotels, where most guests charge their food and beverages to their rooms, a moderate amount of the restaurant's business will still be transacted in cash. Good control of the documents will make it difficult for employees to embezzle cash payments—whether directly or by substitution with charge business. More important, the auditing process relies heavily on an intact audit trail and the integrity of the numerical sequence of the revenue documents.

The guest check is the bill or tab that the customer receives at the end of his or her meal or drink. It is the document that the customer settles or pays, and it is the primary revenue document in food and beverage income (see Exhibit 7.1). Guest checks should be serially numbered accounting documents, and should be ordered, stored,

Exhibit 7.1

Guest Checks

Statler

BANFI'S

NO. 0613		NO. 0509

TOTAL

GUEST SIGNATURE:

COMPANY NAME:

School of Hotel Administration
Cornell University
Ithaca, New York, 14853-7001

As a part of Cornell University and its educational mission, we do not encourage tipping and cannot charge gratuity to your credit card.

NO. **0509** DATE:

AMOUNT: GUESTS:

Banfi's at The Statler Hotel, Cornell University
Ithaca, New York, 13853-2401

Exhibit 7.2

Cashier's Report

Cashier's Record of Checks Distributed to Waiters
Opening and Closing No. of Checks and Waiter's Signature

_____ Cashier   _____ 19____

Waiter No.	Check No.	No. Served	Waiter's Signature	Waiter No.	Check No.	No. Served	Waiter's Signature

WILLIAM ALLEN & CO., N.Y. STOCK FORM 7035

Courtesy: William Allen & Co. Form 7035

issued, inventoried, and audited with the same care and control afforded all such documents. The numerical control used for guest checks, in fact, goes beyond that used for other revenue documents in that there is a "dual level" of control.

The accounting department issues a block of guest checks each day (or meal shift) to each of the various outlets, by serial number. Time and experience will determine the appropriate size of the individual blocks, but they should be large enough so the outlet does not run out of checks during a shift. The outlet cashiers will then issue checks to the individual waitpersons, again by serial number. At the end of each shift, the waitpersons turn in their checks to the cashier, who accounts for each one by serial number. Cashier "shift-report sheets" are useful for this control. They can be purchased as stock items, or they can be custom designed and printed. Simple photocopy versions also work well. Exhibit 7.2 depicts an example of such a document.

Also at the the end of each shift, the outlet cashiers turn in all of the guest checks, used (paid) and unused, to the head cashier along with the cash turn-in. For guest checks that may have been sent to the front office for posting, a receipt portion should be retained and included in the turn-in so that the serial numbers can be accounted for. The accounting department, usually the income controller, or in large operations, a food and beverage controller, audits the checks daily for serial-number integrity. Unused checks should be "re-issued" to the next shift along with whatever number of new checks are necessary. Thus, two levels of numerical control exist: the accounting department to outlet level, and the outlet cashier to wait staff level.

Some of the new electronic POS devices change the role of serially numbered guest checks. Some of the systems use an unnumbered check and, instead, issue a unique serial number for each transaction and print it on the check. Many of the systems eliminate guest checks altogether by using a cut or strip of paper tape from the printer. That approach saves cost in both checks and labor, but suffers in both guest appeal and internal control. Even in the case where unique serial or account numbers are issued by the system, I prefer that the process of using prenumbered checks be retained. Both the document control and the critical division of duties will be enhanced by maintaining traditional guest-check control.

Another important document subject to numerical control is the duplicate check or dupe, used to take orders and as a receipt given to the preparers. Exhibit 7.3 depicts a typical dupe. It is also preferable

EXHIBIT 7.3

Duplicate Check (Captain's Order)

CAPTAIN'S ORDER

WAITER	COVERS	CHECK NO.	ROOM	CAPT.

FORM 574-8L

Courtesy: William Allen & Co. Form 9318

EXHIBIT 7.4

Point of Sale Receipts

```
     ‡‡BANFI'S‡‡
EXPEDITOR PRINTER


                    5 DOUG
--------------------------------
TBL 54     COV    3 04:12 PM
--------------------------------

3 SOUP OF THE D

1 TOSSED GREENS
  BLEU CHEESE

1 TOSSED GREENS
  SIDE DRESSING
  RANCH

1 CAESAR W/CHIC

1 FETTUCCINI

1 FILET MIGNON
  MEDIUM RARE
  BAKED POTATO

1 BROOK TROUT
  GRILLED
  RICE

2 LUNCH DESSERT

1 CHEESE COURSE

--------------------------------
10-FEB-91     GRP 1   CHK 8582
```

```
     ‡‡ROOM SERVICE‡‡
ROOM SERVICE FOOD PRINTER

              114 ROOM SERVICE‡114
--------------------------------
TBL 802    COV    2 03:22 PM
--------------------------------

1 ITHACAN
  APPLE JUICE
  COFFEE

1 ONE EGG
  SCRAMBLED

1 TOAST
  WHEAT
  DRY

1 CROISSANT

1 GRANOLA W/MIL

2 MELON

--------------------------------
10-FEB-91     GRP 1   CHK 8575
```

INTERNAL CONTROL

7

that dupes be serially numbered, controlled, and audited. A wait person who might have access to dupes not numbered or not controlled could conceivably give such a dupe to a preparer and obtain an entree or bottle of wine without a corresponding entry on a guest check. The product could then be consumed or sold fraudulently. That type of fraud is especially prevalent with "add-on" items such as wine, after-dinner drinks, and desserts. Of course, document control alone will not totally prevent such frauds. The entire checking process must be adhered to in addition to document control.

In the case of duplicates, the advent of the new electronic systems also changes the game plan somewhat. Most of the electronic POS systems automatically issue paper receipts that replace traditional dupes. Exhibit 7.4 depicts some of these receipts. They work quite well and eliminate the need for numerical control of dupes. Their role and the nature of how they control product and revenue will be discussed more fully below.

Division of Duties

The four key separations of duties provided by the implementation of the full duplicate-checking system described above greatly enhances internal control in the food and beverage area. The wait staff, the checker, the cashier, and all of the preparation people all have separate duties. Inclusion of all of the preparers into the revenue audit-trail cycle, whether by the old fashioned dupes or the new electronic receipts, adds an immeasurable amount of control.

Additional division of duties is provided by the accounting department, in its document-control and auditing functions, and the head cashier, by interaction with the shift cashiers and control over pick-up and turn-in.

Finally, management has a critical role in ensuring the division of duties in the food and beverage area. Each outlet should have a manager—whether as a sole manager or one with other duties who is assigned to that room for that shift. The room manager is responsible for preparing a "restaurant report" for each shift. The restaurant reports are managerial in nature and thus contain whatever management feels is useful to analyze the operation and make decisions about its conduct. From a control perspective, the daily reports from each outlet should contain a summary of the various revenues by type

Case 7.1

Beat the Checks

The checking system in the restaurant of a full-service hotel was considered impossible to beat, because it was a duplicate-check system. Moreover, the system was used in its most complete form, with two duplicates being required for each order. One dupe was left with the checker, and the other dupe went to the order clerk in the kitchen. Not only that, but the hotel's controller was honest and efficient. He carefully compared all checks and corresponding duplicates, he kept a detailed record for all checks he issued to the wait persons, and he was able to account for each check by its serial number. In short, the hotel's system seemed to offer no opportunity for fraud.

Yet, the food-cost accounting report indicated that something was wrong. The hotel's management investigated every possibility for leakage. As part of the general investigation, the checker was watched, but at all times a check and corresponding duplicate were presented when the wait person took a tray out of the kitchen, and each item was correctly checked. The fact was verified that the order clerk in the kitchen demanded and received a duplicate for every order.

Finally, the food-cost accountant suggested that the head waiter keep an independent record of the actual number of guests served at each meal. A comparison was made of this count with that shown by the restaurant checks. Each day, the controller showed from four to ten fewer guests than that shown on the head waiter's check count.

The accountant then checked the series of checks and duplicates in stock. He found that an entire numerical series of checks and duplicates was missing from the middle of one of the stacks of checks. This particular number series was reserved for extra wait persons. After a severe grilling, the checker confessed that he had a key to the cabinet where the checks and duplicates were stored. He admitted that at different times he removed checks and dupes, and he named the order clerk and one of the waiters as his accomplices.

The *modus operandi* was as follows: Knowing which of his steady customers would pay cash, the waiter would have ready in his pocket a stolen check and dupe that the checker gave him. He would make out the order on the stolen check and, as usual, give the dupe to the checker, who would proceed to check the items as usual. Before leaving for the day, the checker and order clerk would remove and destroy the illegitimate dupes. Hoping to avoid detection, the three conspirators were always careful not to steal more than $40 or $50 per day, which they divided equally after hours. Since the restaurant's sales amounted to about $2,000 per day, such amounts would normally not be noticed, they hoped.

Discussion

The hotel management in this case used a full duplicate-checking system, but did not fully understand many important principles of internal control. Thus, some large loopholes allowed this embezzlement to occur.

First, restaurant checks, like all accounting documents, need to be accounted for by serial number. Under the control of the accounting department, they are ordered, stored, issued, and audited by serial number. As discussed in this chapter, there should be a daily reconciliation of the serial numbers of all checks issued to each outlet, and to each wait person. The inventory of unused checks should be audited by serial number monthly. Such a monthly count, in the present case, would have prevented this fraud.

Second, because collusion is common in food and beverage operations, extra precautions should be taken. For example, head counts were eventually used to detect the fraud, but they should be made on an on-going basis so that they could become preventive rather than detective. Chef counts of entrée items and surprise counts should also be used.

Finally, the dupes should be deposited in lock boxes after they are collected by the food and beverage preparers. The accounting department should collect the dupes and audit them against the checks and the POS readings.

(obtained from register readings or their equivalent), the total of charges sent to the front office for posting, the number of and names of the shift wait staff, cashiers, and checkers, and a "head count" for the shift. This head count of customers should be taken by the management person, as it must be independent of the wait staff or cashiers and checkers.

Independent Revenue Sources

For some inexplicable reason, food and beverage operations suffer far more collusion than most other hospitality areas. For that reason, the notion of independent sources of revenue estimation are even more important than they were in the rooms area.

An independent source of revenue, you recall, is an item used to estimate the revenue or sales that is independent of the normal accounting cycles and audit trails for that revenue. Use of such tools is beneficial for internal-control purposes, but once again they require some caution, because they will usually be far less accurate than the regular "on-line" accounting information. Generally, the farther removed a source is from the regular on-line accounting, the less accurate it will be. But it is that very independence that makes it useful for internal-control purposes.

As in the case of rooms revenue, the correct way to use independent sources is to make estimates of revenue, compare the estimates to the sales recorded by the regular accounting sources, and track the differences. Since the independent sources are estimates, it is assumed that they are less accurate, and differences are to be expected. It is in the long-term tracking and interpretation of those differences that internal-control problems are spotted. The differences that occur should present patterns that become predictable. When a change in the pattern is spotted, we should suspect a possible internal-control problem and investigate further. The rule, by the way, is always to investigate further and not to take drastic action from a single flag like an out-of-line statistic.

The following is a list of independent sources of revenue information for food and beverage operations. The sources are presented in order of increasing independence:

- Restaurant reports,
- Head counts,
- Chef counts, and
- F&B cost-accounting statistics.

Restaurant reports are not particularly independent, since the revenue data on them usually comes from register and POS readings. They are useful, however, for top management's analysis, and for the chief accounting officer to check on the accounting—to see whether the income being read and recorded is the same as the room manager saw it. It is not simply a check against fraud, but rather part of the checks and balances that ensure the accuracy and reliability of accounting data. Restaurant reports are also a good source for head counts, although it is sometimes beneficial to have them turned in separately.

Head counts are the most important of the independent sources of food and beverage revenue. To ensure that they are independent, the counts must be taken by someone outside of the group discussed in the division of duties section—in other words, not a wait person, checker, cashier, or food preparer. An ideal person to make the count is the room manager or a maître d', since the count must be taken over the entire shift. Head counts, essentially similar to cover counts, are counts of the number of customers that patronize the room during the particular shift.

The counts are used by the accounting department in its audit function to make estimates for comparative purposes. The head count can be compared to the cover counts or the number-of-guest counts that are produced by the POS device or are written on guest checks by the wait staff. The head count can simply be multiplied by the average check for the room to estimate sales volume. That estimate can then be compared with the actual sales recorded through the regular accounting cycle.

This last estimate will prove to be the most useful for internal-control purposes. Readers are given three cautions, however. First, the head count must be truly independent. The management employee performing the count should keep it confidential, particularly from wait staff, cashiers, and checkers. Second, the estimate cannot be expected to be precise. Instead, it is the long-term trends and especially changes in those trends that are important. For example, if the estimated lunch revenue in the coffee shop is usually within plus or minus 5 percent of the recorded amount, a sudden drop to minus 15 percent might well indicate a problem. Finally, in case of a variance, investigate further rather than taking immediate or drastic action.

Chef counts or *consumption counts* tally the various entrée and popular appetizer items that are prepared each meal, less what is left over. These counts should be turned in independently to the accounting office, where they can be compared with sales information from the POS or they can be used to estimate revenue by extending them out by their menu prices. Of course, a lot is missing (e.g., salad, dessert, beverages) and the chef counts include spoiled or returned items, so the estimates will be quite crude. Again, as with the other sources, long-term comparisons over time will be the most valuable use of these counts.

F&B cost-accounting statistics are prepared by the accounting department for members of management to use in analyzing the operations. They are the most independent, since they are prepared historically (usually monthly or quarterly) from purchases and other cost data rather than from revenue data. Unexplained changes in food or beverage cost may be symptomatic of internal-control problems.

Auditing: The Accounting Department's Role

Auditing food and beverage income involves tasks that need to be done daily and those that can be done periodically, usually monthly.

Daily Audit. All guest checks must be audited daily. As previously discussed, the daily turn-in includes all guest checks, used and new.

EXHIBIT 7.5

Number Sheet

NUMBER CHECKING SHEET   WHOLE

1	51	101	151	201	251	301	351	401	451	501	551	601	651	701	751	801	851	901	951
2	52	102	152	202	252	302	352	402	452	502	552	602	652	702	752	802	852	902	952
3	53	103	153	203	253	303	353	403	453	503	553	603	653	703	753	803	853	903	953
4	54	104	154	204	254	304	354	404	454	504	554	604	654	704	754	804	854	904	954
5	55	105	155	205	255	305	355	405	455	505	555	605	655	705	755	805	855	905	955
6	56	106	156	206	256	306	356	406	456	506	556	606	656	706	756	806	856	906	956
7	57	107	157	207	257	307	357	407	457	507	557	607	657	707	757	807	857	907	957
8	58	108	158	208	258	308	358	408	458	508	558	608	658	708	758	808	858	908	958
9	59	109	159	209	259	309	359	409	459	509	559	609	659	709	759	809	859	909	959
10	60	110	160	210	260	310	360	410	460	510	560	610	660	710	760	810	860	910	960
11	61	111	161	211	261	311	361	411	461	511	561	611	661	711	761	811	861	911	961
12	62	112	162	212	262	312	362	412	462	512	562	612	662	712	762	812	862	912	962
13	63	113	163	213	263	313	363	413	463	513	563	613	663	713	763	813	863	913	963
14	64	114	164	214	264	314	364	414	464	514	564	614	664	714	764	814	864	914	964
15	65	115	165	215	265	315	365	415	465	515	565	615	665	715	765	815	865	915	965
16	66	116	166	216	266	316	366	416	466	516	566	616	666	716	766	816	866	916	966
17	67	117	167	217	267	317	367	417	467	517	567	617	667	717	767	817	867	917	967
18	68	118	168	218	268	318	368	418	468	518	568	618	668	718	768	818	868	918	968
19	69	119	169	219	269	319	369	419	469	519	569	619	669	719	769	819	869	919	969
20	70	120	170	220	270	320	370	420	470	520	570	620	670	720	770	820	870	920	970
21	71	121	171	221	271	321	371	421	471	521	571	621	671	721	771	821	871	921	971
22	72	122	172	222	272	322	372	422	472	522	572	622	672	722	772	822	872	922	972
23	73	123	173	223	273	323	373	423	473	523	573	623	673	723	773	823	873	923	973
24	74	124	174	224	274	324	374	424	474	524	574	624	674	724	774	824	874	924	974
25	75	125	175	225	275	325	375	425	475	525	575	625	675	725	775	825	875	925	975
26	76	126	176	226	276	326	376	426	476	526	576	626	676	726	776	826	876	926	976
27	77	127	177	227	277	327	377	427	477	527	577	627	677	727	777	827	877	927	977
28	78	128	178	228	278	328	378	428	478	528	578	628	678	728	778	828	878	928	978
29	79	129	179	229	279	329	379	429	479	529	579	629	679	729	779	829	879	929	979
30	80	130	180	230	280	330	380	430	480	530	580	630	680	730	780	830	880	930	980
31	81	131	181	231	281	331	381	431	481	531	581	631	681	731	781	831	881	931	981
32	82	132	182	232	282	332	382	432	482	532	582	632	682	732	782	832	882	932	982
33	83	133	183	233	283	333	383	433	483	533	583	633	683	733	783	833	883	933	983
34	84	134	184	234	284	334	384	434	484	534	584	634	684	734	784	834	884	934	984
35	85	135	185	235	285	335	385	435	485	535	585	635	685	735	785	835	885	935	985
36	86	136	186	236	286	336	386	436	486	536	586	636	686	736	786	836	886	936	986
37	87	137	187	237	287	337	387	437	487	537	587	637	687	737	787	837	887	937	987
38	88	138	188	238	288	338	388	438	488	538	588	638	688	738	788	838	888	938	988

VOI

Courtesy: William Allen & Co. Form 6146

They must be audited for numerical sequence to determine whether any are missing. The numerical control of these revenue documents sounds like a cumbersome job, but it really is not. Clerks can move through a numerical sequence audit very quickly with simple aids such as a numbering sheet (see Exhibit 7.5), file the used checks numerically, and replenish the outlet issue with new checks. In most hotels, an income auditor can do the revenue document audit at a rate of approximately one outlet per hour.

The accounting department must read registers or POS devices for each shift daily and record them indelibly, just as I described in Chapter 2. The newer, fully automated POS devices make this process easier. In some cases, there is an established interface with the general accounting system, and the readings come through automatically. Those readings must be audited for accuracy and reliability, however. In cases where that automatic link proves very reliable over time (few or no errors), this audit can be made periodically instead of daily.

The accounting department picks up the dupes daily, preferably for each meal shift. You'll recall that whoever is responsible for preparing the dupes should place them in lock-boxes whether they are manual documents or machine-prepared tapes.

Matching-Up the Revenue Sources. An auditor matches up the day's on-line revenue sources and notes any discrepancies. Where separate checking and cashiering machines are used, those two totals should match. If POS systems are used, the total settlement should match the sales-mix totals. In either case, the revenue readings must be matched against turn-in information from the head cashier. Thus, the total of cash, checks, credit cards, room charges—the total settlement—is matched daily with the revenue recorded. Any discrepancies must be quickly and vigorously investigated (especially room charges). In some hotels, an income auditor verifies the total settlement against revenue each day, and in some the night auditor does this job.

Periodic Auditing. The appropriate interval for most of the periodic auditing is monthly. Some items, for example comparing the dupes with the checks or the tapes, can be done less frequently. The accounting department must be careful to keep confidential the timing and frequency of such auditing. The guest checks also should occasionally be audited in detail—checking for errors in prices and math and auditing them against the summary documents. Finally, all of the revenue documents must be audited monthly for numerical sequence.

The Effects of Automation

Over the last decade, the effects of automation on the control of income in food and beverage operations has been substantial. The new ECRs and POS devices are near revolutionary in that they have greatly increased capability and speed, while actually bringing down costs. The electronic equipment, for the most part, is far less expensive to install than the electromechanical cash registers of earlier eras.

As I remarked earlier in the chapter, the new POS devices make it easy and inexpensive to return to the full duplicate-checking systems long since abandoned by many hotels and restaurants. Not only is the equipment affordable, but the peripheral needs (i.e., forms, pads, captain's books) have been greatly reduced. More important, because the processing is electronic, much more data can be stored and many more functions can be performed.

For example, the wait person or checker need only open a check for a customer and enter the orders in the POS device. The machine will permanently record the order and the customer's account number, enter the pre-set price, print a guest check, and produce a machine-printed paper receipt for use as the dupe to be given to the preparers. When the time for paying the bill comes, the machine will print a completed check and record the settlement. When the POS machine records the order and prints a receipt, it creates a permanent audit trail. There is no uncertainty to the fact that when an order is on the receipt, it is charged to an account!

The new printed dupes are far easier to read than old-fashioned hand-written ones. Furthermore, since electronic machines have so much more storage and computing capability, the dupes can contain a great deal more information. For example, condiments, cooking preferences, time the order is needed, table number (to keep orders together), and special requests can all be printed on the dupe, making the cooks' and other preparers' jobs much easier. All through the book, I have espoused the theory that if the paperwork is designed to make operational jobs easier, your employees will be willing to use the forms without resenting them. In the food and beverage area in particular, chefs and other preparers resent paperwork as an intrusion on their domain and duties. With the advent of checking receipts that truly help cooks prepare the food, they have become much more willing partners in the internal-control process.

Contemporary POS equipment is also easy to expand, so functions can be divided in a much more efficient manner. Remote printers can be placed at several stations around the kitchen and service bars so that, as the wait person or checker enters the order, the receipt is immediately printed right at the station where the order will be prepared. The additional information available on the receipt can inform the preparer as to when to make (fire) the order. Some manufacturers and hotels have experimented with remote CRT screens instead of printers to transmit order information. From both functional and control perspectives, however, paper printers are better.

Also available are multiple terminals that allow the wait staff to enter orders from various locations around the dining room. That procedure, usually referred to as "pre-checking," accomplishes the same functions as "duplicate checking" through a checker, but does so faster and more efficiently. The retention of a separate checker, however, creates better division of duties and hence better control.

Base your decision regarding which to use on your position on the control versus policy trade-offs, and on cost-benefit analysis.

Automation also has some effects on accounting, auditing, and management. Revenue-document control may be easier with automated equipment. Some systems eliminate the need for pre-numbered checks, and some eliminate checks altogether. But again, I caution you that the paper-tape checks do not have as much guest appeal as traditional hard printed checks. Better internal control is usually achieved by using pre-numbered documents, although some systems have sufficiently robust and easy-to-check audit trails that they are acceptable. Each system must be reviewed and judged on its merits, but the conceptual points of internal control discussed in this book will help the readers make informed decisions.

Another advantage of automated food and beverage systems lies in their ability to produce managerial data. Because processing data electronically is faster, easier, and cheaper, the POS systems can store and analyze a great deal of information. Sales mixes, menu prices, average checks, and even inventory control are routine functions for most of these systems. The increased availability of data, especially information on sales, is very useful to management. One problem that often arises in this environment is the production of too much information and too many reports—to the point where operational managers stop looking at all of them!

A final advantage of many automated food and beverage systems is their ability to connect with such other systems as the front-office system or the hotel's general accounting system. An interface with the front-office system allows food and beverage charges to be posted directly from the F&B outlet to the guest's folio. With this connection, the outlet's cashiers can also check on the authenticity and credit-worthiness of the guest. With an interface to the general accounting system, the process of revenue recording becomes easier and less subject to human error.

Now, a cautionary note: Electronic data processing must be carefully audited even when it has automatic interface. The procedures that ensure that revenue sources, settlements, and guest charges all balance must be maintained in the electronic environment. We may lose fewer charges because the speedy machines post them to the guest's account before he or she checks out, but the electronic era is far from being error or trouble free.

Additional Issues of Importance

Officer's Checks. Officer's checks are used when executives of the hotel make charges in any of the hotel's outlets. Hotel executives usually have the privilege of charging their meals, or making charges for other people for a variety of reasons (public relations, sales, settling a guest's dispute). The right to charge and the level of authority each officer is allowed are policy issues to be decided by top management. There are some important internal-control issues associated with officer's checks, however.

The chief fraud involved with the administration of officer's checks is where wait staff and others substitute the officer's check for a cash customer's order or otherwise use the officer's charges as a way to receive goods fraudulently. The fraud then gets buried in the pile of the officer's charges. The best defense is to set up a system and policy that forces officers to check their charges carefully each month.

Some hotels prefer to use special checks for officers—usually printed in a different color than the regular guest checks. Special forms that "flag" the officer's checks may make it more difficult to make a substitution, but they do not prevent it. Particularly if an officer does not scrutinize his or her checks carefully or does not personally sign them, it is still possible for a wait person to pull the following switch: (1) put an expensive entrée on the officer's check, (2) serve it to a cash-paying customer, (3) put the officer's less-expensive entrée on the guest's check, (4) switch them back after settlement, and (5) pocket the difference. What essentially happened is that the officer's account got charged for the expensive item and the guest got charged the cheaper item, even though he or she paid in cash for the more expensive item!

The best overall approach is to set up an account receivable for each officer. If there are several different types of charges that each officer may make, sub-accounts will be needed for each type. Officers should be compelled to sign for their charges in the same way that guests do, and they should be asked to produce identification. Officers should scrutinize their charges before they sign them and they should retain a receipt copy or stub for their files. As with a business meal, officers should write on the receipt the names of the people they entertained, the purpose of the meal, and so on. Each month, each officer should be sent a regular accounts-receivable statement with a breakdown of each category of charges. The officers should be required to check that the statements are correct, sign them, and return them to the accounting department. The receipts each officer has kept will be helpful to them in checking the statement. The accounting department should investigate any discrepancies and prepare a summary of total officer charges by category and by officer for top management to review.

Control of Bar Revenue

Your hotel's two kinds of bars present different control issues. The service bar, limited to the waitstaff's orders, presents no special problems. That type of beverage service should be handled in the exact same manner as dining room or restaurant service. Pre-checking or "dupes" should be used, and there should be a separate cashier.

In your customers' sit-down bar, however, division of duties is nearly nonexistent. The bartender has complete control of the entire transaction: taking the order, preparing the order, ringing up the order, delivering the order, and settling the tab. Some operations attempt to solve the problem by taking a daily inventory of all alcoholic products in the bar (right down to the tenth of a bottle!) and calculating the daily consumption. The consumption is then used to estimate sales, which are compared to the actual sales. These so called "sales-value" systems are expensive to operate because taking daily inventory requires a lot of labor, and they can encourage frauds through such bad practices as watering the drinks or having the bartenders bring in and sell their own liquor. It is also difficult to estimate fractions of bottles accurately.

I prefer that bar service be treated as much like any other food and beverage service as is practical. If there is enough bar business or if a wait staff is being used, a separate cashier should be brought in to add some division of duties to the transaction. Checks should be issued to all customers with settlement handled the same way it is in the restaurants. Management should also do its part by being "visible" and walking into the bar frequently.

For the retail sales or full-bottle segments of bar operations (e.g., wine and beer), a perpetual-inventory system is highly recommended (see Appendix 4.2). In fact, perpetual inventories should be used for all stored beverages. Additionally, bottle-identification programs, such as stamping the hotel's name or a serial number on each bottle, are useful. Bottle identification makes it easier to document consumption and exchange stock on a bottle-for-bottle basis. I'll discuss this more in Chapter 8 when I deal with banquet service.

Standard Price Schedules

In the same manner as room rates, food and beverage prices have to be fixed and published in standard schedules (i.e., menus). Price changes should be made only with management's approval. When the accounting department audits revenue or audits the individual checks, it should verify that prices are in agreement with the schedules. Any deviations should be accompanied by a duly authorized allowance voucher.

Your hotel should develop a procedure for making price changes. In manual environments, a form should be used to list the old and new prices and to record a management signature. With electronic systems, access to the programming that allows prices to be changed should be limited to management or should require management's involvement. The key issues are the same as they were in the rooms area: namely, we do not want service-level employees or cashiers to have the right to make changes without proper written authorization, including a solid audit trail. The audit trail and division of duties are more important for internal control than the permission component.

Cafeterias and Buffets

The major control problem in a cafeteria involves division of duties. There is no convenient way to bring the preparers (food servers) into the transaction. Generally, the operation must rely on the visual skills of the checker or cashier—usually the sole point of revenue recording—to ensure that all items taken by the customers are recorded and paid for. POS devices with pre-set item keys help reduce errors, but the process is, at best, a poor one. The checker must visually observe the tray, record all the items, and settle the bill with the customer—making change or often having to deal with credit-card verification and voucher preparation.

I strongly recommend that these functions be separated. In other words, separate checkers should observe the trays and enter the items into the POS—producing a receipt or guest-check. The customer would then move on to a settlement cashier. If your operation tries this approach, you will find that internal control is better, errors are reduced, and the line actually moves faster. In my experience, a ratio of approximately 3 to 2 (i.e., three checkers to two cashiers) seems to work well. This approach works very well and is easy to cost-justify in large cafeterias, such as those found in colleges or industrial catering situations. In smaller cafeterias, the separation of checking and settlement may require adding labor—a decision that will have to be made on the usual cost-benefit basis.

Buffets generally entail the same control problem as cafeterias. The food is taken by the guests on the line, making division of duties or bringing the preparers into the transaction quite difficult. Unlike cafeterias, however, the customer is usually charged a single fixed price for the privilege of attending the buffet, and that fact makes control somewhat easier. Some hotels and restaurants run mixed operations—where customers can either purchase the buffet meal or order à la carte. Control becomes very difficult if some members of a table purchase the buffet and some order from the menu. In almost all operations, customers order such extras as beverages à la carte.

The most effective technique for internal control of buffets is to have a manager take an accurate head count for each meal period. At the same time, the regular checking system should be used with dupes for the buffet turned in by the wait staff to the manager or chef. Later, as part of the daily audit process, the income auditor can compare the head counts to the total covers served and the checks settled. Use the technique of tracking discrepancies over time to develop trends and investigating changes in those trends.

Some hotels use a system of having a cashier sell customers buffet tickets that are collected by the wait staff. That approach brings some division of duties, but it inconveniences the guests and fails to address the problems of mixed use or customers' purchasing such extras as beverages or dessert. A strong management presence remains the best control device for buffets.

Glossary

Accuracy versus Independence Trade-off—The principle that revenue estimates are more accurate when they are made most directly from transactions, but the independence of those estimates declines at the same time; the more independent the less accurate and vice versa.

Checking—A comparison of the recorded cash receipts and charges of food and beverage sales against a separately created record of food and beverages actually served.

Chef Counts—A count by the chef of items produced, served, and left over; usually performed for main entrée and appetizer items.

Dupes—Duplicate checks.

Duplicate-Checking System—An approach to checking in which a duplicate check or receipt is prepared for each item, and then given to the preparers as sanction to prepare and release the product; the "dupes" should be designed such that whenever an order is taken it is simultaneously written on or posted to the guest's check.

Electronic Cash Registers (ECRs)—Relatively simple computerized revenue-recording machines; essentially cash registers that operate with electronic processors rather than mechanical ones (compare to POS devices).

Guest Checks—The invoices or sales slips given to restaurant customers.

Officer's Checks—The guest checks used the hotel's managers when they charge food or beverages.

Point-of-sale (POS) Devices—Computerized revenue-recording machines, placed at various sales outlets, capable of recording a large amount of sales detail, and often capable of communicating with other systems, such as the front-office system.

Selected References

Dennis H. Ferguson and Thomas Selling, "Analyzing Food and Labor Costs," *The Cornell Hotel and Restaurant Administration Quarterly,* 24, No. 3 (November 1983), pp. 31-39.

Michael M. Coltman, *Food and Beverage Cost Control* (Englewood Cliffs, NJ: Prentice-Hall, 1977).

Paul R. Dittmer and Gerald G. Griffin, *Principles of Food, Beverage, and Labor Cost Controls for Hotels and Restaurants (4th Edition)* (New York: Van Nostrand Reinhold, 1989).

James Keiser and Elmer Kallio, *Controlling and Analyzing Costs in Food Service Operations* (New York: John Wiley & Sons, 1974).

Douglas C. Keister, *Food and Beverage Control* (Englewood Cliffs, NJ: Prentice-Hall, 1977).

Chapter 8

Banquets and Conferences

Objectives

After completing this chapter, you should understand:

1. **The unique problems encountered with banquet and other group sales.**
2. **The implications of good contract design.**
3. **The internal-control procedures for banquets and other contractual business**

To ensure effective internal control over the revenue from banquets, conferences, and other contractual business, your hotel needs to take precautions beyond the normal internal-control principles. This type of business is especially vulnerable to fraud because of its "custom" nature. Banquets and conferences[1] are usually developed specifically for the client according to his or her special needs. There may be set menu prices for banquets and set room rates for conferences, but the audit trails and recording cycles to account for that business and to settle the bills with the clients is different with contractual business than with individual customers.

With banquets, for example, the meals and drinks served are usually not checked with the same duplicates and division of duties typical of your F&B outlets. Furthermore, most of the products that are to be consumed are usually determined in advance, and the bill for a banquet is settled in total by the group that booked it. These differences require some special internal controls. Compared to the F&B portion of the bill, the rooms business for groups is easy to control. The same folio system and set of audit trails described for individual business are used, with the master bills being simple aggregations. So, I will discuss controls for food and beverage service to groups. The general principles apply, however, to rooms, conference services, or any other type of group revenue that the hotel is capable of generating.

Contracts

The design and implementation of the contracts that are used for this type of business are critical for effective internal control. A well-designed document will deal with contractual obligations (legal and financial) and can also serve numerous practical purposes, from a sales checklist to a function sheet.[2] When designing these contracts, hotels should take this multi-purpose nature into account.

Banquet contracts should be pre-numbered accounting documents. Like all other revenue documents, their distribution is controlled by the accounting department. I'm not advocating that the accounting department usurp the power or jobs of the sales and service departments, but the accounting department should control the supply, flow, and audit history of the documents. They are revenue documents, and thus must be accounted for by serial number, but they also play a much more

---

[1] I'll use the word conferences as a generic term to represent all meetings, conventions, tours, and other types of group business.

[2] A function sheet is the written communication between the persons who develop and sell group business and those who produce and serve it. In addition to function sheet, this communication goes by such names as function report, party order, event order, and tickler sheet.

important role. The entire definition of the product—everything we promise to do for the client, how and when, the prices we charge, and how the account will be settled—is determined and recorded solely by this written contract. It is imperative, then, that the contracts be designed in such a manner that it is absolutely clear to the client and to the various hotel service personnel exactly what has been agreed to by all parties. The best way to accomplish that goal is to design the written contract to contain key line items for the major goods and services that the hotel normally produces, and to also have a check-list format for all possible extras. The form should include the item, a description line, a price line, a quantity line, and a final-amount line. The quantity and final amount will not be filled in until the bill is settled, when you will know how many covers were sold, rooms filled, and so on. Exhibit 8.1 is an example of a stock banquet contract.

It is important that the sales people who are using the contracts fill in every line. If a particular item (e.g., a champagne toast) is not to be included in a particular banquet, the sales rep should write "no" on that line and enter a zero on the price line. If the champagne toast is to be included free as an enticement for booking the banquet, then a "yes" is written on its line and no charge (n/c) is entered on the price line. This procedure is absolutely critical to internal control for this type of business. Never include something by building it into the dinner or other price—even though that might be the intended effect or result to the client. Instead, show it on the contract as having been agreed to, but with a *price of zero*. This approach is similar to the comp-room procedure discussed in Chapter 6. We do not want to give clerks, or in this case banquet or sales people, the power to make price or revenue changes without management oversight. There always must be an authorization that gives permission and preserves the audit trail. By specifying everything in a banquet contract, even zero-price items, the audit trail is maintained.

Permission to change prices should be covered in your operating policy. Each hotel has to decide how much authority to allow for salespeople to "throw in" complimentary items. From the internal-control perspective, the best policy is never to allow such discounts without written management approval. Once those decisions are made, communicate them to all employees, including the accounting personnel. When auditing banquet contracts, the accounting personnel must verify that management approval has been given for price deviations. Such approval can be built into the contract itself, so you

EXHIBIT 8.1

Banquet Contract

MENU QUOTATION AND CONTRACT

NAME OF FUNCTION_____

LOCATION_____

DAY AND DATE_____TIME OF FUNCTION_____TIME OF SERVING_____

NAME OF ORGANIZATION SUBMITTED TO_____

ADDRESS_____PHONE_____

NAME OF REPRESENTATIVE SUBMITTED TO_____

ADDRESS_____PHONE_____

NO. OF GUESTS EXPECTED_____NO. OF GUESTS GUARANTEED_____AMT. OF DEPOSIT $_____

APPETIZERS	PRICE QUOTATION		
	ROOM		
	FOOD, PER COVER		
	WINES AND LIQUORS		
MENU	SOFT DRINKS		
	GRATUITIES		
	SERVICE		
BEVERAGES	TICKETS		
	TICKET COLLECTION		
	DECORATIONS		
	FLOWERS		
	COAT CHECKING		
NOTES AND REMARKS	PRINTED GUEST LIST		
	MENU CARDS		
	FAVORS		
	MUSIC		
	CIGARS-CIGARETTES		
	P. A. SYSTEM		

SEE OTHER SIDE FOR SPECIAL TABLE ARRANGEMENTS

☐ REGISTRATION DESK   _____ TABLES   ☐ MUSIC, ENTERTAINMENT
☐ TICKET COLLECTION   _____ CHAIRS   ☐ P. A. SYSTEM
☐ DECORATIONS   _____ MENU CARDS   ☐ BLACKBOARD
☐ FLOWERS   _____ GUEST LISTS   ☐ FILM PROJECTOR
☐ COAT CHECKING   _____ PROGRAMS   ☐ LECTERN
☐ FLAG   _____ TICKETS   ☐ CIGARS-CIGARETTES
☐ PLATFORM   _____   ☐

TAX

The party making arrangements must guarantee the number of people to be provided for at least 24 hours before the function. If attendance falls below this number, the full guarantee will be paid. No allowance or credit will be made for less than this guarantee. If attendance exceeds this number, the quoted price per person will be paid for each additional cover. By mutual arrangement, the guaranteed number may be increased during this period.

This contract is void if it cannot be performed because of government regulations, accidents, labor trouble, or uncontrollable circumstances. If the food or services specified, cannot be furnished for any of the reasons mentioned, other foods and services may be substituted at prices ordinarily charged for them, but not in excess of the price agreed upon.

It is also agreed that the organization and the person making the arrangements for this function will be responsible for all materials and equipment broken, stolen, or lost. Charges will be based on actual cost of materials and equipment.

DATE SUBMITTED_____   ACCEPTED FOR_____

SUBMITTED BY_____   BY_____

Am. Hotel Register Co., 226 W. Ontario St., Chicago, Ill. 60610   FORM 1255

Courtesy: American Hotel Register Co. Form 1255

won't have to use a separate document (i.e., an approval signature line can be included for items requiring management approval).

The contracts should also include a checklist of extras that is as comprehensive as possible. Before you make your contract design final, conduct a brainstorming session with all of the sales, production, and service personnel to make up the list of extras. The list should include those items generated internally (usually food and beverages, conference services) and those generated externally (e.g., flowers, music, special printing). The extras list should be printed on the contract so that it fulfills the audit-trail function, as well as facilitating sales (by suggesting possible options) and building client communication.

From the internal-control perspective, the contract forms should be at least in triplicate, but for functional reasons, your hotel may wish to add many more copies. The three control copies are for the client, the sales or banquet department, and the accounting department. The accounting copy will be used for confirmation and audit. Any copies beyond these three are function copies to be used for assembling the product.

Determining the contract's design and number of function copies requires serious thought and advance planning. If the banquet contracts are cleverly designed, they can fulfill legal, financial, and internal-control functions and also serve as function sheets to be distributed to all of the necessary hotel departments. Using a single document saves time and paperwork and reduces the chance of transcription errors, but it does pose some other problems. It may be unwise for all departments to see the prices for products and services or to see the fact that an item is served at no charge. Banquet contracts also need to contain certain credit and payment information that should be available only to the accounting department and management. Again, clever design can overcome some of these difficulties. Functional copies may, for example, have carbon only on certain sections so that the recipient sees only the data he or she needs, but does not see the prices or financial information. Or, certain items can be "blacked out" on some copies. With computer-generated documents—such as those in automated sales systems—custom forms are even easier to create.

Division of Duties

In the negotiation, administration, and service of banquet contracts, a six-way division of duties is desirable:

1. Sales,
2. Advance deposits,

3. Confirmation,

4. Service and production,

5. Billing and settlement, and

6. Audit.

Sales are accomplished by the person who meets with the client to discuss and design all arrangements. The salesperson fills in the banquet contract completely, with all details as discussed above, signs it, has the client sign it, and distributes the copies. The three main copies are distributed, one each, as follows:

- To the client,
- To the accounting department, and
- For functional use by the sales department.

If a deposit is required, it should be handled by the hotel's normal cash-receiving stations—namely, a *bona fide* cashier or through the mail. If hotel policy requires an immediate deposit for banquets or other contractual business, the person making the sales contact should escort the client to a cashier (usually in the front office). If immediate payment is not required or desirable, the client should mail the deposit to the hotel. In either case, a credit will be posted to city ledger, and a credit-balance folio will be created.

The accounting department should send the client a written confirmation within 30 days of the contract signing. This confirmation should include the amount of the deposit, the full details of the function including exact prices, and the financial details for final settlement of the bill. The notion of the accounting department's writing to the client sometimes raises some objections by the sales or banquet departments. That confirmation is not designed to take the place of the normal communications between the sales or service personnel and the client. In fact, the client may receive two confirmations, one from sales and one from accounting. The one from accounting will be very specific in nature and deal, in a legal sense, with what each party promises to perform. The one from sales should be informal. I recommend that the sales and accounting departments coordinate their confirmations to avoid duplication. Perhaps the accounting confirmation can be the initial one, since the sales department will usually have several later communications with the client. In any event, the accounting confirmation plays important internal-control roles in the recording of the revenues and in auditing them later.

EXHIBIT 8.2

Consumption Report

GUEST REPORT - CONSUMPTION BAR BY BOTTLE

	Item	Code	B.I	E.I	Usage	Price Bottle	Total
Date	Smirnoff	1 1 4					
EO #	Gordon's	1 1 7					
Guest Name	Bacardi	1 0 7					
	White Horse	1301					
Capt. Name	7 Crown	1 4 0					
	I W Harper	1 3 7					
Comments							
	Absolut	1 1 5					
Liquor Total	Tanqueray	1 1 8					
	Bacardi	1 0 7					
Wines Total	Canadian Club	1 3 8					
	J Walker Black	1 2 8					
Beer Total	Jim Beam	1 3 2					
Soda Total							
Cordial Cart	House white 1.5 L	2 3 8					
	House Red 1.5 L	2 3 9					
Service Charge	House White 750	1 7 9					
$ 50 if less $150	House Red 750	2 0 6					
	Heinekein	1 6 6					
GRAND TOTAL	Budweiser	1 6 2					
	Coors	2 5 0					
	Coors Lite	2 3 0					
	Michelob Lite	1 6 3					
	Beck's	1 6 0					
	Coke	9 2 2					
	Diet Coke	9 2 3					
	Ginger	2 4 2					
	Sprite	4 4 1					
	Tonic	2 4 3					
	Soda	2 4 0					
	La Croix	2 4 1					
	Wines						

The banquet service and production staff can play important internal-control roles. Extra division of duties in most food service is achieved by bringing preparers into the full audit-trail cycle by using duplicates to issue product. The use of dupes would be cumbersome, however, in banquets where the entire party is usually served the same items and where service needs to be continuous and fast. To achieve a suitable audit trail for banquet business, you can use consumption reports instead of dupes. Consumption reports list how much of each product was used for each function. For food and related products, consumption reports should be filled out by the banquet chefs and other preparers and sent directly to the accounting department. They will be quite similar in their requirements to the chef's counts in regular F&B outlets. It is also recommended, where feasible, that banquet covers and sales be rung up on a POS device, thus creating yet another audit trail that can be traced all the way through settlement of the bill.

Beverage consumption and service in banquets present special problems. As with food, duplicate checks are impractical. Consumption reports for wine and other beverages served are essential for internal control and, in some cases, for billing the client. When the price is based on the number of drinks or bottles of wine served, consumption reports will be a main source of billing information. In those cases, they will also have to be prepared quickly and sent to the billing office. Beverage-consumption reports should be filled out by the beverage manager or a member of his or her staff, with a separate copy sent directly to the accounting department. In operations where there is a formal or closed storeroom system, the banquet staff will have to requisition the beverages needed for each party. An audit copy of the requisitions should go to the accounting department. Exhibit 8.2 illustrates a consumption report.

Billing and settlement are also somewhat special with banquets and other contractual business. Billing is accomplished by having folios prepared in advance by the accounting department or sales office and sent to the front office. The folio is prepared from the banquet contract and reflects any advance deposit. The only items missing on the folio are the counts (e.g., number in attendance, number of bottles) and the final calculations. The banquet manager or other representative of the hotel reaches an agreement with the client's representative as to the counts, enters those counts on a guest check, has the client's representative sign the guest check, and then sends it to the front office where it will be used prepare the client's final bill. The desk clerk merely needs to take the counts from the guest check, enter them on the prepared folio, and extend the arithmetic. With automated systems the clerk will need only to post the counts, and the system will automatically calculate and print a completed folio.

Settlement will depend on how the client wishes or is required to pay. The most important internal-control issue is that no payments are made to or accepted by banquet managers, restaurant managers, or any member of the management team. For public-relations or future sales purposes, a manager may wish to accompany the client to the front office or other cashier when payment is made. However, as with all cash receipts, payment can be accepted only at a *bona fide* cashier station, or through the mail, if credit has been properly established.

If the client wishes to pay or otherwise settle at the conclusion of the event, he or she merely does so at the front office (or in the case of small parties, at a food and beverage cashier station). If the client has previously established credit as a direct-bill or city-ledger customer, then he or she may elect simply to look over and sign the folio. In that case, the account will be posted to city ledger, and the client will receive a bill through the normal accounts-receivable process.

Auditing for banquets is similar to other revenue audits in that there are functions that are performed daily and others that can be accomplished periodically. On a daily basis, the accounting department should match its original copy of the signed and confirmed contract with the final bill or folio. This comparison not only helps prevent and detect fraud and embezzlement, but guards against mistakes in billing. The banquet contract contains all the details and the prices promised for each. The daily audit should verify that each item on the contract was billed. Any discrepancies should be flagged and investigated to determine whether, say, an item was deleted by mutual consent with the client or was mistakenly left off the bill.

Similarly, the counts and consumption sheets should be checked against the final bill. The client representative's count, the chef's counts or consumption reports, and head counts taken by the room supervisors should all match and be in agreement with the final bill. The beverage-consumption reports should also match the final bill and should be in agreement with any requisitions from stores.

If these audits cannot be accomplished daily, the verifications should be made within a few days or no more than a week. If they are left to the monthly audit, it may be difficult or embarrassing for the hotel to change a client's bill.

Periodic (monthly) auditing of banquets involves verifying turn-ins, bank deposits, and accounts-receivable postings against the revenues recorded in a similar manner to the monthly audit procedure suggested for rooms income. Additionally, the auditor should analyze the food and beverage cost-accounting statistics, check the hours worked and payroll costs for the banquet department against the business served in dollars and numbers of covers. Again, these "independent" estimates are not precise, but they are useful as indicators. Long-term changes in any of these averages should be flagged for further management investigation.

Extras and Other Issues

Much fraud associated with banquets is due to imprecise definitions of the products or the prices for those products. A common fraud involves padding the client's bill. The hotel receives its revenue, but the client gets ripped off! Certainly, the hotel will pay for such fraud in the long run, and sometimes both the hotel and the client are defrauded.

Padding-type frauds are possible if clients are not fully knowledgeable about the precise details of their contract. For example, the hotel may have a policy of adding a service charge to take care of gratuities. But a staff member can accost the client by saying "the service charge is for the hotel and its labor cost; if you want really good service, we should add another two percent." Many clients will buy this line! If the staff member also collects the bill, particularly if that portion is in cash (or a negotiable check), he or she can pocket the add-on. Not only is the client a victim of embezzlement, but the wait staff never sees a penny of it. Preventing this type of fraud involves writing a precise contract with all details and extras placed on the contract, discussed thoroughly with the client and confirmed in writing. Also, if the other relevant internal-control principles are in place (i.e., payment is accepted only by a cashier or through the mail; checks made out to the hotel are never cashed) padding is nearly impossible.

Examples of internally generated extras are food and beverages—such as champagne toasts, cordial carts, tips, meeting rooms, and so forth. Externally generated extras are supplied by outside vendors. Flowers are a common example, and others include music, special printing, and entertainers. Internally generated extras are added to the contract when the hotel provides the service. Tips are a prime

Case 8.1

The Last Banquet, or: Greed Will Out

The head of a hotel's restaurant department noticed that little attention was paid to the banquet contracts, so he worked out a plan that was personally profitable. Unfortunately, the plan was so successful, that the manager couldn't resist temptation even when he should have.

Here's how the scheme was put together: The manager would make arrangements for a banquet in the usual way, but he would leave the price open on the copy of the contract that he sent to the general manager. The GM paid it little attention and sent it on to the auditing department, where it likewise was given no attention. The restaurant manager would keep his own record, however, made out something like this: Party X—May 1—100 covers at $16.00 each, $1,600.

In his negotiations with the association, he would explain that the $16-per-cover charge was for food only, and he would handle any tips for the waiters. The association representatives would generally add a tip of $100 or $150, including an amount for the head waiter, who was usually the self-same restaurant manager. Then, he would turn to the price of flowers, which he would buy and arrange himself, thus giving his client the benefit of his experience. Next, he would turn the kind of service desired: Did the client wish fast service with plenty of good wait staff? Most association representatives would answer affirmatively, and would agree to an additional charge of $150 for speedy service. The final bill to the association, then would be: Food, $1,600; Service, $150; Tips, $150; and Flowers, $100. Total bill: $2,000.

When it came time to serve the banquet, the restaurant manager would serve a meal worth $14.50. He would turn in a check for 100 covers, which the checker would verify as the correct number served. He would show on the house accounting records a price of $14.50 per cover, or $1,450 total, an amount that would satisfy the chef, who knew he had served a $14.50 meal. Meantime, the association representatives had in mind that the entire package was $20 per person, or $2,000, an amount that the association would usually pay by check on the spot. The manager would give a receipt for $2,000, payment in full for 100 meals, including flowers, tips and food.

The restaurant manager would take the check to the front office to be cashed. No matter that the bill was paid by cash or check, it was a simple matter for the restaurant manager to turn in $1,450 to the restaurant cashier and keep the remainder. He would pay the usual ten wait persons $25 each and would pay the florist about $60 for the flowers. Those expenses of $310 would leave him $240 in clear profit, but he would add $100 to that amount by applying in a few days to the general cashier for the waiters' extra money for the party. His list of waiters would agree with the original listing turned in to the cashier for special functions, so the $100 would be paid with no questions, and the records closed. The restaurant manager would be a total of $340 richer from the function.

Even the best scheme can fall afoul of an accident. The restaurant manager was out of town for a few days when the representative of an association told the general manager that his group thought they should get a better rate for their next banquet. The hotel manager made the arrangements on the spot, quoting a rate of $15.50 per cover or $1,550, inclusive of service, food, and flowers. Upon his return, the restaurant manager found out about the arrangement, and undoubtedly should have simply let it stand. But his greed was too great, and he tried to make the association representative pay for the usual extras. When the representatives took the matter up with the hotel manager, the scheme was finally brought to light and the goose that laid the golden eggs was finally laid to rest.

Discussion

This seemingly complicated case of fraud has a simple solution: properly designed and executed banquet contracts. In this case, the hotel received its due, but the customers were subject to fraud. Of course, the hotel would pay for that in the long-run by way of lost goodwill.

A well-designed contract, showing all possible banquet items and offering a simple way to check them off or charge for them, would set up an environment where the customer would know precisely what goods and services he or she will receive and how much they will cost. Having numerical control on the contracts allows for an audit trail and ensures that the accounting department is informed of every contract and all details.

Having the accounting department send a written confirmation to the customer—including all promised details and costs—will add division of duties and prevent the type of guest fraud we saw in this case. The confirmation letter should state that any changes or additions will also be confirmed in writing.

Also, management employees should never be allowed to accept payment. Payment is received only at *bona fide* cashier stations, or, with proper credit, through the mail. The check-cashing and exchange procedures explained in Chapter 1 were also violated in this case.

---

example, and as stressed before, they should always be put on the payroll. There may be strong employee objections to that policy (particularly with banquet wait staff), but from the internal-control, audit-trail, and legal perspectives, it is the only way to conduct business.

With externally generated extras, both quality control and internal control are important issues. The hotel should develop specifications for each product type, evaluate vendors, and pick designated suppliers with negotiated and fixed prices. Those vendors should supply the products as needed, leave invoices that can be posted to the clients' folios, and mail monthly statements detailing each client delivery. The hotel should pay the vendors monthly, through the regular documented and controlled accounts-payable process (see Chapter 4). In that way there are clear and traceable audit trails for all extras. The hotel collects revenue for them and pays for them through normal channels. Many of the extras, in fact, can become legitimate profit sources for the hotel since they are sold to the client at a fair retail price, and the hotel should be able to buy them at a wholesale price.

A final point related to extras and of some importance to both internal control and general client relations is who can authorize adding extras to the contract, particularly during the function. Your internal controls should never be so rigid as to prevent additional business. It is important, however, to have duly authorized client's representatives to approve the final bill and to approve extras during the event. In the latter case, normal revenue procedures should be used, with the client's representative signing the guest checks as evidence that he or she approved the purchase.

Designating the approved clients' representatives and introducing them to the key hotel service and production staff is good business as well as good internal control. The banquet staff should never accept orders or changes from someone in the function who is not a duly designated client representative.

Effects of Automation

The banquet and other contractual-business segments of hotel operations are beginning to use automated systems. As the rooms and food and beverage areas of hotels become fully automated, the banquet and conference segments must conform. Furthermore, automated selling and administration software systems are being developed, many of which can achieve interface with property management and accounting systems.

All of the principles discussed above are easily adaptable to automated systems. In fact, many are greatly facilitated by automation. The internal-control principles for automated systems are discussed in detail in the next chapter.

Glossary

Client's Representative—An official of a group holding a banquet or other function at the hotel who has the legal permission of the group to authorize the final bill, including any additional charges or services.

Conferences—Meetings, symposia, or any group function held at a hotel that will require special services.

Confirmation—Official notice, preferably in writing, from the hotel to a guest or group spelling out, in detail, future services to be provided, the prices, and the methods of settlement; any deposit required or paid should also be included.

Consumption Reports—Documents filled out by the food and beverage preparers listing items made and served at banquets and other large parties; used to prepare and audit invoices.

Externally Generated Extras—Services from outside the hotel requested and consumed by guests and added to their folios; examples are flowers, theater tickets, and car rentals.

Function Sheets—Documents prepared by the sales or banquet departments that list all of the details for each function or party to be performed by the hotel or restaurant.

Internally Generated Extras—Services requested and consumed by guests, performed by the hotel, and added to the folios; examples are room service, telephone calls, parking, and gratuities.

Chapter 9

Internal Control with Electronic Data Processing

Objectives

After completing this chapter, you should understand:

1. **Environmental changes when data and accounting are processed electronically.**

2. **The special problems and risks of loss encountered in an electronic environment.**

3. **The general and administrative controls that management can institute to reduce the risks of loss.**

4. **The procedures needed to back-up and protect files and data.**

A New Environment

Data processing is not a new concept or function in hotels. From the moment the first guest signed the first registry pad, data were being processed. All accounting is data processing. What is new today is the manner in which data are processed. Over the years data processing has evolved from pen and ink to mechanical to electromechanical and, finally, electronic—with the modern computer.

There are several reasons why hotels have difficulty adjusting to electronic data processing (EDP) and why EDP adds to internal-control vulnerability. First, the entire style, look, and feel of the data and their source documents are different in an EDP environment than a manual one. Many entries and most pieces of stored data are invisible with EDP. They are stored on an electronic or magnetic medium and cannot be readily seen by eye or retrieved without a machine. Second, even when data or programs are translated into a readable form, they are not always understandable.

Third, the storage media—usually magnetic disks or tapes—are far more fragile than the old fashioned pen-and-ink or machine-printed files. A fire or flood might destroy the old fashioned media as easily as the new electronic ones. But the new ones are sensitive to even moderate temperature deviations, dust, smoke, dampness, and stray magnetism. Fourth, the storage efficiency of the new media means that an enormous amount of data can be stored in a relatively small space. That phenomenon, called concentration, vastly increases the risk of losses, whether fraudulent or accidental. All of the hotel's guest-accounts receivable, for example, will fit on a single disk. If that disk is destroyed or otherwise rendered unreadable, the hotel may instantaneously lose its entire set of guest accounts! Finally, many managers don't understand computers and data processing, and, perhaps even more disturbing, computers are often a mystery to the outside auditors on whom the hotel often relies to "check" that all is well.

Weaknesses in EDP Operations

In addition to the differences in mechanical and environmental characteristics referred to above, most EDP operations contain some inherent weaknesses that do not exist with more traditional means of accounting. They are:

- Accessibility and curiosity,
- Speed of implementation,
- Frequent and rapid change,
- Difficult audit trails,
- Abandonment of traditional controls, and
- Expense of good EDP controls.

Because they are still new and exciting in many hotels, EDP installations are often the **center of attention**. Managers are proud of their modernization and often include the computer room on tours of the hotel. There is nothing wrong with tours of the facility, but hotels must begin to understand the vulnerabilities of these centers and products, and the need to increase security commensurate with the increased risks. Access must be restricted to authorized personnel only.

Most EDP installations are **implemented as crash programs**. Once the decision to automate is finally made and the equipment arrives on the scene, the actual installation and change-over from earlier systems is usually done on a rush basis, and it is always chaotic and frenetic. EDP systems require considerable training. That fact, the anxiety felt by the staff, and the fragile nature of the media all contribute to the anxious and frenzied pace of most installations.

The modern computer and its peripheral equipment **change more frequently** and rapidly than any other items previously used by hotels. The change with the most implication for control is the continual drop in cost and resulting rapid proliferation of computers and computerized systems in hotels. Every year, hotels that previously could not afford automated systems now find them cost justified. This almost exponential increase in use often leaves internal control in the dust.

The audit trails are **more difficult to follow** in automated environments. Because the media are often invisible, managers might find it more difficult to "check" on an item.

Many of the packaged systems have built-in checks and balances. The staff are required to go through elaborate procedures, complete with "secret" passwords, simply to operate the system. The apparent control by password often leads to the relaxation of traditional internal-control measures. The problem is that the built-in controls are often inadequate and the lapsed traditional controls are often still necessary.

Finally, **it is expensive** to ensure that an EDP installation is well controlled. Since cost justification is an important issue in automation, controls are sometimes sacrificed as the EDP applications are being pared down to reduce expenses and make a project more feasible.

As a consequence, EDP installations can actually contribute to an increased risk of loss, whether from fraud or simply from equipment breakdown. In either case, a hotel that does not take proper precautions can find itself in great difficulty. Before discussing those precautions, a brief discussion on computer fraud is in order.

Computer Fraud

The computer has added a new motivation for fraud. A computer thief can be psychologically motivated. He or she is usually young, intelligent, and not particularly interested in economic rewards.* The mental challenge of "cracking the system" is what turns on this new breed of thieves. Breaking into a business computer and successfully completing some manipulation is the ultimate computer game.

How can hotels protect against these computer criminals? The answer for computer fraud is the same as for any other kind of fraud— namely, preclude the opportunity. Little can be done to change the needs of the would-be thief, but you can eliminate the opportunity. Some of the steps to accomplish that may be different in the electronic arena, but the general concept is the same.

The feature of computers that makes access possible for computer hackers is connection to networks. Hotels have been connected to networks through their reservations systems for decades. What has changed recently is the advent of modern networks where two-way communication is feasible. While such communication ability can be very useful and efficient, it makes hotels liable to hacking. Although the internal-control measures to combat unauthorized access to external networks are beyond the scope of this book, I will, however, deal with control of access on premises.

Types of Computer Crime. Computer crimes and frauds can be classified into five types:

• Financial crime,

---

*For example, see: Donn B. Parker, *Crime by Computer* (New York: Charles Scribner's Sons, 1976), Chapter 5.

- Property crime,
- Information crime,
- Theft of service, and
- Vandalism.

Financial crime involves traditional fraud and embezzlement whose goals are financial reward. In hotels, such frauds are often "back-of-the-house" schemes carried out with the payroll or payables. Some financial frauds have been perpetrated at the front of the house, usually involving rate changes or other allowances.

Property crime is similar to financial crime, but the target is merchandise, inventory, or other property instead of money. It often involves the diversion of shipments and deliveries, and is thus more common in industries where inventory, purchasing, and ordering are fully automated. This type of crime is not yet common in the hotel industry, but as automation progresses in the industry, so will the exposure to property crime.

Information crime involves the theft or unauthorized use of mailing lists, proprietary programs (software), classified data, or any other information "owned" by the hotel. With their guest histories, banquet lists, and other mailing or marketing lists, hotels are extremely vulnerable to this type of crime. Unfortunately, a computer embezzler who gains access to a hotel's repeat guest list will discover that he or she can find many potential buyers among the hotel's competitors.

Theft of service is unauthorized use of the computer. For example, an employee may use the company's computer to do a moonlighting or consulting job for which he or she gets paid, but for which the company gets nothing. This type of crime is more common around universities and manufacturing or research companies where large computers exist. It is not too common at hotels yet, but as technology marches forward, so will theft of service. Many hotels, for example, are extensively using desk-top publishing to produce menus and other marketing programs. That type of software-hardware combination allows great flexibility and produces nice work. Unfortunately, it also affords hotel employees the opportunity to go into the printing business for themselves.

Vandalism, the destruction of computer data, can be the most serious of the computer crimes. Disgruntled employees or other miscreants can do large amounts of damage to a data base with very little effort. While the incidence of such crime is not high, most of the control measures and preventative steps required to preclude them or to recover from them are equally useful for accidental losses. In other words, it is not important how the loss occurs. What's important is the fact that preventative and back-up steps have been taken.

Computer Controls: Some Background

EDP Auditing versus EDP Controls. There are two distinct and equally important fields in the arena of prevention and detection of computer fraud and embezzlement. *EDP auditing* is the process by which auditors, usually external to the company, check on and attest to the accuracy and validity of the programs and computer systems that are being used to process the company's data. An audit is critical to the prevention of unauthorized manipulation and use of the accounting and other programs in place at your hotel. EDP auditing is an extremely complex field, the discussion of which is far beyond the scope of this book.[1] Later in this chapter, however, I will briefly discuss the external auditor's role and give suggestions for the most efficient means to check on and validate the hotel's programs and data processing.

EDP controls are the internal processes and principles used to preclude opportunity and prevent fraud and embezzlement in the electronic processing of data. This chapter focuses on EDP controls.

Applications Controls versus General and Administrative Controls. *Applications controls* are the checks and balances, tests of reasonableness, and limits that are imbedded in programs to ensure control of input, processing, and output. The controls entail a system of "self-checking" that should take place whenever the program is used. Applications controls need to be designed and built-in at the time a program is developed and written. Most hotel companies do not use programmers to create original applications. Even the chain hotels use already prepared or packaged programs. For that reason, and because of their highly technical nature, applications controls are considered beyond the scope of this book.[2]

General and administrative controls are those processes and principles that can be applied at the hotel to prevent frauds and other losses

---

[1]For an excellent discussion of EDP auditing, see: Michael A. Murphy and Xebia Ley Parker, *Handbook of EDP Auditing (Second Edition)* (Boston: Warren, Gorham & Lamont, 1989).

[2]For example, see: AICPA Computer Services Executive Committee, *The Auditor's Study and Evaluation of Internal Control in EDP Systems* (New York, American Institute of Certified Public Accountants, 1977).

from occurring. They are as critical to ensuring fraud protection in a hotel's computing and data processing as are applications controls and EDP auditing. There are five general and administrative EDP controls that hotel managers should know, understand, and implement:

- Physical security,
- Division of duties,
- Documentation,
- File protection, and
- Audit—Internal and External.

Physical Security. As the term implies, physical security involves the mechanical and administrative security of the space, equipment, and files for the hotel's data processing. It is preferable to have the location of the computer room and, especially, the storage areas for files, data, and programs be as inconspicuous as possible. Doors should be securely locked at all times, and access to keys should be strictly limited to those who need to work in each area. The new electronic locks are excellent for the EDP areas. Many lock systems have the ability to record and print out the last 20 or so entries (i.e., exactly which key was used and when). All entrants should be required to sign in and out and log the times of entry and exit. In large installations, you might want a door guard to observe and check the traffic in both directions. Most hotels will find it hard to cost-justify such a guard, however.

There are some aspects of the physical security that deal with the environment and the extreme sensitivity of the equipment and media. If the hotel is sprinklered, it is critical that any water sprinklers in the computer rooms and data storage areas be replaced with approved chemical ones that are designed for electrical use. Since both the equipment and storage media are sensitive to temperature and moisture changes, you should install temperature and humidity alarms. These alarms should be designed to notify the front desk if any problems arise with the heating or air-conditioning systems.

Both computers and storage media are sensitive to power surges (voltage changes) and interruptions, so all equipment should be plugged into power-surge protectors. Uninterruptable power supplies (UPS) and emergency power systems are likewise important for EDP installations. UPS systems provide automatic and instantaneous battery operation for the computer for a designated time period, or until emergency power takes over. Emergency power systems provide for generators to start up automatically in the event of a power failure. Emergency power and UPS systems are quite expensive. Hotels should look at the emergency power requirements for their EDP systems along with the bigger picture of hotel-wide emergency power—some of which may be required by code or law. One way to provide for cheaper interruption-free operation is to have a less expensive UPS that will give you enough time to save all the files and create enough records to shut down the computer and operate manually until full power is restored.

Labeling of programs, documentation books, files, and data-storage media should also be inconspicuous. Some operators have all such items labeled in code—to make it more difficult for a person attempting to perpetrate a fraud or create damage. Strict rules should exist for the careful destruction of old matter when any changes are made. Tapes, disks, and other magnetic media should be completely erased (and used over); paper items should be shredded. Old documentation, in particular, has often been used by perpetrators to gain access or to learn about certain operations. Most files are secured by passwords and keywords, which should be memorized by the staff and never written in documentation or logs. The better designed password devices are those that require frequent (e.g., monthly) changing.

For a more extensive discussion of EDP physical security, see Appendix 9.1, adapted from a pamphlet produced by the accounting firm Pannell Kerr Forster.

Division of Duties. The concept of separating functions so that no one individual has complete control over a transaction applies as much to EDP environments as it does to manual environments. As an operation moves from a manual environment to automation, the need to divide functions remains—and sometimes even intensifies. The data-processing department or group should report to top management. In hotels that means the manager of data processing (often called information systems) should be at the executive-committee level and report to the general manager. In smaller hotels, the EDP manager may report to the controller (who is part of top management).

The degree of separation of duties depends to a large extent on the size of the data-processing effort. Size always affects division of duties, but it has an even larger impact in EDP since it governs the type of installation that you will be able to have. Smaller organizations almost always use packaged software, whereas larger operations with internal programmers have the choice of using packaged programs or writing their own. With an in-house staff also comes some danger: the ability to write programs means the ability to modify or alter programs—a factor that can lead to fraud or embezzlement. At the minimum, a three-way division of duties is required:

- Systems planning and programming,
- Machine operation, and
- Data and file maintenance.

The three-way separation operates on the premise that a fraud perpetrated through the actual computer operation requires unauthorized programming or data-entry changes. If employees who can program are separated from those who operate and have access to the programs and data, such changes would be extremely difficult. Similarly, if the operators cannot program, they cannot make unauthorized changes. If they make fraudulent entries, it does them no good, for they have no access to the files (or cash and other assets).

Systems planning involves the initial design of the programs that an operation will use, together with any ongoing modifications and changes that may be needed over time. Programming is writing and maintaining the programs. In larger operations, it is desirable to separate these two functions so that the people who plan and design (usually called systems analysts) are not the same ones as those who write and implement the programs (called programmers—see Exhibit 9.1). In small operations, there may not even be any programmers. All programming may be done by the vendor or by an outside consultant. In those cases, the separation of duties is already accomplished! If a smaller operation has someone with programming skills, that person should not be involved with initial system design or making major changes. Those duties should be handled by persons outside the hotel. All programming should be kept separate from machine operation and the custody of the programs and data.

Machine operation, of course, involves various employees operating the computers and other components of the EDP system. People who are charged with actual machine operation should not have access to the program code. They may need to "mount" the programs physically to run them, but they should not have sufficient access to make changes or modifications. The operators should also be denied access to the storage of data files. In large operations machine operators have no other responsibilities.

Exhibit 9.1

Organization Charts for Data Processing

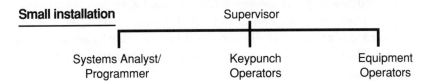

Small installation

Supervisor
- Systems Analyst/Programmer
- Keypunch Operators
- Equipment Operators

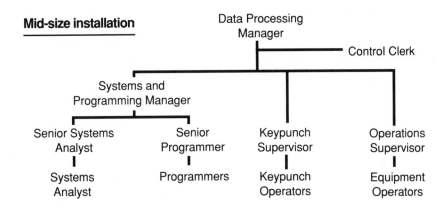

Mid-size installation

Data Processing Manager
- Control Clerk
- Systems and Programming Manager
  - Senior Systems Analyst
    - Systems Analyst
  - Senior Programmer
    - Programmers
- Keypunch Supervisor
  - Keypunch Operators
- Operations Supervisor
  - Equipment Operators

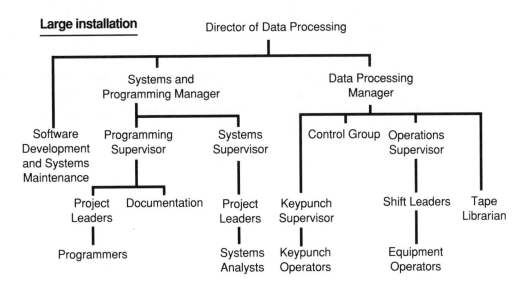

Large installation

Director of Data Processing
- Systems and Programming Manager
  - Software Development and Systems Maintenance
  - Programming Supervisor
    - Project Leaders
      - Programmers
    - Documentation
  - Systems Supervisor
    - Project Leaders
      - Systems Analysts
- Data Processing Manager
  - Control Group
  - Operations Supervisor
    - Keypunch Supervisor
      - Keypunch Operators
    - Shift Leaders
      - Equipment Operators
    - Tape Librarian

Adapted from: Canadian Institute of Chartered Accountants, *Computer Control Guidelines* (Toronto, Ontario: CICA, 1973), pp. 29-30.

In smaller operations (including most hotels), the machine operators are employees who operate the computer in the normal course of their regular duties (e.g., front-desk clerks, food and beverage shift cashiers, accounting clerks). The use of regular hotel employees as the computer operators makes the division of duties easier to accomplish. However, they should have no access to the programs and only limited access to data storage.

Data and file maintenance, often called the library function, is a key area for separation of duties. It includes custody of the programs themselves and of all the data files, including back-ups. Every operation, large or small, requires an EDP librarian. Only large operations, however, can afford to have a separate employee by that designation. In most operations, the custodial function is delegated to an employee with other duties—usually an accounting-department or front-office employee. Top management should also maintain an archival copy of all programs, including modifications, which can be used for auditing comparisons.

Documentation. Documentation is the process of substantiating existing facts with documents. Because you can't really see EDP entries, documentation is vital for all aspects of an EDP system. In simple terms, documents are created that describe, explain, and diagram the individual components of the EDP systems, while providing blueprints or road maps for operators, programmers, and others to follow. The ideal test of well-prepared documentation is whether it is clear enough and complete enough for an outsider with some EDP knowledge to come in cold, pick up the documentation, study it, and then proceed to program, repair, or operate the system. In other words, the documentation consists of detailed manuals that fully describe the functioning of each part of the information system. It is almost unfortunate that it took automation to force many hotels to document procedures. In truth, well-operated hotels should have clear, accurate, and concise documentation for all operations and procedures—automated or not. Documentation should be developed for all services and all operating departments.

Division of duties must be maintained at the documentation level. EDP documentation should be stratified so that each level and each group of employees has separate access only to the manuals covering their portion of the system. In that way, a machine operator, for example, will not have access to the programming section of a manual that may cover the operation of his or her machine.

The various pieces of EDP documentation have many different names. It seems that every author and every operation makes up document names. To review all the different documents would be beyond the scope of this book. Some of the references at the end of the chapter, however, have excellent sections on documentation and its design.*

To demonstrate and discuss a key piece of EDP documentation, a sample "Master Manual" appears below. A manual of this type would be prepared for each major EDP or accounting function (e.g., payroll, payables, sales journals, guest accounting):

Master Manual for _____:

    A. Description of the purpose of the program;

    B. Complete set of flow charts;

    C. Assembly listing of the program;

    D. Operating instructions;

    E. Program-testing instructions;

    F. Description of all input and source documents; and

    G. Sample of all output and reports.

The *purpose of the program* should be a fairly simple description of what the particular program will accomplish and how it will do so. The *flow charts* are schematic diagrams of all of the processes, flows, documents, and files that will be used or required in the function the program is performing. These charts are critical tools for a programmer who is attempting to write a program. In some ways, flow charts are analogous to blueprints if we think of the programmer as a builder constructing a building. Flow charts also play important diagnostic and auditing roles.

When computer programs are written, they consist of specific instructions to the computer, written in a code known as a language. Those instructions are listed, in the code of the language, line by line. After the program is written, tested, and debugged, it is permanently entered into the memory of the computer or recorded on some medium such as magnetic disks or tapes for use-by-use entry. The computer will be able to print out a *listing of the program codes* known as the assembly listing. As we will see later, the assembly listing of computer

---

*For example, see: W. Thomas Porter and William E. Perry, *EDP Controls and Auditing (Fifth Edition)* (Boston: Kent Publishing Co., 1987).

code in the documentation plays an important audit role in checking for unauthorized changes, or "patch" programs. Patch programs are illicit mini-programs within the main program that have been placed there to accomplish a fraud. An example of a difficult but feasible one is a patch that instructs the payroll program to send the writer two paychecks each period and to destroy the evidence of the second.

The *operating instructions* are detailed, step-by-step instructions for the machine operator to run the program. These same instructions usually appear in the other documentation, such as the operator's manual. The instructions should also include a listing of all necessary inputs, stating where, from whom, when, and how often the operator should expect those inputs. *Program-testing instructions* are similar in scope to the operating instructions. They are intended for programmers and auditors to use in debugging, testing, and ultimately checking on the actual performance of the program.

The last two items of documentation, the *description of all inputs and source documents* and *samples of all output and reports*, are especially useful in emergency situations, for training, and for analyzing how well the program has accomplished its purposes.

The role of documentation in internal control is greatly enhanced if archive copies of all key documentation are kept by top management— preferably in the general manager's safe. The documentation must be updated whenever any changes are made, and it should be available to internal and external auditors for use in their testing work.

Legitimate changes. Documentation and procedures should be established so that any changes to programs or other parts of the information systems are made only with management's specific written authorization.

File protection. The fragility of modern electronic files and the increase in the concentration of data mean that lost data files can be catastrophic to a hotel. To guard against the loss of data—whether from willful destruction, an environmental problem, or a mechanical breakdown—hotels should develop an on-going file-protection program. Such a program should include the five following elements:

- Separate library function,
- Labeling,
- Periodic saving and dumping,
- Redundancy, and
- Record reconstruction.

As I remarked earlier, only very large operations can justify separate, dedicated employees for a *file library*. All EDP operations, however, should separate the library function from the other data-processing tasks. Access to the EDP library of data and files should be strictly limited.

A good *labeling program* for data and software merely involves a common-sense approach as to how to identify each file. Files should be labeled in code so that the identity of each one is not readily apparent to an unauthorized user. In that way, a person gaining unauthorized access will have difficulty identifying the files he or she is trying to harm or steal. Back-up files should have labels different from the originals they are copied from. That feature not only adds protection to the back-up process, but may disguise the fact that back-up exists—thus foiling the efforts of a would-be vandal.

A program of *periodic saving or backing up* is essential to file protection. Since electronic files (e.g., the memory in the computer) are fragile, all employees that operate the systems must be trained to save files regularly and frequently. Saving a file means recording it on another medium—presumably one less fragile. The internal memory of most computers, for example, will be completely erased if there is a power failure, or even if the employee accidentally hits the on-off switch. If the material in fragile electronic memory is frequently saved to a disk or tape file, such losses can be avoided. This concept should be extended to making additional back-up copies and to "dumping" to hard copy. A *program of dumping* simply means that files are periodically printed out to hard or paper copy. In other words, the electronic and magnetic files are transformed to a less fragile and more readable paper format. The problems associated with the periodic printing out of the files are that it is slow, expensive, and creates mountains of paper. (The paper can be recycled, at least.) All of these costs have to be weighed against the benefits of safety and back-up.

There are no set rules for which files should be printed out and how frequently to print them. Hotel managers have to work that out for themselves on a case-by-case basis depending on the importance of the data to the hotel's survival and operations. For example, I usually recommend that the guest-accounts receivable from the front-office system (i.e., the guest folios) be printed to hard output every four to six hours. With the overnight period excluded, that means three or four paper files each day! That much printing may represent some overkill, but if there is a system crash or a power failure, the front office can continue to operate and settle guest accounts by hand. The clerks need only to go back to the time of the last print-out, look for any new charges, post them by hand, and hand tally the guest's bill. Check-in and other operations can also be done by hand during a down period.

Redundancy, as contrasted with saving and dumping, means having extra back-up copies. In some instances that means designing the system so it will simultaneously record data to more than one file. In other cases, a procedure must be instituted and followed whereby employees periodically make special copies (often also referred to as "making a save" or "saving"). In either case, it is a good idea to have at least one or two back-up copies of all important files. The only significant expense is in the employee time required to make the copies. The media themselves, tapes or disks, can be continually used and re-used.

Internal control will be enhanced if the employees making the saves (or storing and using them in the case of automatic saves) are not the computer or machine operators. Accounting personnel can usually be assigned to make these copies since the time required is brief (e.g., the night auditor can make the late shift copies). In the case of critical files, one extra copy might well be stored separately from the others, perhaps off-premises. That extra precaution helps with vandalism, but is also good insurance with environmental or mechanical problems.

Record reconstruction is a process that re-creates files if they are somehow lost. Most accounting procedures take place in regular cycles or generations—sometimes the length of a generation is a month, a quarter, or, in the case of the front office, a night. This cyclical or "generational" characteristic of accounting is probably why many auditors refer to this process as the "grandfather-father-son principle" (although I prefer the gender-neutral "grandparent-parent-child").

In the course of normal accounting tasks, a complete generation of records is developed by adding new entries to the already established records. Those new entries are made with information from source documents. In an EDP environment, payroll records may be contained on a magnetic medium such as a disk. That disk would contain all of the year-to-date payroll information on each employee, including the current period's paycheck. The new cycle involves updating the last pay-period's disk with the new pay-period's information, taken from source documents such as time-cards and pay-change forms. The result is a new payroll, new paychecks, and a new updated disk.

If somehow that record (the "child") should be lost or destroyed, it could be completely re-created by simply going back to the last generation (last period's payroll, i.e., the "parent"), taking the current period's source documents, and re-running the payroll (without the pay checks, of course). If the process goes back one more cycle, we get the "grandparent" records that could be used for updates. A generation, then, is the record of the previous cycle combined with the current cycle's source documents. The three-generation process of record reconstruction involves the separate retention of each generation and its source documents. Three generations are sufficient, so, for the fourth generation, the media used for the first generation can be reused. Some operators prefer to store one generation off-premises. That additional precaution adds expense, but it may be cost-justified in the case of very important records.

Auditing

External Auditing. In the introduction to this chapter, I pointed out that EDP is not always well-understood by external auditors. In all fairness to the auditing profession, that situation has improved over time. Early in the history of automation, the '50s and '60s, external auditors would essentially ignore the computer. They would test and check the transactions, source documents, journals and ledgers, and the actual assets and liabilities. There was some validity to their thinking—after all, what was the difference if a human bookkeeper made the journal entries or a machine made them? The auditor's job was to check for validity and to look for mistakes, not to worry about the means of how the mistake was made. This approach to auditing in an EDP environment came to be known as "auditing around the computer." As computing and EDP became more sophisticated and more pervasive, it became clear that auditing around the computer was not going to be sufficient. During the '70s, the major national accounting firms started hiring computer experts, insisting on computer literacy and some expertise for all of their auditors, and, most important, developing "test-packages." These test packages were designed to check whether the computer and the program it was running were accomplishing their goals. This type of auditing came to be known as "auditing through the computer." The tests auditors ran through the computer could check for accuracy and validity and could compare programs to check for fraudulent changes. By the late '70s and early

'80s the major accounting firms all had good capability to audit EDP, and most could detect even highly sophisticated patches in programs. In the last half of the '80s, with the proliferation of portable personal computers, the auditing process itself became automated. The '90s bring two new challenges for auditors. One is to extend computer expertise and sophistication throughout the entire profession. Smaller audit firms, upon whom many hospitality firms must rely, do not always have computer expertise or the testing capability.

Second, the proliferation of the personal computer has sparked an explosion of "end-user" computing. End-user computing means that the users themselves—the managers and supervisors in the hotel—are doing a lot of computing on their own rather than relying on the EDP department to do it for them. That situation is replete with issues like ensuring the accuracy and validity of the data they are using to make important business decisions, the authorization for them to obtain the data, and control of the data once they are released. Increased end-user computing will continue to create many challenges for the auditing profession and for management.*

The role of the external auditor in EDP, then, is to apply his or her sophisticated testing capability to the hotel's computers and programs and to look for unauthorized changes and other illicit processes. The hotel's management should insist that this take place. If the hotel's audit firm does not have such capability, the hotel management should discuss with the auditor the feasibility of occasionally bringing in an outside firm (sub-contractor) to "audit through the computer." If that cannot be arranged and the hotel is heavily automated, it should consider changing audit firms.

Internal Auditing. Like all other auditing tasks, auditing of the EDP by the hotel's accounting department is divided into daily and periodic tasks. Most of the daily auditing tasks for EDP are the same as those for the audit of revenue and exceptions such as allowances. It is critical that traditional controls, such as the allowance-voucher procedure (complete with the paper audit trail) be maintained in an automated environment.

In addition to the normal daily audit of revenue, the accounting department should check the following each day:

- Prescribed saves are completed on schedule;

---

*For further discussion of end-user computing, see: R. Ryan Nelson, *End-User Computing: Concepts, Issues, and Applications* (New York: John Wiley & Sons, 1989).

- Dumps (to hard output) are completed on schedule;
- Computer-room access logs are filled in properly; and
- Back-up media are stored properly and at their correct locations.

Periodic auditing, usually monthly, should consist of a program of general and specific checks including:

- Checks of all programs for unauthorized changes;
- Checks of all exception reports;
- Checks for traditional control measures, documents, and audit trails;
- Checks for numerical control and calculations; and
- Checks that all passwords are changed at reasonable intervals.

Checking programs for *unauthorized changes* or other alterations is difficult unless the auditor has a high level of computer-programming skill. That is why I recommended that hotels insist on annual, professional, through-the-computer testing. The hotel's accounting department, however, can and should do some interim testing. By comparing a print-out (an assembly listing) of the currently operating versions of a few key programs to the assembly listings in the manager's archival copy of the documentation, the auditors can make a crude but effective check. If the auditor has some programming skills, a side-by-side comparison of the two versions of the program should point up differences. If none of the auditors has any programming ability, a "quick and dirty" approach to program testing is simply to count the number of lines of code (instructions to the computer) in the two versions. While that approach is not always conclusive, any variance should be immediately investigated further by an outside auditor or a consultant. Often, perpetrators of computer fraud assume that non-computer people would never check the program code or that the auditors would assume that the currently running version of the program is the only one. These quick and simple program checks often yield interesting results.

All *exception reports*—rate-variance reports, allowance vouchers, transfers, error corrections, over- and under-rings—should be reviewed in detail each month by the accounting department. Those containing important managerial information, allowance vouchers, for example, should be passed on to top management for their review, initialing, and return. The exception reports should also match up with all discrepancies found in the normal income-audit processes. An auditor must be able to verify that no exception or change can be made without a solid audit trail, consisting of the change itself, how much it was, when it was made, to which accounts, and by whom. The questions of why they were granted and who authorized them can be answered by looking at the hard-paper documents.

Finally, the *numerical sequence* of documents must be verified even though numerical entry or assignment is part of the data-processing routine. Auditing is meant to detect fraud and non-routine events. For that reason, even mathematical accuracy must be occasionally verified in an EDP environment. Computers may not make mathematical errors, but embezzlers often inadvertently cause such errors. Also, the column of numbers may look correct, but the total may be wrong because of intentional omissions or fraudulent additions. So, periodic math and serial-number checking play useful EDP-audit roles.

Specific Control Issues for Hospitality Packages

The internal-control features of many of the packaged systems for hotels, particularly front-office or property-management systems, are generally good.[1] Some, however, are very bad or lack key elements. A system-by-system review of all of the available packages would be beyond the scope of the book and would probably have a "shelf-life" of only three months. Some of the references at the end of the chapter may be helpful in reviewing the various systems, although none concentrates on the issue of internal controls.[2] The best way for a hotel operator to review the internal-control strengths and weaknesses of any particular system is as follows: List the key control elements of the functions the system must manage or operate (e.g., front office, restaurant, etc.). In other words, using the key concepts covered throughout this book, design or illustrate the important internal-controls elements as if a manual environment existed. Then take that list of controls and investigate whether or how well the system in question handles the

---

[1]Property-management systems are broader versions of front-office and guest-accounting systems that incorporate communications to and from the telephone, housekeeping, and food and beverage departments into the front-office operation.

[2]For example, see: Joseph A. Marko and Richard G. Moore, "How to Select a Computer System," *The Cornell Hotel and Restaurant Administration Quarterly*, 21, No. 1 (May 1980), pp. 60-71, and 21, No. 2 (August 1980), pp. 8-18.

Case 9.1

New Computer, Old Tricks

To improve the efficiency of the front desk, the management of a 350-room roadside inn installed an on-line computer. Reservations were no longer lost, room status was always current, check-ins were fast and correct, the cumbersome room rack was eliminated, posting machines and pits for room folios were no longer needed, and errors were rare. Moreover, the hotel needed fewer front-desk clerks, since one clerk could now handle a greater volume of transactions. Because it was no longer necessary to post room charges and taxes and to check laboriously all department totals and folio balances, the night audit now consisted of producing a wider variety of pertinent managerial information. The only difficulty was the relatively minor one of training the clerks in the proper use of the machine. In short, the computer was a tremendous asset.

The night auditor could produce a list of transactions by key, and the auditor would review these the following day. Any unvouchered corrections, adjustments, transfers, paid-outs, or other unusual transactions would be investigated. Figures from the daily report, which was produced by the front-office accounting system, were entered directly into an automated back-office system. This transaction updated the general-ledger revenue accounts. Little human intervention was needed.

In the midst of this automated system, the front-desk clerks were given the authority to make minor adjustments (under $10) to customers' bills. This authorization proved to be too tempting for one clerk and the night auditor.

The two decided to try an old and proven rip-off technique on the new computer system. To them, it seemed that the new technology made the manipulation that much easier. The only requirement was that the guest pay cash on check-out. The desk clerk would hand the guest a computer-printed bill that showed the correct amount of his or her charges. As the guest was paying, the clerk would pretend that the computer was temporarily malfunctioning and so it would be impossible to prepare a new folio showing a zero balance. He would give the guest a copy of the folio marked "paid in full."

After the guest departed, the clerk would take the "paid" bill, reduce the balance, and keep the difference. The clerk would do this by one of three methods available to him: **(1)** transfer part of the balance to a large outstanding customer account on city ledger; **(2)** make an allowance or adjustment on the bill; or **(3)** simply make a correction to lessen the balance shown. Corrections presented no problem. Allowances had to be $10 or less, and he was careful to keep the amounts of city-ledger transfers small while choosing customers who would be unlikely to notice a minor increase in their bills.

Although he was careful never to wipe out any guest's balance completely, the clerk was able to credit falsely and pocket between $60 and $100 per day. Occasionally, however, greed overcame him and he would make allowances in excess of his $10 authority. To hide his manipulations, he relied on the ingenuity of the night auditor. This industrious fellow had access to the system's programming manual and was able to write a patch program that prevent the computer from printing any transaction that carried with it a particular voucher number. Dollar amounts corresponding to the entry of the false voucher number were, nevertheless, accumulated by the machine and were included in the totals print-out in the computer reports.

The night auditor also learned a way to take advantage of another of the computer system's features—namely, automatic check writing. The hotel had long paid commissions to travel agents for generating certain types of business. But problems with this policy had arisen in the past because the agents frequently were not paid as promptly as they wished. In turn, some agencies had refused to send patrons to this hotel. The computer resolved the time-lag problem. Each agency was assigned an account number. When a guest was referred to the hotel by an agency, the appropriate index number was entered on the folio during registration. When the guest checked out, the agent's account was credited with the commission payable. At the end of the month, this money would be including with other accounts payable, and the back-office system would print and send out checks.

The auditor learned how to create a fictitious travel-agency account. He set up a post-office box and a checking account for the phony agency and gave his accomplice, the front-desk clerk, the number for the "new" agency. The desk clerk would enter the "agency's" number occasionally as guests checked in, usually when they were walk-ins, and the computer did the rest.

The two schemes did not immediately call attention to themselves, because the amounts were small and there was no visible audit trail to reveal the missing transactions. All good things must come to an end, however, and these schemes went the way of all flesh when the income auditor decided one day to add up the columns of adjustments, allowances, and transfers to check them against the totals at the bottom of the sheet. Before this time, the auditor had merely checked off vouchers against transactions listed to make sure that all of the vouchers had been posted. After all, he reasoned, the computer would total all the columns correctly. To his surprise, he found that even when all the vouchers were recorded, the totals did not correspond to the tape he was running on his adding machine. When he checked the print-out sheets for the past several months, he discovered that this discrepancy appeared repeatedly.

The hotel called in a public-accounting firm knowledgeable in EDP auditing, which ran a test program through the computer. The test uncovered the unauthorized patch program, and suspicion immediately centered on the night auditor. To avoid prosecution, the auditor admitted his complicity in the fraud and offered the hotel information on the mechanics of the travel-agency manipulation. Management dropped criminal charges against him and took immediate steps to prevent these problems from recurring.

Discussion

Much of the fraud in this case occurred because traditional controls became lax in the computerized environment. Managerial approval for allowances, numerical control of vouchers, audit of all vouchers and other transfers, testing of mathematical columns, verification of the legitimacy of travel agents, and management involvement in disbursements were all let go.

With respect to the travel-agent portion of the embezzlement, all travel agencies should be checked in industry source books for legitimacy, and documentation, such as a copy of the guest's folio, should accompany the disbursement check. Management should verify and cancel the documentation and supervise the mailing of the checks (as with all disbursements).In addition to the failures of some traditional controls, this hotel also failed to implement some basic computer controls—division of duties, for example. Computer-operating personnel should not have access to programs or program documentation, and programmers should not have access to the computer operations and files.

All programs, and especially changes in those programs, should be documented. Management should maintain an archive copy of the documentation, and periodically compare it to the current operating version to verify that no unauthorized changes have been made. The comparisons can be accomplished through sophisticated testing programs, or even simple approaches such as counting lines of code.

Finally, hotels should never rely on guests for internal control. It is perfectly understandable that a guest might not question a full charge balance on his or her fully paid folio printout (rather than a zero balance), especially if the folio is stamped: "paid in full."

(Note: Rosalind Rustigian, an M.P.S. graduate, assisted with the preparation of this case.)

---

elements on the list. Internal-control performance is only one of several criteria by which an operator must judge a system, albeit an important one.

If an otherwise attractive system has some **internal-control weaknesses**, the operator may wish to point them out to the vendor and discuss possible modifications to the system to correct them. Another approach is to see whether controls can be added to or used alongside the system. A system should be rejected, however, if it has too many control weaknesses or if its weaknesses cannot be overcome, even if that system seems feasible in most other ways.

Access is an important area to investigate. Some key issues are: Is it possible to set up stratified access levels? How many strata are possible? How is access to the various strata controlled? Can we be sure that certain key functions performed at the managerial level are prohibited at lower levels of access? Other important issues to consider when looking at access are the ease (or difficulty) of making such non-programming changes as menu-item and price changes and room-rate changes; the existence and degree of permanence of the audit trail for those changes; and the ability to make changes to the actual operating programs. Most packaged hospitality systems have programs that cannot be changed without vendor support. From the internal-control perspective, that is not a bad feature as it adds some division of duties and provides control against internal embezzlement. On the other hand, having to rely on vendor support for major changes may disrupt or impede operations—another example of the trade-off between control and policy.

Interface means that the various components of the system are connected or can "talk" with each other. A recent and important interface developed by package vendors is the one between the various food and beverage POS devices and the front-office or guest-accounting system. In other words, a restaurant cashier can electronically send a guest charge directly to the front office for posting. In many of the systems, the outlet cashier can actually post the charge. Some even allow the cashier to verify the credit-worthiness of the guest prior to accepting the charge. While these innovations bring much-needed progress to some important operating problems—such as non-guests posing as guests to make charges, or charges arriving at the desk after a guest has checked out—they bring some new internal-control problems.

The fact that an employee outside of the front office can gain access to guest folios may be dangerous. The level of that access must be carefully scrutinized and, perhaps, limited. If the communication goes in two directions, the problem becomes even more serious. The idea of a food and beverage cashier's being able to enter a guest's room folio and change the room rate is disturbing. Fortunately, most of the currently available systems do not allow that level of two-way communication. Most of the current interfaces only allow charges to be sent from the outlets to the desk, and information such as posting authorization to be received by the outlets. Even that limited information exchange brings some risks, because it allows a larger pool of employees to have access to information about who our guests are, which rooms they are in, and their credit limits. Having this level of information available to employees will require better screening and training for more employees.

Training gains importance in an EDP environment. Not only is the technology new and different, but the operations actually change. Some processes that may have previously been standard operating procedure may now be eliminated. Moreover, you'll have to counter your staff's tendency to focus on their computer terminals at the expense of friendly guest contact and good controls. Training must reinforce both traditional hospitality and the thoroughness of the control procedures. The computer must be only a tool.

A related issue is planning, preparing, and training for "crash" or **back-up situations.** After converting to automation, many hotels completely mothball all their hand-operated systems. The staff members soon forget that they ever existed. With high turnover, your hotel soon becomes populated with many employees who have never worked with manual documents and controls at all. When a system crashes, the hotel may come to a virtual standstill. Therefore, you must have on hand a set of back-up procedures, including all documents and supplies for each automated function of the hotel. Employees must be trained to switch immediately to the back-up as soon as a problem surfaces. Better operations drill their employees with "test" crashes. Examples for front-office operations include manual check-in procedures, manual folios and paper charge slips for all the various types of charges (numerically controlled, of course), and a manual check-out procedure. These manual procedures will work only if the policy of periodically "dumping" guest accounts to hard paper print-out is strictly followed so that current guest-account balances will be available without the computer.

In the food and beverage area, numerically controlled hand duplicates and guest checks must be available to take over if the pre-check or POS systems break down. Not only are internal controls affected, but when the food and beverage preparers become accustomed to printed receipts, they find it very difficult to work, produce orders, and keep track of them without a substitute.

Appendix 9.1

Computer Security:

Controlling the Computer Environment

by Pannell Kerr Forster

Problems of Computer Security

Computer security is an essential consideration in the design and operation of any computer system. The many hazards that might corrupt data or destroy the computer facility must be explicitly considered. Having good safeguards in one respect while lacking in any other could still result in the loss you are trying to prevent. We suggest that only by carefully examining all possible hazards will you obtain a balanced set of precautions, whose cost is commensurate with the loss that you might sustain.

The probable hazards vary from one installation to another, but most will be subject to the following risks:

- sabotage,
- fraud,
- theft,
- fire,
- flooding,
- equipment malfunctions,
- power failure,
- software error,
- accidental incorrect operation, and
- overloads.

The results of breaches in computer security can vary from mere inconvenience to a complete and permanent breakdown in business operations. Even if recovery is possible, it may cost more than your business can afford and still survive.

Categories for Consideration

For convenience, we can consider security under two main headings, namely:

- physical security, and
- operational security.

In practice, these headings overlap to some extent, and they must not be considered in isolation. They require completely different approaches to the problems they attempt to cover. They involve skills as diverse as those of an engineer, accountant, and computer programmer. The intention of this appendix is to indicate the areas to which attention should be paid and the type of problem that should be anticipated, regardless of the type or size of computer installed.

Mainframes, Minis, and Micros

Mainframes. In a large installation, it is possible to have a highly organized system of security, involving division of duties in the computer department and having the computer situated in a separate area so that physical access is restricted to authorized staff. A librarian may control access to files and documentation, and the user department can act as the final control over the completeness and accuracy of the data processed.

Minis and micros. It is harder to establish the same high standards of organized security controls usually associated with large installations for mini- and micro-computer installations.

A small computer may be located in the accounting department, with all operations being carried out by a few members of the staff. Under these circumstances, internal control and internal checks in the department may be minimal. Minis and micros are subject to additional security hazards because immediate access to source programs may be possible and the operators have direct use of the disk media. The user-friendly nature of these machines can also render them "hazard friendly," as their ease of use can permit unauthorized persons to examine or change data if precautions are not taken to restrict access to computer files, manuals, and particularly to the machine. It is entirely possible for the computer itself to be stolen.

Despite these problems, security precautions for mini- and micro-computers are just as necessary and are practical to implement. For example, use of computer terminals and of certain programs or routines can be restricted by password protection, and the equipment location can be such that all activity can be observed by management.

Strong external controls are particularly important. Care should be taken that staff members who have programming knowledge are not given the opportunity to make any unofficial alterations to programs and, if possible, are not used as operators.

Controls over disks, cassettes, and other highly portable forms of storage should be used to guard against unauthorized removal and against damage. Back-up copies and records of such copying should be kept.

Physical Security

The purpose of physical security, as the term suggests, is to protect the equipment itself from damage. The increasing reliance on the computer and the information stored on its files means that computer equipment out of action for any reason can have a serious effect on the future of the company.

Physical hazards include fire, sabotage, flood, magnetism, heat and humidity, the effects of strikes or industrial actions, and the theft of computer data, equipment, and software. In reviewing security requirements at a particular computer installation, you should consider what the likely hazards are, what their consequences might be, and what practical precautions can be taken.

The following are the main points to be considered:

1. Access to the computer room,
2. Fire detection and prevention,
3. Storage of files on magnetic media, and
4. Off-site storage of security copies of data.

Position of the Computer Room

In light of some of the more dramatic breaches of computer security that have occurred in the past, one might think that the computer should ideally be installed in an underground concrete bunker, surrounded by four high walls, and protected with a strict security check on admitted personnel. While such a suggestion is impractical, it high-lights the fact that the policy of a number of companies that placed their computers in easy view and access was wrong.

The choice of a sensible location for the computer must involve consideration of the following:

- domestic hazards (e.g., water pipes, boiler rooms),
- susceptibility to burglary and casual visitors,
- suitability of environment (e.g., floor strength, ventilation),
- accessibility for fire services, and
- local hazards (e.g., floods).

Access to the Computer Room

There should be no direct access to the computer room from outside the building. While you might want to make it easy to install and move computer equipment, access should only be via several outer offices (e.g., data preparation, control), each of which should make entry by unauthorized persons increasingly difficult. Emergency exits should not create a loophole in these precautions.

Only authorized employees (operators on duty, the librarian, and data-processing managers) should have access to the computer room. Some form of magnetic key is probably the best way of restricting access. Visitors should be strictly controlled. Cleaners invite the possible risk of espionage and environmental problems resulting from the use of inappropriate cleaning methods (i.e., generating dust).

When it is impractical to isolate the computer and limit access (e.g., a micro-computer terminal), other measures should be considered to protect against unauthorized use. These precautions may include the following:

- password protection against unauthorized use of the computer itself or of particular programs, files, and utilities;
- location of the computer and terminals so that users can be observed;
- clear indications to the staff of who is authorized to use the computer (e.g., signs, memos); and

- printing audit trails as a routine matter.

Fire Precautions

Protection against fire is vital. Consideration should be given to the following:

- Siting the computer away from possible fire hazards;
- Access for fire-fighting services;
- Suitable fire-fighting equipment (e.g., CO_2 extinguishers);
- Alarm systems (e.g., smoke detectors);
- Procedures and training for staff;
- Fire safes and other protection for files, equipment, and documentation;
- Emergency power controls in the computer area;
- Regular maintenance of all equipment;
- Drainage facilities if water is used to fight fire (e.g., raised floors);
- Back-up provisions for files, programs, and documentation at a remote location; and
- Stand-by arrangements to use another computer in the event of equipment loss or breakdown.

Storage of Magnetic Files

In addition to the fire precautions, care should be taken to protect magnetic records against other possible hazards. The following should be considered:

- Air conditioning of storage areas;
- Control over access to files;
- Static electricity;
- Magnetic interference;
- Care in handling disks; and
- Instructing staff on file storage.

Files are usually kept separately by a librarian in larger installations, so that access to the files can be controlled to prevent unauthorized use. Tape files can have outside visible records for identification purposes, and magnetic header labels to enable the computer to recognize the correct file. Disk packs should also have external labels.

If your installation is too small to justify a full-time librarian, files should be stored in a suitable location and locked up to guard against unauthorized access. If your storage is on floppy disks, make sure they are not bent or otherwise damaged by casual mishandling. The rigid 3.5-inch disks appear sturdier than the flexible 5.5-inch disks, but both are easily damaged by careless handling. If a disk malfunctions for any reason, copy what data you can from it and discard it. Never attempt to reuse a disk that has malfunctioned.

If a computer is destroyed, most manufacturers may be able to supply a replacement within a few days, but if programs or files are destroyed, recovery may be completely impossible or take so long that you may be forced into bankruptcy. As a general rule, companies that have suffered casualty losses have failed due to the loss of irreplaceable records and not the loss of physical property. The records to store are application programs, master files, and copies of the transaction files.

Regardless of the size of your installation, the most effective security against loss of files is to store back-up files at a separate location outside your property. A possible alternative to remote storage is the use of fireproof safes. These safes, however, have their own disadvantages—namely, they are expensive and give you no protection when they are standing open, as they typically are when you are using materials inside them.

Storage of Documentation

Physical security is required for documentation just as much as for magnetic files. Use the following precautions:

- Fireproof safes,
- Remote storage of copies,
- Restricting access to documentation,
- Cataloguing and review of documentation to ensure its adequacy, and
- Access control.

Back-Up Copies of Magnetic Files

As a precaution against physical hazards, back-up copies of magnetic files should be stored at a location entirely separate from the computer installation. These can be used in the event of destruction of files at the installation. Back-up storage involves the following:

- Cataloguing and regular updates of remotely stored files;
- Control over access to files (especially ensuring that no one person has access to all copies of essential files);
- Care in transportation to avoid damage; and
- Regular testing of back-up arrangements to ensure that they work.

Stand-By Facilities for Computer Processing

The provision of stand-by facilities for computer processing can act as a precaution against hazards ranging from a temporary cut in the power supply to complete destruction of an installation. If possible, you should have an agreement in writing and test the back-up before you need it. The back-up installation must have a similar configuration and support the same system software as your main installation.

For back-up arrangements to be effective, there must be enough available time at the stand-by installation to accommodate your data-processing needs. It may take a month or more to restore your home installation. Since computer systems are time-critical, any break in processing would probably prove disastrous if the back-up installation has insufficient time available. In practice, stand-by facilities can be difficult to use. Therefore, you must have set, documented procedures that are regularly checked and rehearsed.

It is impossible to obtain effective stand-by facilities for some systems. A large installation with many terminals and many operators, possibly at remote locations, could not be relocated at a stand-by installation. In these circumstances, it is necessary to look at alternative back-up procedures, such as spreading the workload over two back-up systems, so that one can take over if the other breaks down. An in-house generator for back-up power supply or an uninterruptible power supply may also be appropriate.

You should have a plan that clearly explains all actions so that there is a smooth transition from main facility processing to stand-by facility processing. The plan must include the following:

- personnel procedures,
- prioritization of systems,
- methods for testing prior to production,
- transference of programs and files from main facility or off-site facility,
- a means of communications from users to the system, and
- additional back-up.

Equipment Maintenance

Maintenance of equipment must be preventative as well as curative. As with any equipment, computers will break down if they are not regularly maintained. Worse, they may appear to be running but incorrectly process the data.

Maintenance contracts are invariably offered when you buy a system or machine. It is important to make sure that effective, fast maintenance service is available.

Operational Security

The procedures laid down for operating a computer installation should give maximum protection to both the installation and the information within the system.

Staffing and Division of Duties

To protect against sabotage, fraud, theft, and error, the various functions of employees should be segregated as far as the size of your installation allows. In particular, the user and the data-processing departments should be separate. If possible, the functions of computer operations should be separated from system development and planning.

In a large installation, it may be possible to separate completely the functions of data preparation, data control, systems development and programming, computer operation, librarian, and data-processing management. When shifts are involved, however, attention should be paid to staffing, as procedures may lapse at certain times, owing to lack of supervision. Access to the computer and data-preparation areas should be restricted to operations staff and the data-processing manager only. Systems and programming staff should be allowed access only under supervision.

In smaller installations, one individual may perform more than one function. In this case, take care in the allocation of duties, and introduce independent controls and checks wherever necessary. No transaction, file, or processing run should be under the sole control of any one person without review by others holding supervisory positions.

These controls should be supported by comprehensive audit trails.

Systems Development and Testing

All systems development should be properly sanctioned and should involve the active participation of the user departments to ensure that the finished system is both acceptable and appropriate.

Operational controls should be incorporated into the system's design at an early stage to save the prohibitive cost of subsequent changes. Procedures should be established to ensure that no new systems or programs are used operationally until their reliability has been proved by testing and they have been formally accepted. Developments should be properly documented, and the documentation should be kept up to date.

Documentation

Documentation of systems, programs, operator, and user procedures is important for the following reasons:

- It ensures continuity in the event of staff changes;
- It allows ease of system maintenance; and
- It maintains clear reference material for staff to consult whenever necessary.

Procedures should be established to ensure that documentation is updated whenever changes are made (for example, amendment records). The procedures should cater both to changes by employees and changes by a software supplier.

Access to documentation should be restricted when practical to those who need to use it (for example, operating instructions restricted to operations staff).

Implementation

When a new system is being implemented, consideration should be given to a suitable method of conversion from old to new to prevent disasters resulting from unexpected bugs in the installation of a the new system. Different methods of conversion include:

- parallel running,
- pilot running, and
- direct changeover stage by stage.

The conversion should be planned and controlled and will examine:

- staff requirements for any increased workload,
- degree of training necessary,
- controls over system and program testing,
- controls over file creations or conversion, and
- the production of manuals.

Only when the system is wholly acceptable should the implementation of the new system be initiated.

Access to Applications Software

The precautions that should be used to prevent unauthorized access to applications software will depend on the computer system in use and the degree of confidentiality necessary.

In large systems, siting the computer in a separate room, separation of duties, and library controls over files and documentation can be used to restrict access to authorized users.

In systems using terminals located away from the computer room or in small installations where no separate computer room exists, access to applications software can be controlled by the following means:

- predefinition to the system of actions or entries permissible via particular terminals;
- access-control methods, such as passwords, hardware locks, and badge readers (with particular attention to maintaining confidentiality of passwords); and
- access to files being restricted by software routines allowing access only to authorized users.

When confidential information is entered into the system, the equipment should be situation in a place where access and visibility is restricted.

Remote Terminals

The security hazards connected particularly with remote terminals are as follows:

- interruption or corruption of communication lines,
- remote terminals that can access data without authorization, and
- wire tapping or misrouting that results in unauthorized access.

For highly confidential data, it may be necessary to encrypt or code the transmission.

Particular care should be taken with systems using the public telephone network. It may be possible for a user on a time-sharing service to close down a line without logging off the system, so that someone could then dial in and gain access to the user's files without any log-on security procedures.

Control of Computer-Based Systems

As a general principle, the control of computer systems should be the responsibility of the user departments. User-operated controls should be designed to detect any computer misprocessing, whether deliberate or accidental, within an acceptable time period.

The accounting systems and internal controls should be designed to achieve the following control objectives:

- All computer input documents accurately reflect source documents (for instance, using source documents as input documents and showing evidence of checking);
- All computer input documents reach the computer input stage (for example, batch controls established by user departments, sequence checks on input documents,

input document stamped as evidence of input, and cut-off and effective-date controls);
- Only authorized documents are accepted for input (e.g., authorizations on all input documents, authorizations checked, and access to input forms restricted);
- All data are completely and accurately entered (e.g., batch value and hash-control totals checked by data preparation staff and user departments, edit and validation checks in input programs);
- Errors in processing are detected and corrected (e.g., results of processing checked to precalculated totals, programmed checks on control totals, proof listings of all transactions, full management and audit trail, and error and exception listings);
- All errors and rejections are acted upon (for example, errors recorded in a control book and computer system monitors and ages errors);
- All reports will reach the due recipients and will be appropriately dealt with (e.g., reports distribution lists, sequential numbering of reports,and evidence of action taken by users where appropriate);
- All changes to the master that are duly authorized by management are correctly processed (for instance, prenumbered forms, authorization evident on input forms, batch-control totals, record counts established, input and edit controls, one-for-one check of reported changes by originator, sequence checks for completeness, and adequate segregation of duties);
- No unauthorized changes to the master are made (e.g., access to forms restricted, sequence checks on input forms, and verification of standing data by periodic review); and
- Overall correct processing is confirmed by user reconciliations (e.g., such run-to-run controls as reconciling control totals from one processing cycle to the next, or system-to-system controls, like ensuring different applications are in agreement with each other).

Operating System Software and Utilities

Unrestricted access to the operating system may enable computer users to examine information that should be confidential and to use all the utilities offered by the system. Therefore, access to system software must be restricted.

In larger installations where systems-development staff are employed, these controls are particularly important. Monitors can sometimes be built into the system software to verify that only permitted programs from the system library are executed and that neither application programs nor the operating system itself is altered to permit unauthorized operation.

It is possible to manipulate the operating system and possibly also the monitor. While this is a remote possibility, regular review of the monitors and logs to check for such a situation will help detect any unauthorized activity.

In smaller installations, it is unlikely that employees will have the knowledge necessary to manipulate the operating system. The possibility should, however, be borne in mind when you decide who has access to the computer.

Program Changes

Control procedures should ensure that all program changes are properly authorized and that documentation is kept up to date. Proposed changes should be channeled through a routine to ensure that alterations will

- genuinely improve the system,
- meet a definite need,
- be economically viable,
- not interfere with controls or other user requirements,
- be properly tested before use in live operations, and
- be adequately documented.

Insurance

Many security hazards (e.g., fire, flood, theft) can be covered by insurance. Assessing the value of such items as loss of data can be difficult, however. In all cases, suitable coverage should be obtained. Shopping around with different insurance companies to determine which ones offer the most comprehensive terms and competitive premiums is a worthwhile exercise.

Glossary

Applications Controls—The checks and balances, tests of reasonableness, and limits embedded in computer programs to ensure the control of inputs, processing, and output.

Assembly Listing—A copy of the currently running program, listed by the computer line-by-line, usually written in a programming language.

Computer Code—Instructions to the computer, usually written in a programming language.

Concentration—The increased storage efficiency of electronic and magnetic media that allows vast amounts of data to be stored in relatively small spaces.

Documentation—The process of putting in writing all of the procedures for a given task or function in such detail that someone unfamiliar with the task could perform it from the written record alone.

Dumping—Periodic printing out of data to hard (paper) output.

EDP Auditing—The process of checking and verifying that computer programs are performing their prescribed tasks correctly and that they are not performing illicit or other non-valid tasks.

EDP Controls—Procedures and principles applied, usually by management, to preclude opportunity for fraud and embezzlement in computer-processed functions.

Electronic Data Processing (EDP)—Operating accounting and other data systems by computers rather than by hand.

Emergency Power Systems—Back-up electrical power usually provided by diesel or gasoline generators that turns on automatically in a power failure.

End-user Computing—A description of the environment in which persons other than the information-systems employees, usually most of the top executives of the hotel, use computers to manipulate data and support decision making.

File Protection—A general and administrative computer control focusing on the security, back-up, and, if necessary, reconstruction of the electronic files containing programs or data.

Flow Chart—A schematic diagram depicting the flow of information and documents between components or persons in a particular function; an important first step in designing programs.

General and Administrative Controls—The procedures and principles that can be applied by the hotel's management to prevent frauds and other losses from occurring.

Hacking—Unauthorized entry to any computer network.

Interface—A mechanical or electronic process whereby one system is connected to or able to communicate with another.

Library Function—The task involving the custody and protection of data files and program copies.

Magnetic Disks or Tapes—Electronic storage media for data that operate by magnetic recording.

Patch Program—An illicit mini-program placed within the main computer program whose purpose is to accomplish fraudulent tasks.

Periodic Saving—A file-protection procedure that involves periodically copying data from a fragile medium, like the computer's memory, to a more stable medium, like magnetic disks.

Peripheral Equipment—Data-processing equipment other than the computer itself; examples are printers and storage media like hard-disk drives.

Programmer—A person who writes computer programs that instruct the computer in how to operate.

Programming Language—a code system that is used to write instruction for a computer.

Property Management System (PMS)—A term describing a broad-purpose hotel-computing system that incorporates front-office accounting with communications and management of the housekeeping, telephone, and food and beverage departments.

Proprietary Programs—Computer programs (software applications) that have been created by a software company and purchased or leased by the hotel.

Record Reconstruction—Re-creating or re-building data files that are lost or destroyed.

Redundancy—A file-protection procedure that involves creating automatic back-up files to replace data files if they should become lost or destroyed.

Software—The aggregated instructions or programs that tell the computer what to do for each task or function.

Systems Analyst—A person who designs computer applications to fit the needs of the various functions (engages in systems planning).

Systems Planning—The process of designing computer applications to fit the needs of the various functions.

Uninterruptable Power Supply (UPS)—A power source for EDP equipment, usually supplied by continuously charged battery packs, that automatically cuts in when the regular power fails or fluctuates.

Vandalism—The willful destruction of property.

Selected References

AICPA Computer Services Executive Committee, *The Auditor's Study and Evaluation of Internal Control in EDP Systems* (New York, AICPA, 1977).

AICPA Computer Services Executive Committee, *Computer Services Guidelines* (New York, AICPA, 1977).

John G. Baab, Stephen M. Paroby, and William H. Marquard, "A Three-Dimensional Look at Computer Fraud," *Financial Executive*, October 1984, pp. 21-28.

The Canadian Institute of Chartered Accountants, *Computer Control Guidelines* (Toronto, Ontario: CICA, 1973).

The Canadian Institute of Chartered Accountants, *Computer Audit Guidelines* (Toronto, Ontario: CICA, 1975).

A. Neal Geller, "Tracking the Critical Success Factors for Hotel Companies," *The Cornell Hotel and Restaurant Administration Quarterly,* 25, No.4 (February 1985), pp. 76-81.

A. Neal Geller, "The Current State of Hotel Information Systems," *The Cornell Hotel and Restaurant Administration Quarterly,* 26, No. 1 (May 1985), pp. 14-17.

A. Neal Geller, "How to Improve Your Information System," *The Cornell Hotel and Restaurant Administration Quarterly,* 26, No. 2 (August 1985), pp. 19-27.

Kevin Wayne Kelley, "Applying Technology to Internal Controls in Hotels," (Ithaca, NY: Cornell University Monograph, 1985).

Joseph A. Marko, "A Practical Guide to Automated Property Management Systems for the Lodging Industry," (Ithaca, NY: Cornell University Monograph, 1980).

Joseph A. Marko and Richard G. Moore, "How to Select a Computer System," *The Cornell Hotel and Restaurant Administration Quarterly,* 21, No. 1 (May 1980), pp. 60-71); and 21, No. 2 (August 1980), pp. 8-18.

Michael A. Murphy and Xebia Ley Parker, *Handbook of EDP Auditing (2nd Edition)* (Boston: Warren, Gorham & Lamont, 1989).

R. Ryan Nelson, *End-User Computing: Concepts, Issues and Applications* (New York: John Wiley & Sons, 1989).

Donn B. Parker, *Crime by Computer* (New York: Charles Scribner's Sons, 1976).

John Patterson and Roy Alvarez, "Computer Systems for Food-Service Operations," *The Cornell Hotel and Restaurant Administration Quarterly,* 26, No. 1 (May 1985), pp. 132-141.

W. Thomas Porter and William E. Perry, *EDP Controls and Auditing (5th Edition)* (Boston: Kent Publishing, 1987).

Chapter 10

An Overview of Internal Control

Objectives

After completing this chapter, you should understand:
1. **The role of external auditors.**
2. **Management's responsibilities for good internal control.**
3. **Application of the book's internal-control principles to other areas or future developments.**

Role of External Auditors

At the beginning of this book, I recommended frequent external audits as one of the general principles of internal control. I pointed out the importance of an outside, objective look at the hotel's operations, accounting practices, and books. In this chapter, I will elaborate on the external audit and try to explain a possible paradox.

When external auditors are called in to audit a firm, they examine the books and accounts that represent the assets, liabilities, equities, revenues, expenses, gains, and losses of the firm. The output of those auditing efforts is an opinion expressed by the audit firm as to how well the books, accounts, and statements that were examined present the financial condition and results of operations of the firm, as they were found by the auditors. The terminology found in the auditor's opinion letter, if no additional disclaimers (e.g., "except for"; "subject to") are present, is that the financial statements "present fairly" the financial position. Such an unqualified opinion is known familiarly as a "clean opinion."

People have misconceptions about the audit process that should be addressed. First, there is no such thing as a certified statement. That terminology is slang that has evolved over time. There are "certified public accountants" (CPAs), the term for accountants who are duly licensed by their states to practice their profession publicly. The only adjective that should be applied to financial statements is "audited." Audited financial statements are the firm's own financial statements, produced by its management, subjected to the audit process above, upon which the outside auditor has expressed an opinion.

The second misconception involves the objectives of the audit process. Too often, the public and even the management of the firm being audited believe that the main objective of the audit process is to certify that "all is well"—whatever that means. Such is not the case! In fact, the main objective of the auditing process is for the external auditor to prepare himself or herself to express an opinion. The testing and checking performed in the audit process are for the auditors to satisfy themselves that the financial conditions reported in the statements are a good representation of (present fairly) the actual conditions observed by the auditor, and that they are free of material misstatement. The typical language of opinion letters demonstrates those facts: "We believe that our audits provide a reasonable basis for our opinion."[1] The audit firm itself decides, under broad professional guidelines,[2] what auditing should be done and how much and how

---

[1] From the opinion letter by Arthur Andersen & Co. regarding the annual report of Hilton Hotels Corporation. See Appendix 10.1.

[2] A discussion of the accounting profession's auditing rules are beyond the scope of this book. They are referred to as generally accepted auditing standards. See: *Statements of Auditing Standards* (American Institute of Certified Public Accountants, 1211 Avenue of the Americas, New York, NY 10036).

deeply items should be checked. That approach is probably all right. After all, the audit firm is expressing an opinion and is liable if that opinion is wrong. The process of deciding how much and what type of auditing is deemed necessary in the circumstances is called "setting the scope" of the audit, a process that has a great deal of importance to internal control.

When the external auditor sets the scope of the audit, one of the first tasks that is performed is to evaluate the internal controls of the firm being audited. The relative strength or weakness of the client's internal controls will have great impact of the breadth and depth of the audit process. If the client has extensive, strong internal controls, then random and "spot" checking may be enough. The internal controls themselves should be ensuring the accuracy and reliability of the accounting data. If the client's controls are weak, the auditors will have to do substantial testing and checking. Transactions must be traced and possibly even re-created. Missing source documents, for example, are often symptoms of weak internal controls. If the internal controls are really poor or non-existent, the auditor may not be able to complete a valid audit. In that case, a "disclaimer of opinion" letter is written, stating that the auditor could not express an opinion due to the audit's limited scope.

One of the first tasks performed by audit firms when assessing the relative strengths and weaknesses of a client's internal controls is to administer an "internal-control questionnaire." That questionnaire is designed for use by the auditors as an input to the process of evaluating a hotel's internal control. The questionnaire is quite detailed and contains many items that would not be useful to management. I believe, however, that readers can learn a lot from examining such a questionnaire. Appendix A shows a sample internal-control questionnaire. By looking it over, hotel managers can learn how auditors evaluate their operation's controls and see the relative importance of the various control elements.

For hotel managers, the point is to understand the objectives of the external-audit process, and to be able to put it into perspective. External audits are essential to the goal of having an operation with good internal control. With the inside view of the process, however, it should be apparent why audits do not guarantee that a hotel is fraud-proof. The auditor is not looking for fraud—he or she is looking for information upon which to base his or her opinion. In the process, however, fraud may be uncovered. More important, since the auditor evaluates the hotel's internal control, managers can use that process to improve the operation further. Managers should discuss internal control with the outside auditors. They should ask about the auditor's evaluation of the hotel's internal control. Managers should insist that the auditors clearly spell out any and all weaknesses that they found, so that the hotel can take steps to correct and improve those weaknesses. In the future, that should mean a reduced scope and lower audit fees!

Management's Responsibilities

For hotels to have truly successful internal controls, there must be a strong commitment and involvement of management—from the top to the bottom. The key elements of management responsibility for internal control are:

- The buck stops at the top;
- Management must be completely committed;
- Management must foster an appropriate attitude;
- Resources must be adequate;
- Management must be involved; and
- Employees must be trained.

The "buck stops at the top" implies that **final responsibility** for problems rests with the chief executive. In other words, the person at the top cannot rely on excuses or explanations for what went wrong, but rather must face and accept the consequences. In hotels, that person is the general manager. In fact, this book was built on the assumption that the general manager is honest and the controls are designed from that top person down.

With internal control, however, more than top-down design is necessary. Top management must embrace and endorse the control principles, and must publicly espouse their importance to the hotel. Furthermore, management must be an active participant in the controls, in the ways that have been demonstrated in detail throughout the book.

Complete management commitment means that top managers not only wish good controls throughout the hotel, but work hard to ensure their implementation and success. Honesty, sound internal controls, adherence to rules, and respect for the importance of the audit trails—all must become ingrained in the hotel's culture. Those results can be achieved only with a healthy attitude, displayed continually in a manner that makes it clear to all employees that top management is serious about internal control.

Top management must also be willing to **commit resources** continuously to good internal control. While that usually means financial resources, particularly for adequate payroll for proper division of duties, it can also mean other resources. In smaller hotels or when budgets are very tight, managers can make up for inadequate financial resources by becoming more personally involved in the control processes.

Top-management involvement includes several key internal-control roles for operations of all sizes—such as checking the documentation and signing the checks for accounts payable, paychecks, petty cash, and other appropriate activities. In smaller operations, however, management's role can increase dramatically. All of the internal-control principles must be observed if proper internal control is to be ensured. In smaller operations there are usually not enough resources to implement all of the controls—particularly division of duties that requires more employees than a small hotel can afford. The solution is for top management to assume more of the day-to-day accounting or other clerical tasks. In that way, the duties remain separate, the controls remain intact, and the hotel does not overspend its budget simply for the sake of controls. The main management objections to such a plan—that the tasks are too menial, or that top managers do not have time for them—are usually less critical in small operations where managers are more "hands-on" anyway.

Finally, management must bear the responsibility for **on-going training** of employees. Good training programs are essential for well-run hotel operations. They are equally important for good internal control—particularly in today's environment of increasing automation and continuously changing technology. The more automated hotel operations become, the more essential effective training becomes. Not only is on-going training necessary to ensure that the hotel employees master and stay on top of the technological changes, but also to ensure that they continue to provide good service and hospitality in spite of the technology. The nature of automation in front-desk operations or food and beverage operations is such that it is easy for employees to focus on their computer terminals and entry tasks, and to forget the warm human contact with the guests, which still is the most essential ingredient for good hospitality! That problem can only be overcome by effective and continual training.

Areas of Internal Control Not Covered

Several areas of hotel operations were not specifically covered in the book. Examples are: mini-bar control, automated room-key control, automated inventory-management and purchasing systems, and automated housekeeping-control systems. As time and technology march forward, even more automated systems will be developed. In each of those areas or systems what is required for good internal control is the application of the same sound principles advocated throughout the book. The principles outlined here should be used as a blueprint. All of the plans and guides for successful internal control are in it. As new systems evolve and new applications are developed, the same tried and true internal-control principles need to be applied. The context or the tools may change, but the concepts are the same. You now have the understanding of the necessary tools to design and implement good programs of internal control.

I want to reiterate that although the book used hotels as the primary model, such segments as free-standing restaurants or clubs also can follow these principles. The internal controls designed for hotel food-service outlets are similar to those needed in free-standing restaurants. In fact, all of the chapters of the book, with the possible exception of the discussion of rooms revenue, are relevant and directly applicable to restaurateurs.

For club operators, the entire book is relevant. Some specific areas of club management (e.g., membership and dues management, assessments, golf-course operations) are not covered in the book. The application of the internal-control principles espoused throughout the book will work well in those areas, however.

Finally, casino operations and casino control were not discussed in the book. The internal control of gaming operations is similar in nature to all other internal control. Casinos are quite complex, however, and adequate internal-control design for them is beyond the scope of this book.

Glossary

Audited Financial Statements—A process whereby a company has its books and financial statements examined by an independent accounting firm that expresses an opinion as to how well those statements represent the financial condition it found in its examination.

Auditor's Opinion Letter—A letter written by the auditor of financial statements, expressing an opinion as to how well those statements present the financial condition found in the audit.

Disclaimer—A letter written by the auditor of financial statements stating that he or she cannot express an opinion on those statements, usually because of limited scope.

Scope of the Audit—A blueprint or description of the level of testing and checking that an auditor plans to perform in an audit; related to, among other factors, the relative strength or weakness of the client's internal controls.

Unqualified Opinion—A "clean" opinion; one expressed without any qualifications or exceptions by an auditor as to how well the financial statements present the financial condition found in the course of an audit.

Appendix 10.1

Auditor's Opinion Letter

To the Board of Directors and Stockholders of Hilton Hotels Corporation:

We have audited the accompanying consolidated balance sheets of Hilton Hotels Corporation (a Delaware corporation) and subsidiaries as of December 31, 1989 and 1988, and the related consolidated statements of income, stockholder's equity, and cash flows for each of the three years in the period ended December 31, 1989. These financial statements are the responsibility of the Company's management. Our responsibility is to express an opinion on these financial statements based on our audits.

We conducted our audits in accordance with generally accepted auditing standards. Those standards require that we plan and perform an audit to obtain reasonable assurance about whether the financial statements are free of material misstatement. An audit includes examining, on a test basis, evidence supporting the amounts and disclosures in the financial statements. An audit also includes assessing the accounting principles used and significant estimates made by management, as well as evaluating the overall financial statement presentation. We believe that our audits provide a reasonable basis for our opinion.

In our opinion, the financial statements referred to above present fairly, in all material respects, the financial position of Hilton Hotels Corporation and subsidiaries as of December 31, 1989 and 1988, and the results of their operations and their cash flows for each of the three years in the period ended December 31, 1989, in conformity with generally accepted accounting principles.

ARTHUR ANDERSEN & Co.
Los Angeles, California
February 2, 1990

Selected References

Alvin A. Arens and James K. Loebbecke, *Auditing: An Integrated Approach (4th Edition)* (Englewood Cliffs, NJ: Prentice-Hall, 1988).

Alon Ben-Gurion, "Internal Control for the Hospitality Industry" (Ithaca, NY: Cornell University Monograph, 1981).

A. Neal Geller and Raymond S. Schmidgall, "The Hotel Controller: More than a Bookkeeper," *The Cornell Hotel and Restaurant Administration Quarterly,* 25, No. 2 (August 1984), pp. 16-22.

Henry R. Jaenicke, *Evaluating Internal Control* (New York: John Wiley & Sons, 1980).

W. Thomas Porter, Jr., and John C. Burton, *Auditing: A Conceptual Approach* (Belmont, CA: Wadsworth, 1971).

Statements of Auditing Standards (New York: American Institute of Certified Public Accountants).

J.J. Willingham and D.R. Carmichael, *Auditing Controls and Methods* (New York, McGraw-Hill, 1971).

Appendix A

Internal-Control Questionnaire

by Pannell Kerr Forster

Cash

1. General
    A. Is control of all accounting records other than cash receipts and disbursements vested in persons other than the cashier?
    B. Are all bank accounts and signers authorized by the Board?
    C. Are all bank accounts in the client's name recorded in control accounts in the general ledger or subsidiary ledger?
    D. Are transfers from one bank account to another under accounting control (i.e., are charges and credits passed through a ledger account)?
    E. Are persons who hand cash bonded? What is the amount of the bond?

2. Cash on Hand
    A. Are cash funds maintained on an imprest basis?
    B. Is primary responsibility for each fund vested in only one person?
    C. Are cash funds limited to reasonable amounts for the needs of the business?
    D. Are individual petty-cash expenditures limited to a maximum amount?
    E. Are petty-cash tickets prepared in such a manner as to make alteration difficult?
    F. Are petty-cash tickets signed by the person who received the cash?
    G. Are supporting vouchers attached to petty-cash tickets?
    H. Are advances to employees made only for regular business purposes?
    I. Are petty-cash reimbursement checks made payable to the custodian?
    J. Are petty-cash slips presented to the check signer for inspection when the reimbursement checks are presented?
    K. Are petty-cash slips supporting the disbursements impressed with a "paid" stamp or perforated by, or under the direct supervision of, the check signer to prevent their irregular use in support of fictitious or duplicate payments?
    L. When checks are cashed to accommodate employees:
        i. Are such checks deposited or otherwise sent to the bank for prompt payment?
        ii. Has the bank been instructed not to cash checks payable to the company?
    M. Are post-office postage-meter receipts checked to meter readings and cash disbursement by the controller or other responsible person?

3. House Banks
    A. Is there a procedure to verify that departmental cashiers deposited their daily receipts in the safe? Describe.

B. Is withdrawal of envelopes from the safe witnessed?
C. Are checks stamped on the back to show exchange and on account?
D. Are receipts on hand for all house accounts?
E. Are receipts given for interchange of funds between general and other cashiers?
F. Are front-office petty-cash disbursements approved?
G. Is there a daily bank-count report from each cashier?
H. Is there adequate control of house banks when they are not in use?
I. Are duplicate safe-deposit keys, if any, under proper controls? Describe.
J. Who has the combination to the safe?
K. Is there a separate sheet or book for each cashier at the front office?
L. Who has authority to cash checks?
M. Is the number of times the front-office machine is cleared recorded on the "D" card?
N. Who is accounting verifies numerical control?

4. Bank Reconciliations
   A. Are bank accounts reconciled by a person who does not sign checks or handle or record cash?
      i. General Accounts
      ii. Payroll Accounts
      iii. Any Other Accounts
   B. Is a separate exchange account maintained?
   C. Are bank accounts reconciled regularly?
   D. Are bank statements and paid checks delivered in unopened envelopes directly to the employee preparing the reconciliations?
   E. Do the company's reconciliation procedures provide for all steps considered essential to an effective reconciliation, particularly:
      i. Comparisons of checks with cash disbursements?
      ii. Examination of endorsements?
      iii. Comparison with general-ledger balances?
   F. Does an official who is not responsible for the receipt of cash disbursement review all reconciliations and question unusual reconciling items? Who?

5. Cash Receipts
   A. Is mail opened and distributed by a person or department other than cashier or accounting? Who?
   B. Is a list of receipts prepared by the mail opener?
   C. If so, is such a list effectively used as a check against the deposit?
   D. Are cash receipts forwarded directly to the cashier before being handled by:
      i. Accounts-receivable clerk?
      ii. Credit manager?
      iii. Anyone having responsibility for bookkeeping or billing functions?
   E. Is a restrictive endorsement placed in incoming checks as soon as they are received?
   F. Are cash-remittance advices, letters, or envelopes that accompany receipts separated and given directly to the accounting department?
   G. Are cash receipts deposited intact daily?
   H. Is effective control provided over cash sales and other "over the counter" currency receipts through the use of cash registers, pre-numbered sales slips, receipts, and

the like?

I. Is effective control provided over unapplied remittances pending investigation?

J. Is a duplicate deposit ticket prepared by the cashier and receipted by the bank?

K. Is such a deposit ticket returned by the bank directly to a person other than the cashier and compared with the cash-receipts record? Who?

L. Are returned checks charged back on the bank statements?

6. Cash Disbursements

    A. Are the following approvals by properly authorized persons required before vouchers are submitted for payment:

        i. Approval of prices?

        ii. Approval of receipt of goods?

        iii. Approvals of footings, extensions, and discounts?

        iv. Approval of account distributions?

        v. Final approval of payment?

    B. Does the procedure require that at least one check signature and final approval for payment be made by different individuals?

    C. Does at least one person signing the check (other than persons responsible for preparing the check) scrutinize supporting data at the time of signing?

    D. Are signed checks delivered directly to the mail room without their being handled by persons who requested, prepared, or recorded them?

    E. Is the responsibility fixed for seeing that all cash discounts are taken?

    F. Are vouchers and supporting papers effectively cancelled upon payment?

    G. Is there a prohibition on the signing of checks, in advance of their being completely filled out?

    H. Are facsimile signatures used only on checks covered by blanket approval? Particularly:

        i. Is their use limited to payrolls or general disbursements of relatively small amounts?

        ii. Are such facsimile plates or stamps properly safeguarded?

        iii. Is there a log book kept of the meter readings?

        iv. Is the number of checks issued checked against the increase in the meter reading?

        v. Does an independent party verify the logbook reading to the check-writer meter?

    I. Are spoiled and voided checks properly accounted for?

    J. Is the supply of unused checks adequately safeguarded?

Payroll

1. Personnel Records

    A. Are properly approved authorizations maintained on file for:

        i. Personnel changes, increases, and the like?

        ii. Salary and wage rates or union classifications?

        iii. Payroll deductions?

    B. If so, are these files maintained independently or are they inaccessible to persons who:

        i. Prepare payrolls?

        ii. Approve payrolls?

iii. Distribute payrolls?
C. Do procedures provide that all authorizations, particularly notices of separations from employment, be transmitted promptly to the payroll department?
D. Do personnel records contain the employees' signatures?

2. Time Records
   A. Are the time records and other data from which the payrolls are prepared maintained independently of the employees who prepare the payrolls?
   B. Are overtime hours and other special benefits approved by employees who supervise the activities but who do not:
      i. Prepare payroll?
      ii. Distribute payroll?
   C. Do timekeepers cover all shifts in all departments?

3. Preparation and Checking of Payroll
   A. Are the persons who prepare the payroll independent of the hiring and firing functions?
   B. Are those persons excluded from the distribution of payroll?
   C. Are names added to the payroll only upon written authorization from responsible persons outside the payroll department?
   D. Are individual wage- or salary-rate changes made only upon written authorization from responsible persons outside the payroll department?
   E. Is the payroll checked?
   F. Is the payroll approved by a responsible employee or officer?
   G. Is the accounting distribution of the payroll charge examined by someone not in the payroll department?
   H. Are banquet tips paid to employees recorded as payroll?

4. Payment
   A. Is the payroll made by employees:
      i. Who take no part in and do not control the preparation of the payroll?
      ii. Who are not responsible for hiring and firing employees?
      iii. Who do not approve time reports?
   B. Are persons distributing payroll rotated from time to time? How often?
   C. Is the payroll bank account reconciled regularly by an employee who has no connection with the:
      i. Preparation of the payroll?
      ii. Distribution of paychecks?
   D. Are endorsements compared, at least on a test basis, with signatures on file?
   E. Are unclaimed wages returned to the cashier or a department other than the payroll department?
   F. Is a report of unclaimed wages made direct to the accounting department by the employee who made the payroll?
   G. Are payments of unclaimed wages at a later date made only upon:
      i. Presentation of appropriate evidence of employment?
      ii. Approval by an officer or employee who is not responsible for the preparation of the payroll or for reporting time?
   H. Are W-2 forms accounted for and placed in the mail by persons who take no part in:

    i. Approving payroll?
    ii. Preparing payroll?
    iii. Distributing payroll?
  L. Are W-2 forms that are returned by postal authorities forwarded for investigation directly to persons who took no part in:
    i. Approving payroll?
    ii. Preparing payroll?
    iii. Distributing payroll?
  J. Is vacation and sick pay verified by persons other than the department head? Describe.
  K. If payroll is prepared by computer, are batch totals used to verify input? Describe.

Inventories

1. Recording and Handling
  A. Are perpetual inventories maintained for:
    i. Liquor?
    ii. Supplies?
    iii. Linen, china, glass, and silver?
  B. Are they kept as to both quantity and value?
  C. If so, are they balanced to general-ledger controls monthly?
  D. Are inventories taken monthly? By whom?
  E. Does the accounting department participate in taking the inventory?
  F. Are inventories safeguarded against loss by theft? How?
  G. Are inventories adequately insured? How much?
  H. Is merchandise issued only against requisitions?
  I. Are cost ratios to sales reasonable compared to other hotels?
  J. Is food checked or weighed as received and listed on receiving reports?
  K. Is each employee required to obtain a pass to remove packages from the premises?
  L. Is inventory reviewed for slow-moving items?

Cash Disbursements and Accounts Payable

1. Purchasing
  A. Are formal written purchase orders required for all purchases (in excess of a low floor amount)?
  B. Does the accounting department compare the invoice quantities, prices, and terms with the purchase order?
  C. Are competitive quotations obtained for vendors?
  D. Are market lists used?
  E. Is there a purchasing agent? Who?

2. Receiving
  A. Are written receiving reports prepared by the receiving department for all materials received?
  B. Does a copy of the receiving report go directly to the accounting department?
  C. Does the accounting department match the receiving report to the invoice?
  D. Do procedures ensure filing of claims against vendors for shortages of damaged materials?

3. Paying
   A. Is the person or department finally approving vouchers for payment functioning independently of:
      i. The purchasing department?
      ii. Other persons requesting the specific expenditure?
      iii. The cashier or persons signing the check?
   B. Are invoices not involving materials or supplies (such as advertising, fees, rentals, and utility bills) approved by department heads prior to payment?
   C. Are such invoices reviewed for reasonableness and necessity and approved by a responsible employee outside of the originating department?
   D. Does the company have a satisfactory procedure for approving reimbursements to employees for travel and other expenses?
   E. Is an employee designated to maintain a record of payments of recurring charges (e.g., rentals, utility bills) and approve such charges to prevent duplicate payments, skipped payments, and the like?
   F. Is indication of payment effectively noted on the invoice?

4. Recording
   A. Is the account to be charged indicated on the purchase authorization by the person requesting the purchase?
   B. Is the distribution of charges reviewed in the accounting department by a person competent to pass judgment on the propriety of the distribution?
   C. Does the accounting department check extensions and footings on invoices?
   D. Is an accounts-payable trial balance taken and balanced to the general-ledger control at least monthly?
   E. Are monthly statements from vendors regularly reconciled to open vouchers or accounts-payable ledgers?
   F. Is there an adequate record of open purchase orders and commitments?

Cash Receipts and Revenue

1. Recording
   A. Is there a separation of duties between accounts-receivable clerks and cashiers?
   B. Are accounts-receivable control accounts balanced with detail monthly? By whom?
   C. Are monthly statements mailed on all accounts? By whom?
   D. Are bad-debt write-offs approved by management? By whom
   E. Are allowances approved by management? By whom
   F. Are accounts-receivable balances aged periodically and reviewed by an official who:
      i. Has no access to company checks and currency?
      ii. Takes no part in approving credits?
      iii. By whom?
   A. Is the housekeeper's report used in the accounting office to verify room sales?
   B. Is a check made to verify approved room rates against rates actually charged?
   C. Is total room revenue balanced to a room-count sheet? By whom?
   D. By whom is the night-audit tape checked to guest bills? How frequently?
   E. Who verifies rates per count sheet to approved rates? How frequently?
   F. Who approves rates other than established rates?

G. Are allowance vouchers examined and approved daily?

H. Are transfers to and from city ledger reviewed daily for management's approval?

I. Are guest accounts transferred to city ledger signed by the guest and approved?

J. If the property has no credit manager, are questionable accounts given three-day bills by the controller?

K. Are advance payments controlled?

L. Are reservation deposits controlled?

M. Are earnings for permanents pro-rated and controlled?

N. Are complimentary rooms controlled?

3. Food and Beverage Control

A. Is a numerical control of food and beverage checks maintained for all locations? By whom?

B. Is total food and beverage revenue balanced with register readings or other independent accumulation of charges? By whom?

C. Are the supply and issuance of guest checks controlled?

D. Are the pricing and addition of guest checks verified?

E. Is there a check of possible alterations of totals?

F. Are employee's meals controlled?

G. Is a check made for every meal? Particularly:

  i. For all employees?

  ii. For private parties?

H. Are all extras (e.g., flowers) recorded on banquet checks?

I. Is there a signed contract for every banquet?

J. Is the banquet contract copy verified with the check for each function?

K. Is there a food and beverage controller?

L. Are covers and corkage charges controlled?

M. Are banquet tip disbursements reconciled to the sales journal?

N. Are bottle sales segregated from drink sales?

O. Are cashiers' overages and shortages controlled?

P. Are cashiers required to make up shortages and deposit overages?

Q. Do guests sign restaurant and room-service checks?

R. Do checkers and cashiers come under the controller's supervision?

S. Does the property have service supervisors checked by an outside agency?

4. Telephone

A. Is the telephone bill for tolls checked to revenue records?

B. Is there control of house calls? Describe: _____

C. Is a schedule or work paper maintained for toll and pay-station commissions?

D. Who checks traffic sheets or telex slips to daily earnings?

5. Stores and Concessions

A. Are percentage-rent computations made by the controller's office?

B. Are store sales audited were applicable?

C. Are store sales tested to the trend of hotel income?

D. Are rents per leases checked to revenue periodically? How often?

E. Are monthly sales statements in support of percentage rentals received from lessees?

F. Does the accounting department receive copies of all leases and revisions thereof?

Glossary

Accounting Controls—Procedures that are concerned with safeguarding assets and ensuring the accuracy and reliability of financial records *(Chapter One)*.

Accounting Documents—Forms that are numbered serially, have multiple parts or copies, whose distribution is controlled by the accounting department, and are accounted for periodically by serial number *(Chapter One)*.

Accounts Payable—Monies owed by the hotel to its suppliers and vendors for goods and services received *(Chapter Four)*.

Accounts Receivable—A claim or debt due to the hotel from a guest or customer for services rendered *(Chapter Two)*.

Accounts Receivable—Control—The balance sheet (general ledger) account representing the total accounts receivable due to the hotel; the sum of all the individual (subsidiary) accounts receivable *(Chapter Three)*.

Accounts Receivable—Subsidiary—The individual guest accounts representing the monies each individual owes the hotel; the sum of the subsidiary accounts receivable equals the control account *(Chapter Three)*.

Accounts-Payable Clerk—An accounting department employee whose major responsibilities include compiling and checking the purchasing and receiving documentation, posting the accounts payable and appropriate inventory or expense accounts, and drawing the checks for payment of the accounts payable *(Chapter Four)*.

Accuracy versus Independence Trade-Off—The principle that revenue estimates are more accurate when they are made most directly from transactions, but the independence of those estimates declines at the same time; the more independent the less accurate and vice versa *(Chapter Seven)*.

Administrative Controls—Procedures that are concerned with ensuring operational efficiency and adhering to management's policies *(Chapter One)*.

Advance Deposits—Payments made by guests to the hotel in advance of their stay to hold specific space; advance deposits are recorded as a liability until they are earned by having the guest actually use the hotel's services *(Chapter Six)*.

Aged Accounts Receivable—A listing of the accounts receivable—control account, stratified by age, usually from current to over 120 days *(Chapter Three)*.

Allowance Voucher—A pre-numbered accounting document used to post and record allowances; allowance vouchers have both permission and audit-trail roles *(Chapter Six)*.

Allowance—A credit, rebate, or discount given to a guest that lowers the rate, price, or revenue to the hotel; allowances are often issued in response to a guest complaint *(Chapter Six)*.

Applications Controls—The checks and balances, tests of reasonableness, and limits imbedded in computer programs to ensure the control of inputs, processing, and output *(Chapter Nine)*.

Assembly Listing—A copy of the currently running program, listed by the computer line-by-line, usually written in a programming language *(Chapter Nine)*.

Audit Trail—The path or road (consisting of entries and accounting documents) of history left by accounting transactions, which can be followed, mapped, recreated, or traced *(Chapter One)*.

Audited Financial Statements—A process whereby a company has its books and financial statements examined by an independent accounting firm that expresses an opinion as to how well those statements represent the financial condition it found in its examination *(Chapter Ten)*.

Auditor's Opinion Letter—A letter written by the auditor of financial statements, expressing an opinion as to how well those statements present the financial condition found in the audit *(Chapter Ten)*.

Automated Front-Office System—The generic term for computerized guest-accounting or front-office systems; also used to describe the broader property-management systems *(Chapter Six)*.

Bad Checks—Customers' checks that the hotel has accepted and deposited in the bank but that have been returned by the bank as uncollectible, usually because of insufficient funds *(Chapter Three)*.

Bad Debts—Past-due accounts receivable that have become old (over 90 or 120 days), and are probably uncollectible *(Chapter Three)*.

Billing—The portion of the accounts-receivable process concerned with typing or producing statements from the subsidiary accounts receivable, and mailing those statements to the customers *(Chapter Three)*.

Blind Receiving—A description of the style of receiving of goods whereby the receiving clerk does not see a copy of the purchase order in advance *(Chapter Four)*.

Blind Turn-In—The process of having cashiers count and list their total cash drawer, subtract the original bank, and turn in the balance—all without having access to the readings of their shift totals *(Chapter Two)*.

Bona fide—Sincere or genuine; made in good faith *(Chapter Two)*.

Book (Theoretical) Inventory—The amounts, in dollars and units, of the goods that should be in inventory, based on the postings of the perpetual-inventory records; often compared with actually counted or physical inventory *(Chapter Four)*.

Bucket (bin, tub, or tray)—The guests' accounts receivable, or total charges incurred by guests currently in the house, as represented by their folios. Also used to describe the physical files containing the guests folios *(Chapter Three)*.

Cash Management—A systematic and scientific approach to the control of inflow, outflow, borrowing, and investment of cash and other short-term assets so as to minimize cost and maximize return *(Chapter One)*.

Check-In—The process of registering a guest and issuing him or her a room *(Chapter Six)*.

Check-Out—The process of settling the bill (folio) with the guest *(Chapter Six)*.

Checking—A comparison of the recorded cash receipts and charges of food and beverage sales against a separately created record of food and beverages actually served *(Chapter Seven)*.

Chef Counts—A count by the chef of items produced, served, and left over; usually performed for main entrée and appetizer items *(Chapter Seven)*.

City Ledger—Hotel jargon for the subsidiary accounts receivable of guests who have settled their folios by transferring them to prior-approved direct billing. It is probable that the historical origin of "city ledger" evolved from use of the hotel's facilities by local customers (i.e., those from the "city") *(Chapter Three)*.

Client's Representative—An official of a group holding a banquet or other function at the hotel who has the legal permission of the group to authorize the final bill, including any additional charges *(Chapter Eight)*.

Collection—The process of attempting to receive payment from customers on past-due accounts or bad checks *(Chapter Three)*.

Collection Agency—An outside firm that specializes in collecting bad debts or bad checks for the hotel for a fee usually based on a percentage of the amount collected *(Chapter Three)*.

Competitive Bids—The solicitations used in a procedure for purchasing in which suppliers formally reply to specified requests for goods; usually responses from two, three, or more suppliers are required to make the bids competitive *(Chapter Four)*.

Complimentary Room—A guest stay where the price for a room-night is zero, usually for reasons such as public relations or sales *(Chapter Six)*.

Computer Code—Instructions to the computer, usually written in a programming language *(Chapter Nine)*.

Concentration—The increased storage efficiency of electronic and magnetic media that allows vast amounts of data to be stored in relatively small spaces *(Chapter Nine)*.

Conferences—Meetings, symposia, or any group function held at a hotel that will require special services *(Chapter Eight)*.

Confirmation—Official notice, preferably in writing, from the hotel to a guest or group spelling out, in detail, future services to be provided, the prices, and the methods of settlement; any deposit required or paid should also be included *(Chapter Eight)*.

Consumption Reports—Documents filled out by the food and beverage preparers listing items made and served at banquets and other large parties; used to prepare and audit invoices *(Chapter Eight)*.

Control/Policy Trade-off—A description of the conflict that develops between ideal internal control and management's operating policies. Often one can be improved only at the expense of the other *(Chapter One)*.

Cost of Goods Sold (CGS)—An income-statement expense representing the cost of sales or dollar cost of the goods that have been sold *(Chapter Four)*.

Credit Manager—A member of the hotel's management team whose responsibilities center around the formulation and administration of credit policy, as well as the collection of accounts *(Chapter Three)*.

Credit Policy—Those aspects of the hotel's operating policies that deal with the extension of credit to guests, and the procedures, rules, and training required to successfully accomplish that extension of credit *(Chapter Three)*.

Custody of Assets—Having physical control or guardianship of assets; also used in the context of having responsibility for the assets *(Chapter One)*.

Custody of Stores—The responsibility for goods in inventory in the store-rooms; usually the function of the storeroom clerk *(Chapter Four)*.

Cut-off Statements—Statements (usually checking-account or bank state-ments) prepared at a random or specially selected time other than the end of the month *(Chapter Two)*.

Daily Audit Process—The accounting process of checking and verifying all of the documentation and audit trails for rooms revenue; may include portions of what were traditionally called the night audit and the morning audit *(Chapter Six)*.

Daily Intact Deposit—The procedure of depositing each shift's receipts separately and daily in the hotel's bank *(Chapter Two)*.

Daily Transcript (of accounts receivable)—A summary document of all live or active guest folios, ranging from the older hand-prepared versions to computerized spreadsheets *(Chapter Six)*.

Delivery Tickets—A shipping invoice or copy of the invoice that will ac-company the actual shipment of goods; it usually contains the quantity shipped, the weights and counts, product descriptions, and sometimes the prices *(Chapter Four)*.

Deterrence—The process of preventing, discouraging, or inhibiting an act, usually by intimidation or fear of the consequences *(Chapter One)*.

Direct Purchases—Items, usually perishable, that are received and sent directly to kitchens or other user areas rather than to stores *(Chapter Four)*.

Disclaimer—A letter written by the auditor of financial statements stating that he or she cannot express an opinion on those statements, usually because of limited scope *(Chapter Ten)*.

Division of Duties—The segregation or separation of tasks among several employees so that no single individual has complete control over an entire transaction or process *(Chapter One)*.

Documentation—The process of putting in writing all of the procedures for a given task or function in such detail that someone unfamiliar with the task could perform it from the written record alone *(Chapter Nine)*.

Documentation—The process of writing down all of the procedures for a given task or function in such detail that someone unfamiliar with the task could perform it from the written record alone *(Chapter Two)*.

Dumping—Periodic printing out of data to hard (paper) output *(Chapter Nine)*.

Dupes—Duplicate checks *(Chapter Seven)*.

Duplicate-Checking System—An approach to checking in which a duplicate check or receipt is prepared for each item, and then given to the preparers as sanction to prepare and release the product; the "dupes" should be designed such that whenever an order is taken it is simultaneously written on or posted to the guest's check *(Chapter Seven)*.

EDP Auditing—The process of checking and verifying that computer programs are performing their prescribed tasks correctly and that they are not performing illicit or other non-valid tasks *(Chapter Nine)*.

EDP Controls—Procedures and principles applied, usually by management, to preclude opportunity for fraud and embezzlement in computer-processed functions *(Chapter Nine)*.

Electronic Cash Registers (ECRs)—Relatively simple computerized revenue-recording machines; essentially cash registers that operate with electronic processors rather than mechanical ones (compare to POS devices) *(Chapter Seven)*.

Electronic Data Processing (EDP)—Operating accounting and other data systems by computers rather than by hand *(Chapter Nine)*.

Embezzlement—The act of an employee or other insider fraudulently converting property to his or her own use; employee theft *(Chapter One)*.

Emboss—To press in a manner as to leave a raised imprint. In financial transactions, to imprint a credit card on a hotel document or record of charge *(Chapter Two)*.

Emergency Power Systems—Back-up electrical power usually provided by diesel or gasoline generators that turns on automatically in a power failure *(Chapter Nine)*.

End-User Computing—A description of the environment in which persons other than the information-systems employees, usually most of the top executives of the hotel, use computers to manipulate data and support decision making *(Chapter Nine)*.

Exchange—The act of trading one item for another. In hotels, trading customer's checks that the hotel cashed as a courtesy for cash to replenish the house banks *(Chapter Two)*.

External Audits—Having the firm's accounting books and documents periodically examined by an outside accounting firm *(Chapter One)*.

Externally Generated Extras—Services from outside the hotel requested and consumed by guests and added to their folios; examples are flowers, theater tickets, and car rentals. *(Chapter Eight)*.

Fidelity Bond—A casualty-insurance policy that insures the firm against employee dishonesty *(Chapter One)*.

File Protection—A general and administrative computer control focusing on the security, back-up, and, if necessary, reconstruction of the electronic files containing programs or data *(Chapter Nine)*.

Float—In the internal-control context, the original stake or initial cash given to a cashier for use in his or her shift. In a cash-management context, to describe the difference in cash balances between the company's books and the bank's books *(Chapter One)*.

Flow Chart—A schematic diagram depicting the flow of information and documents between components or persons in a particular function; an important first step in designing programs *(Chapter Nine)*.

Fraud—The intentional distortion of the truth to acquire property that belongs to another; the intent to deceive; trickery *(Chapter One)*.

Front Office—The front desk and all guest-accounting operations of a hotel *(Chapter Six)*.

Front-Office Accounting—Guest accounting, or all of the processes involved in checking a guest in, accumulating his or her charges, and settling the bill upon check-out *(Chapter Six)*.

Function Sheets—Documents prepared by the sales or banquet departments that list all of the details for each function or party to be performed by the hotel or restaurant; also known as function reports, event orders, and tickler sheets *(Chapter Eight)*.

General and Administrative Controls—The procedures and principles that can be applied by the hotel's management to prevent fraud and other losses from occurring *(Chapter Nine)*.

Guest Accounting—Front-office accounting *(Chapter Six)*.

Guest Checks—The invoices or sales slips given to restaurant customers *(Chapter Seven)*.

Guest Folio—An individual guest's account with the hotel, or the amount the guest owes the hotel at any point in time, usually evidenced by a written document or computer file *(Chapter Six)*.

Guest-Accounts Receivable—The total charges-to-date incurred by and posted to the folios of guests currently in the house *(Chapter Three)*.

Hacking—Unauthorized entry to any computer network *(Chapter Nine)*.

Head Cashier—The hotel's chief cash-handling employee, in charge of all cash handling and custody, banking, and management of shift cashiers *(Chapter Two)*.

Housekeeper's Report—A document prepared daily by the housekeeping staff that lists the rooms status for the previous night; an inventory of rooms occupied *(Chapter Six)*.

Imprest—A fund, such as petty cash, where the amount is held constant *(Chapter Four)*.

Indelible—Unable to be erased *(Chapter Two)*.

Independent Sources of Revenue—Data sources that are not part of the revenue-recording documents but that allow estimation of the revenue; examples are the housekeeper's report for rooms, or cover counts in restaurants *(Chapter Six)*.

Interface—A mechanical or electronic process whereby one system is connected to or able to communicate with another *(Chapter Nine)*.

Interface—A mechanical process whereby one system is connected to or able to communicate with another *(Chapter Six)*.

Internal Control—The methods and measures adopted within a business to safeguard its assets, check the accuracy and reliability of its accounting data, promote operational efficiency, and encourage adherence to prescribed managerial policies *(Chapter One)*.

Internally Generated Extras—Services requested and consumed by guests, performed by the hotel, and added to the folios; examples are room service, telephone calls, parking, and gratuities *(Chapter Eight)*.

Inventory Management—A systematic and scientific approach to the purchasing, storing, and issuing of inventories so as to minimize cost and maximize return *(Chapter One)*.

Invoice—The official bill or notice from a supplier stating the items purchased by, shipped to, and received by the hotel, and the dollar amount for which the hotel is indebted; it is usually received in the mail, but occasionally may accompany the shipment *(Chapter Four)*.

Lapping—A type of embezzlement where assets or other resources from one period are used to cover shortages or manipulations from another period. A fraud of "over-lap" *(Chapter Two)*.

Library Function—The task involving the custody and protection of data files and program copies *(Chapter Nine)*.

Magnetic Disks or Tapes—Electronic storage media for data that operate by magnetic recording *(Chapter Nine)*.

Management by Exception—The process whereby key items, such as out-of-line numbers, are flagged for management's special attention; items not considered exceptional are assumed satisfactory and management's time is not spent on them *(Chapter Four)*.

Manual Environment—In the rooms-revenue context, a front-office or guest accounting system that is posted and prepared by hand *(Chapter Six)*.

Mini-Bar—In-room vending of food and beverage items *(Chapter Six)*.

Morning Audit—The portion of the daily audit of rooms revenue that is traditionally performed during the morning following the transactions *(Chapter Six)*.

Night Audit—The portion of the daily audit of rooms revenue that is traditionally performed during the night following the transactions *(Chapter Six)*.

Off-Line—In the context of revenue, an item of data that is not part of the revenue-recording cycle or documentation *(Chapter Six)*; in data processing, a piece of equipment that is not communicating with the central processing unit *(Chaptetr Nine)*.

Officer's Checks—The guest checks used the hotel's managers when they charge food or beverages *(Chapter Seven)*.

On-Line—In the context of revenue, those items that are part of the official revenue-recording cycle or documentation *(Chapter Six)*; in data processing, a piece of equipment that is communicating with the central processing unit *(Chaptetr Nine)*.

One-Write" System—A pen-and-ink hand bookkeeping system that uses carbons and inserts to allow one writing of the numbers or data to be simultaneously recorded on several records. These systems are quite useful for repetitive tasks such as payroll, accounts payable, and accounts receivable *(Chapter Five)*.

Opportunity—In the current context, a set of circumstances allowing or facilitating embezzlement *(Chapter One)*.

Patch Program—An illicit mini-program placed within the main computer program whose purpose is to accomplish fraudulent tasks *(Chapter Nine)*.

Paymaster—A hotel employee whose responsibilities include the control of payroll, the analysis of payroll expense, and handing out paychecks; the paymaster should be separate from the payroll clerk, who prepares the payroll and the checks *(Chapter Five)*.

Periodic Inventory—The inventory valuation and cost-of-sales system whereby an actual counted or physical inventory is taken each period, priced out, and used for the balance sheet and cost of goods sold *(Chapter Four)*.

Periodic Saving—A file-protection procedure that involves periodically copying data from a fragile medium, like the computer's memory, to a more stable medium, like magnetic disks *(Chapter Nine)*.

Peripheral Equipment—Data-processing equipment other than the computer itself; examples are printers and storage media like hard-disk drives *(Chapter Nine)*.

Perpetual Inventory—The inventory valuation and cost-of-sales system whereby permanent records are kept for each item in inventory; such records are posted for each receipt of new goods, and each issue to users, with the latter yielding cost of goods sold, and the sum of the total inventory yielding the theoretical balance-sheet inventory *(Chapter Four)*.

Petty Cash—A fund (usually small) of cash on hand that is kept for odd-hour, last-minute, or emergency purchases *(Chapter Four)*.

Pick-Up—The procedure whereby hotel cashiers obtain their starting banks and other supplies and sign-in for their shift *(Chapter Two)*.

Point-of-Sale (POS) Device—A register or terminal where sales are recorded and bills are settled with customers, specifically, a computerized revenue-recording machine, placed at various sales outlets, capable of recording a large amount of sales detail, and often capable of communicating with other systems, such as the front-office system *(Chapter Seven)*.

Price Quotation—The process of soliciting prices from several suppliers, usually by telephone, to facilitate purchasing decisions *(Chapter Four)*.

Price—The exchange value of a unit of good or service, usually expressed in dollars; with quantity and quality, one of the three key attributes for purchase control *(Chapter Four)*.

Probable Cause—A reasonable ground for supposing that a criminal charge is well-founded *(Chapter One)*.

Programmer—A person who writes computer programs that instruct the computer how to operate *(Chapter Nine)*.

Programming Language—A code system that is used to write instructions for a computer *(Chapter Nine)*.

Property Management System (PMS)—A term describing a broad-purpose hotel-computing system that incorporates front-office accounting with communications and management of the housekeeping, telephone, and food and beverage departments *(Chapter Nine)*.

Proprietary Programs—Computer programs (software applications) that have been created by a software company and purchased or leased by the hotel *(Chapter Nine)*.

Protest—The legal procedure necessary to establish evidence of the fact that a returned check is officially uncollectible. Usually performed by the hotel's bank and evidenced by a notarized document *(Chapter Three)*.

Purchase Orders—Documents issued by the hotel to authorize a purchase and to bind the hotel to pay for it; purchase orders are numerically controlled accounting documents, limited in use to those with prior authorization *(Chapter Four)*.

Purchasing Department—A hotel department whose job is to purchase the best quality of needed goods and services at the lowest prices; serves as part of internal-control process *(Chapter Four)*.

Quality—A subjective judgment as to the degree of acceptability of goods and services received by the hotel; the degree to which goods and services match their specifications; with quantity and price, one of the three key attributes for purchase control *(Chapter Four)*.

Quantity—Refers to the counts, weights, or measures of the amount of goods and services; may refer to amounts ordered or received; with quality and price, one of the three key attributes for purchase control *(Chapter Four)*.

Rationalize—To cause an act, such as theft or fraud, to seem reasonable, plausible, or appropriate *(Chapter One)*.

Rebate—A discount or allowance given to a guest *(Chapter Six)*.

Receiving Report—A document sent by the receiving department to the accounting department itemizing the receipt of goods and services, and verifying their quantity and quality *(Chapter Four)*.

Record Keeping—The process, usually attributed to a hotel's accounting office or department, of analyzing data and making entries or recording transactions into the accounting records *(Chapter One)*.

Record Reconstruction—Re-creating or re-building data files that are lost or destroyed *(Chapter Nine)*.

Redundancy—A file-protection procedure that involves creating automatic back-up files to replace data files if they should become lost or destroyed *(Chapter Nine)*.

Registration Cards—Documents that are used at check-in to capture information about the guest, his or her credit worthiness, and his or her stay *(Chapter Six)*.

Replenishment—To refill or re-stock; used in the context of petty-cash purchases for the process of turning in paid vouchers to draw a check to repay the fund for depleted cash *(Chapter Four)*.

Requisitions—A document sent by storeroom clerks to the accounting department to itemize the goods that were issued to user departments; a key document in the perpetual-inventory system for valuation and cost of goods sold *(Chapter Four)*.

Room-Rate (Tariff) Schedule—A fixed and published listing of the various room rates charged by the hotel *(Chapter Six)*.

Rooms Revenue—Sales, in dollars, by the rooms department *(Chapter Six)*.

Rooms-Sold Inventory—A daily listing of rooms occupied *(Chapter Six)*.

Scope of the Audit—A blueprint or description of the level of testing and checking that an auditor plans to perform in an audit; related to, among other factors, the relative strength or weakness of the client's internal controls *(Chapter Ten)*.

Signature-on-File—The procedure whereby hotels post charges to a guest's credit-card account without the guest's actually having signed a charge voucher. Generally that guest's account number and signature were otherwise obtained—for example, on the registration card *(Chapter Two)*.

Software—The aggregated instructions or programs that tell the computer what to do for each task or function *(Chapter Nine).*

Source Documents—The documents of evidence associated with transactions, usually with outside parties: typically, sales slips, invoices, register tapes, time cards, and receipts *(Chapter Two).*

Specifications—A formal list of attributes that fully describes goods and services; used by vendors to supply bids or price quotations *(Chapter Four).*

Standard Operating Procedures (SOPs)—Methods of completing tasks and functions within the operation that have become routine or have been stated in formal rules *(Chapter One).*

Steward's Sales—A procedure whereby hotels sell products to their own employees so that the employees obtain the benefit of better quality or lower price *(Chapter One).*

Storeroom Issues—The goods delivered from storerooms to users; evidenced by a document called a requisition *(Chapter Four).*

Storeroom—A secure place where inventory is received, kept, and issued *(Chapter Four).*

Stratified Authority—An approach to management authority whereby decisions are separated into levels, and lower-level decisions are permitted at lower levels of management; stratified authority allows for more efficient use of management time *(Chapter Five).*

Systems Analyst—A person who designs computer applications to fit the needs of the various functions (engages in systems planning) *(Chapter Nine).*

Systems Planning—The process of designing computer applications to fit the needs of the various functions *(Chapter Nine).*

Tariff—*See* Room-Rate Schedule.

Theoretical (Book) Inventory—The amounts, in dollars and units, of the goods that should be in inventory, based on the postings of the perpetual-inventory records; often compared with actually counted or physical inventory *(Chapter Four).*

Time Cards—The documents upon which the time worked by employees is recorded, usually measured in hours; most time-recording systems are mechanical or electronic and thus use some type of card to record the time *(Chapter Five).*

Timekeeper—An employee whose responsibility is to observe hourly employees as they punch in and out (record their time), to verify their identity and the veracity of the hours recorded *(Chapter Five).*

Trade-Off—A balance. In this case, the balance between committing scarce resources and achieving optimum internal control *(Chapter One).*

Travel-Agency Commissions—The fees paid to travel agents for sending business to the hotel; usually a percentage of room sales generated by the travel agent's client *(Chapter Six)*.

Turn-In—The procedure whereby hotel cashiers deposit their accumulated receipts, starting banks, charge vouchers, and excess supplies with the head cashier and sign-out for their shift *(Chapter Two)*.

Unclaimed Wages—Paychecks that are not picked up by the employees who are entitled to them; unclaimed wages are sometimes symptomatic of internal-control problems *(Chapter Five)*.

Uninterruptable Power Supply (UPS)—A power source for EDP equipment, usually supplied by continuously charged battery packs, that automatically cuts in when the regular power fails or fluctuates *(Chapter Nine)*.

Unqualified Opinion—A "clean" opinion, one expressed without any qualifications or exceptions by an auditor as to how well the financial statements present the financial condition found in the course of an audit *(Chapter Ten)*.

Vandalism—The willful destruction of property *(Chapter Nine)*.

Write-Off—A process consisting of internal accounting entries whereby a hotel removes uncollectible accounts (assets) from the books and transfers them to expense (through an allowance account) *(Chapter Three)*.

Yield Management—A systematic approach to managing room rates so as to maximize total revenue *(Chapter Six)*.

Index

About the Author

A. Neal Geller is a professor on the faculty of the Cornell University School of Hotel Administration. He obtained a B.S. in 1964 and an M.B.A. in 1974 from Cornell University, and a Ph.D. in accounting from Syracuse University in 1977. Professor Geller also has extensive experience in the management of resorts and hotels. His current research interest is in financial management and accounting applications for the hospitality industry, and he has published numerous articles on those topics. Professor Geller is also a consultant to many hospitality companies. His consulting work involves operational and financial analysis. He is a member of the American Accounting Association, the Financial Management Committee of the American Hotel & Motel Association, and the Association of Financial-Management Educators.

During a sabbatical leave from Cornell in 1983-84, Professor Geller worked for the international accounting firm, KMPG Peat Marwick. On a subsequent sabbatical leave in 1989, he served as chief financial officer of the newly opened Statler Hotel and J. Willard Marriott Executive Education Center, located on the Cornell Campus.

In addition to this book, Professor Geller is the author of *Executive Information Needs in Hotel Companies* (1984).